OXFORD IB DIPLOMA PROGRAMME

AUTHORITARIAN STATES

COURSE COMPANION

Brian Gray
Sanjay Perera
Verity Aylward
Mariam Habibi

OXFORD
UNIVERSITY PRESS

OXFORD
UNIVERSITY PRESS

Great Clarendon Street, Oxford, OX2 6DP, United Kingdom

Oxford University Press is a department of the University of Oxford.
It furthers the University's objective of excellence in research,
scholarship, and education by publishing worldwide. Oxford is a
registered trade mark of Oxford University Press in the UK and in
certain other countries

British Library Cataloguing in Publication Data
Data available

978-0-19-831022-8

5 7 9 10 8 6

Paper used in the production of this book is a natural, recyclable
product made from wood grown in sustainable forests.
The manufacturing process conforms to the environmental
regulations of the country of origin.

Printed in India by Manipal Technologies Limited

Acknowledgements

p13: AP Photo; p18: AFP/Getty Images; p21: AP Photo; p23: Keystone-
France/Gamma-Keystone/Getty Images; p27: Abd Al-Samee'a; p31:
Nasser Bibalex; p51: Keystone-France/Gamma-Keystone/Getty Images;
p37: Owen Franken/Corbis; p38: Hurst & Co Publishers; p43: Mary
Evans; p44: Przemyslaw "Blueshade" Idzkiewicz; p48: Mary Evans;
p49: STR/AFP/Getty Images; p61: Keppler, Udo J/Library of Congress;
p64: DIZ Muenchen GmbH, Sueddeutsche Zeitung Photo/Alamy; p67:
AFP/Getty Images; p72: Corbis; p73: Pictures From History/Bridgeman
Images; p76: Bettmann/Corbis; p80: Magnum Photos; p83: Cuban
School (20th Century)/Private Collection/Prismatic Pictures/Bridgeman
Images; p82: Ullstein bild/Getty Images; p89: AP Photo; p90: Photo12/
UIG/Getty Images; p92: Bettmann/Corbis; p93: Underwood Archives/
Getty Images; p96: Art Directors & Trip/Alamy; p97: U.S. Coast
Guard; p102: Independent Picture Service/Alamy; p111: Chris Hellier/
Corbis; p112: The Print Collector/Print Collector/Getty Images; p117:
Corbis; p120: Interfoto/Alamy; p123: Granger Collection; p127:
Mondadori Collection/UIG/Rex Features; p133: Bettman/Corbis; p142:
ChinaFotoPress/Getty Images; p143: Photo 12/UIG/Getty Images; p146:
Pictures From History/Bridgeman Images; p150: Jacquet-Francillon/
AFP/Getty Images; p156: Landsberger Collection/International
Institute of Social History; p165: Gareth Jones; p174: History Archives/
Alamy; p178: Alamy; p179: Alpha History; p187: Heidelberg University
Library; p188: United States Holocaust Memorial Museum; p190:
United States Holocaust Memorial Museum; p191: Heidelberg
University Library; p192: Heidelberg University Library; p193:
Heidelberg University Library; p219: Süddeutsche Zeitung Photo;
p223: War Posters/Alamy.

Cover illustration by Karolis Strautniekas, Folio Illustration Agency.

Artwork by QBS Learning and OUP.

The authors and publisher are grateful for permission to reprint the
following copyright material:

Sebastian Balfour: *Castro (Profiles in Power)* (London: Routledge, 2009)
© Sebastian Balfour 1990, 2009. Reproduced by permission of Taylor
and Francis.

R Bessel: *Life in the Third Reitch* edited by R Bessel (1987) 94 words from
Chapter 'Social Outcasts in the Third Reitch' by J Noakes, pp 83-84, 90
& 93. By permission of Oxford University Press.

Michael Burleigh: Excerpts from "Among the Believers" from THE
THIRD REICH: A NEW HISTORY, Picador. Copyright © 2000 by
Michael Burleigh. Reprinted by permission of Hill and Wang, a
division of Farrar, Straus and Giroux, LLC, Macmillan Publishers and
The Wylie Agency on behalf of the author.

L Coltman: *The Real Fidel Castro* (New Haven: Yale University Press,
2003). © L Coltman 2003. Reproduced by permission of the author c/o
The Andrew Lownie Literary Agency.

Steven A Cook: *The Struggle for Egypt: from Nasser to Tahrir Square* (2012)
147 words from pp. 46, 50, 67-8, 78 & 92. By permission of Oxford
University Press / By permission of Oxford University Press, USA.

David Crew: *Hitler and the Nazis: A History in Documents* (2006) 101 words
from p.93. By permission of Oxford University Press, USA

Frank Dikotter: *The Tragedy of Liberation*, 29 August 2013, Bloomsbury
Publishing Plc. Reproduced by permission.

Jonathan Fenby: A table from *The Penguin History of Modern China*, (Allen
Lane, 2008, Penguin Books, 2009) Copyright © Jonathan Fenby, 2008.
Reproduced by permission of Penguin Books Ltd.

Peter Gay: THE WEIMAR CULTURE: THE OUTSIDER AS INSIDER.
Copyright © 2001, 1968 by Peter Gay. Used by permission of W. W.
Norton & Company, Inc.

N Gregor: *Nazism* edited by N Gregor (2000) 204 words from pp. 244-
246, 257-258 & 284. By permission of Oxford University Press.

R Griffin: *The Nature of Fascism*, © Roger Griffin. Routledge, London,
1991. Published with the permission of the author.

Jane Jenkins and Edgar Feuchtwanger: *Hitler's Germany*, Hodder
Murray (December 30, 2000). Reproduced by permission of Edgar
Feuchtwanger.

Ian Kershaw 'Der 30. January 1933, Ausweg aus der Krise und Anfang
des Staatsverfalls' (from Winkler, H. A., *Die deutsche Staatskrise* 1930-
33, Oldenbourg Verlag, Munich 1993.

Ian Kershaw: extracts from 'Der Spiegel, The Fuhrer Myth: How Hitler
Won Over the German People'. Copyright © Ian Kershaw 2008, used
by permission of The Wylie Agency (UK) Limited.

Kurt G W Lüdecke: *I Knew Hitler: The Lost Testimony by a Survivor from
the Night of the Long Knives* edited and introduced by Bob Carruthers.
Reproduced by permission of Pen and Sword Books.

Mohammad Naguib: *Egypt's Destiny* (London: Gollancz, 1955).
Reproduced by permission of the Copyright Clearance Center on
behalf of ABC-CLIO Inc.

J Noakes and G Pridham: *Nazism 1919-45*, Vol 2, University of Exeter
1984. Reproduced by permission of Liverpool University Press.

David Quentin and Brian Baggin: transcribers of *Problems of War and
Strategy* (November 6, 1938), Selected Works, Vol. II, p. 224 from
Selected Works of Mao Zedong. https://www.marxists.org/reference/
archive/mao/works/red-book/ch05.htm.

Extracts from the Selected Works: https://www.marxists.org/
reference/archive/mao/selected-works/index.htm). Reproduced by
permission of the Marxists Organization Reference Archive.

Detlev J. K. Peukert: Excerpt taken from Die Weinmarer Republik.
Krisenjahre der Klassischen Moderne. © Suhrkamp Verlag Frankfurt
am Main 1987. All rights with and controlled through Suhrkamp
Verlag Berlin. *The Weimar Republic: The Crisis of Classical Modernity*
(Penguin Books 1993) Copyright © Detlev J K Peukert, 1992.
Reproduced by permission of Penguin Books Ltd and Farrar Straus
Giroux.

A Speer: *Inside the Third Reich*, Sphere Books London.

Jonathan Spence: THE SEARCH FOR MODERN CHINA. Copyright ©
1990 by Jonathan D. Spence. Used by permission of W. W. Norton &
Company, Inc.

Roderick Stackelberg and Sally A. Winkle (eds): *The Nazi Germany
Sourcebook: an Anthology of Texts* (First published in 2002 by Routledge).
© 2002 Roderick Stackelberg and Sally A Winkle. Translated into
English by Sally A. Winkle. Reproduced by permission of the
translator.

A J P Taylor: *The Course of German History* (Methuen, London, 1978).
Reproduced by permission of David Higham Associates.

John Waterbury: *The Egypt of Nasser and Sadat: The Political Economy of
Two Regimes* (Princeton: Princeton University Press, 2014). Reproduced
by permission.

Although we have made every effort to trace and contact all copyright
holders before publication this has not been possible in all cases.
If notified, the publisher will rectify any errors or omissions at the
earliest opportunity.

Links to third party websites are provided by Oxford in good faith
and for information only. Oxford disclaims any responsibility for
the materials contained in any third party website referenced in this
work.

Course Companion definition

The IB Diploma Programme Course Companions are resource materials designed to support students throughout their two-year Diploma Programme course of study in a particular subject. They will help students gain an understanding of what is expected from the study of an IB Diploma Programme subject while presenting content in a way that illustrates the purpose and aims of the IB. They reflect the philosophy and approach of the IB and encourage a deep understanding of each subject by making connections to wider issues and providing opportunities for critical thinking.

The books mirror the IB philosophy of viewing the curriculum in terms of a whole-course approach; the use of a wide range of resources, international mindedness, the IB learner profile and the IB Diploma Programme core requirements, theory of knowledge, the extended essay, and creativity, activity, service (CAS).

Each book can be used in conjunction with other materials and indeed, students of the IB are required and encouraged to draw conclusions from a variety of resources. Suggestions for additional and further reading are given in each book and suggestions for how to extend research are provided.

In addition, the Course Companions provide advice and guidance on the specific course assessment requirements and on academic honesty protocol. They are distinctive and authoritative without being prescriptive.

IB mission statement

The International Baccalaureate aims to develop inquiring, knowledgable and caring young people who help to create a better and more peaceful world through intercultural understanding and respect.

To this end the IB works with schools, governments and international organizations to develop challenging programmes of international education and rigorous assessment.

These programmes encourage students across the world to become active, compassionate, and lifelong learners who understand that other people, with their differences, can also be right.

The IB learner Profile

The aim of all IB programmes is to develop internationally minded people who, recognizing their common humanity and shared guardianship of the planet, help to create a better and more peaceful world. IB learners strive to be:

Inquirers They develop their natural curiosity. They acquire the skills necessary to conduct inquiry and research and show independence in learning. They actively enjoy learning and this love of learning will be sustained throughout their lives.

Knowledgable They explore concepts, ideas, and issues that have local and global significance. In so doing, they acquire in-depth knowledge and develop understanding across a broad and balanced range of disciplines.

Thinkers They exercise initiative in applying thinking skills critically and creatively to recognize and approach complex problems, and make reasoned, ethical decisions.

Communicators They understand and express ideas and information confidently and creatively in more than one language and in a variety of modes of communication. They work effectively and willingly in collaboration with others.

Principled They act with integrity and honesty, with a strong sense of fairness, justice, and respect for the dignity of the individual, groups, and communities. They take responsibility for their own actions and the consequences that accompany them.

Open-minded They understand and appreciate their own cultures and personal histories, and are open to the perspectives, values, and traditions of other individuals and communities. They are accustomed to seeking and evaluating a range of points of view, and are willing to grow from the experience.

Caring They show empathy, compassion, and respect towards the needs and feelings of others. They have a personal commitment to service, and act to make a positive difference to the lives of others and to the environment.

Risk-takers They approach unfamiliar situations and uncertainty with courage and forethought, and have the independence of spirit to explore new roles, ideas, and strategies. They are brave and articulate in defending their beliefs.

Balanced They understand the importance of intellectual, physical, and emotional balance to achieve personal well-being for themselves and others.

Reflective They give thoughtful consideration to their own learning and experience. They are able to assess and understand their strengths and limitations in order to support their learning and personal development.

A note on academic honesty

It is of vital importance to acknowledge and appropriately credit the owners of information when that information is used in your work. After all, owners of ideas (intellectual property) have property rights. To have an authentic piece of work, it must be based on your individual and original ideas with the work of others fully acknowledged. Therefore, all assignments, written or oral, completed for assessment must use your own language and expression. Where sources are used or referred to, whether in the form of direct quotation or paraphrase, such sources must be appropriately acknowledged.

How do I acknowledge the work of others?

The way that you acknowledge that you have used the ideas of other people is through the use of footnotes and bibliographies.

Footnotes (placed at the bottom of a page) or endnotes (placed at the end of a document) are to be provided when you quote or paraphrase from another document, or closely summarize the information provided in another document. You do not need to provide a footnote for information that is part of a 'body of knowledge'. That is, definitions do not need to be footnoted as they are part of the assumed knowledge.

Bibliographies should include a formal list of the resources that you used in your work. The listing should include all resources, including books, magazines, newspaper articles, Internet-based resources, CDs and works of art. 'Formal' means that you should use one of the several accepted forms of presentation. You must provide full information as to how a reader or viewer of your work can find the same information. A bibliography is compulsory in the extended essay.

What constitutes misconduct?

Misconduct is behaviour that results in, or may result in, you or any student gaining an unfair advantage in one or more assessment component. Misconduct includes plagiarism and collusion.

Plagiarism is defined as the representation of the ideas or work of another person as your own. The following are some of the ways to avoid plagiarism:

- Words and ideas of another person used to support one's arguments must be acknowledged.

- Passages that are quoted verbatim must be enclosed within quotation marks and acknowledged.

- CD-ROMs, email messages, web sites on the Internet, and any other electronic media must be treated in the same way as books and journals.

- The sources of all photographs, maps, illustrations, computer programs, data, graphs, audio-visual, and similar material must be acknowledged if they are not your own work.

- Works of art, whether music, film, dance, theatre arts, or visual arts, and where the creative use of a part of a work takes place, must be acknowledged.

Collusion is defined as supporting misconduct by another student. This includes:

- allowing your work to be copied or submitted for assessment by another student

- duplicating work for different assessment components and/or diploma requirements.

Other forms of misconduct include any action that gives you an unfair advantage or affects the results of another student. Examples include, taking unauthorized material into an examination room, misconduct during an examination, and falsifying a CAS record.

Contents

Extra resources for this book can be found at www.oxfordsecondary.com/ib-history-resources.

YOUR GUIDE TO PAPER 2

The information in this book relates to key figures or events but is not prescriptive. For example, any relevant leader can be referred to in an answer on Authoritarian States in the 20th century. While authors have chosen well-known world leaders and events in this book, there is also an opportunity to explore your own regional history using the book as a guide as to the necessary concepts to know and to understand.

The aim of this book is to:

- provide in depth knowledge of a world history topic
- introduce key historical concepts
- develop skills by providing tasks and exercises
- introduce different historical perspectives related to key events/ personalities.

The content in this book is linked to the six key IB concepts.

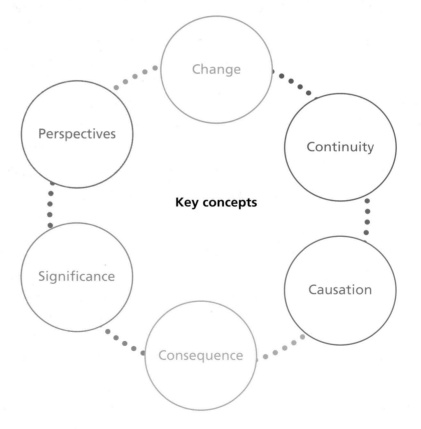

Key concepts

Change

Continuity

Causation

Consequence

Significance

Perspectives

How to use this book

This book contains sections relating to key aspects of *Authoritarian States in the 20th century* as outlined in the prescribed content section of the IB syllabus, for example, conditions that contributed to the emergence of authoritarian leaders in the 20th century.

You should use this book in the following ways:

- To gain more detailed knowledge about a significant event or leader

- To gain insight and understanding of different perspectives (explanations) of an historical event

- Use the exercises to increase your understanding and skills, particularly the skill of analysis when contributing to the formulation of an argument

- Consider the exam-style questions at the end of each chapter and think how you would apply your knowledge and understanding in an essay in response to the question.

As you work through the book make sure you develop strategies to help you learn, retaining the information and understanding you have acquired. These may be in the form of timelines (where chronology is important), spider diagrams, cue cards and other methods to suit your individual learning style. It is better to consolidate knowledge and understanding as you go along; this will make revision for the examination easier.

What you will be expected to do

There are 12 world history topics and the course requires you to study two of them. You should learn about a range of factors in the prescribed content relevant to each topic area, as shown in this table for Topic 10: *Authoritarian States (20th century)*.

Topic	Prescribed content
Emergence of authoritarian states	- Conditions in which authoritarian states emerged: economic factors; social division; impact of war; weakness of political system - Methods used to establish authoritarian states: persuasion and coercion; the role of leaders; ideology; the use of force; propaganda
Consolidation and maintenance of power	- Use of legal methods; use of force; charismatic leadership; dissemination of propaganda - Nature, extent and treatment of opposition - The impact of the success and/or failure of foreign policy on the maintenance of power
Aims and results of policies	- Aims and impact of domestic economic, political, cultural and social policies - The impact of policies on women and minorities - Authoritarian control and the extent to which it was achieved

Make sure you understand all the terms used under the heading "prescribed content" because these terms will be used to structure examination questions. If you have a clear understanding of all these terms, you will get the focus of your answers right and be able to select appropriate examples.

- If you are studying "The causes and effects of 20th-century wars", an exam question may focus on "political or economic causes", which is in the prescribed content.

- If you are studying Authoritarian States, you may get a question dealing with the topic "Emergence of authoritarian states". When the focus is on the "use of force", this relates to "methods used to establish authoritarian states" In the prescribed content.

- If you are studying the Cold War and the topic area is "Rivalry, mistrust and accord", you may get a question that focuses on "two Cold war crises each chosen from a different region and their impact on the Cold War", as stated in the prescribed content.

The Paper 2 examination is an essay test in which you are expected to answer two questions in 90 minutes in two different topic areas. You *must* choose questions from two different topics. This amounts to 45 minutes per question – not much time for answering what can be rather broad questions on two different subjects. One of the most critical components in succeeding in this examination, therefore, is good time management.

The best ways to improve your essay-writing skills are to read examples of effective, well-structured essays and to practise writing them yourself. In addition to timing, you must understand the skills you need to produce a good answer.

What the exam paper will look like

The will be 24 questions with two questions set for each of the twelve topics. There will be clear headings identifying the topics and the questions will focus on different aspects of the topic as outlined in the prescribed content.

The questions will be "open" questions (with no specific names or events mentioned). This will allow you to apply your knowledge and understanding in response to the question set. Some questions may ask you to refer to events or leaders, "each chosen from a different region".

Preparing for Paper 2

Make sure you understand what the command terms used in essay questions are asking you to do. The most common command terms are:

- **Compare and contrast**
  Identify similarities and differences relating to a specific factor or event

- **Discuss**
  Review a range of arguments

- **Evaluate**
  Weigh up strengths and limitations. In an essay question this is often expressed as "successes and failures"

- **Examine**
  Consider an argument or assumption and make a judgment as to the validity of either

- **To what extent**
  This usually refers to a quotation or a statement, inviting you to agree or disagree with it

Essay skills

Understanding the focus of a question is vital as this is one of the skills and examiner looks for. There are usually two or three **focus words** in a question.

The focus words are identified in the examples below:

Example 1

Evaluate the *significance* of *economic factors* in the *rise to power* of one 20ᵗʰ century authoritarian leader.

The question is asking about the importance of economic issues and crises in the rise to power of an authoritarian leader.

A good answer would be expected to include a range of factors (popularity, threat of force and weakness of existing political system) not just economic factors, before making a judgment on the importance of economic factors in the rise to power of the chosen leader.

Example 2

The *outcome* of Civil war is often *decided* by the *actions of Foreign powers*. To what extent do you agree with this statement with reference to **two** civil wars *each chosen from different regions*.

The question is asking you to consider whether the end of civil wars is usually decided by foreign powers. Again you should consider a range of factors relevant to your chosen examples. It is quite possible that the statement applies to one of them but not the other.

Example 3

Evaluate the *social and economic challenges* facing one newly independent state and how *effectively* they were dealt with.

The question is asking you to do two things — identify social and economic problems and then assess the success and failures of attempts to solve those problems.

The command term tells you what you have to do and the focus words tell you what you have to write about. Make it clear in your answers that you understand both of these and you will show the examiner that *"the demands of the question are understood"* – a phrase that is used in the markbands for Paper 2.

Markbands

Marks	Level descriptor
0	Answers do not reach a standard described by the descriptors below.
1–3	There is little understanding of the demands of the question. The response is poorly structured or, where there is a recognizable essay structure, there is minimal focus on the task. Little knowledge of the world history topic is present. The student identifies examples to discuss, but these examples are factually incorrect, irrelevant or vague. The response contains little or no critical analysis. The response may consist mostly of generalizations and poorly substantiated assertions.
4–6	The response indicates some understanding of the demands of the question. While there may be an attempt to follow a structured approach, the response lacks clarity and coherence. Knowledge of the world history topic is demonstrated, but lacks accuracy and relevance. There is a superficial understanding of historical context. The student identifies specific examples to discuss, but these examples are vague or lack relevance. There is some limited analysis, but the response is primarily narrative or descriptive in nature rather than analytical.
7–9	The response indicates an understanding of the demands of the question, but these demands are only partially addressed. There is an attempt to follow a structured approach. Knowledge of the world history topic is mostly accurate and relevant. Events are generally placed in their historical context. The examples that the student chooses to discuss are appropriate and relevant. The response makes links and/or comparisons (as appropriate to the question). The response moves beyond description to include some analysis or critical commentary, but this is not sustained.
10–12	The demands of the question are understood and addressed. Responses are generally well structured and organized, although there is some repetition or lack of clarity in places. Knowledge of the world history topic is mostly accurate and relevant. Events are placed in their historical context, and there is some understanding of historical concepts. The examples that the student chooses to discuss are appropriate and relevant, and are used to support the analysis/evaluation. The response makes effective links and/or comparisons (as appropriate to the question). The response contains critical analysis, which is mainly clear and coherent. There is some awareness and evaluation of different perspectives. Most of the main points are substantiated and the response argues to a consistent conclusion.
13–15	Responses are clearly focused, showing a high degree of awareness of the demands and implications of the question. Responses are well structured and effectively organized. Knowledge of the world history topic is accurate and relevant. Events are placed in their historical context, and there is a clear understanding of historical concepts. The examples that the student chooses to discuss are appropriate and relevant, and are used effectively to support the analysis/evaluation. The response makes effective links and/or comparisons (as appropriate to the question). The response contains clear and coherent critical analysis. There is evaluation of different perspectives, and this evaluation is integrated effectively into the answer. All, or nearly all, of the main points are substantiated, and the response argues to a consistent conclusion.

Common weaknesses in exam answers

Many answers demonstrate knowledge often in great detail; these answers tell the story but make little or no analytical comment about the knowledge shown. This is a narrative answer that will not reach higher markbands.

Other answers often consist of statements which have some focus on the question but with limited or inaccurate factual evidence; what examiners often describe as unsubstantiated assertion.

Here are some frequent comments by examiners on answers:

These types of comments mean that the answers do not contain enough evidence to answer the question or support analysis. This is one of the most common weaknesses in exam answers.

Other comments:

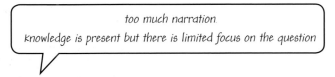

These types of comments mean that the candidates know quite a lot but are not using knowledge to answer the particular question. Answers do not make clear links to the focus of the question.

Writing good essays

Good essays consist of a combination of three elements:

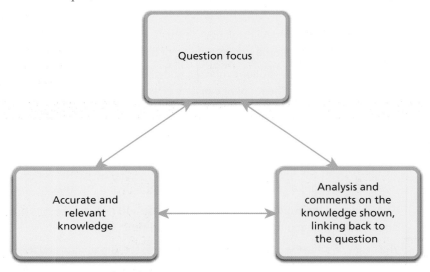

A good essay structure will ensure that you don't miss out key factors, keep your line of argument clear and your focus on the question at all times.

More information on essay skills can be found in the Skills sections at the end of each authoritarian state leader.

1 EGYPT – NASSER

The global context

The victors in the Second World War had put an end to one form of authoritarianism – the totalitarian regimes of Germany and Italy – but other types of authoritarian regime persisted throughout the globe, and others would also emerge in the post-war world.

Authoritarianism is a system of government that restricts or eliminates pluralism, censors the press and represses all forms of opposition. Participation in political activities is limited and is only permitted as long as it does not threaten the authority of the ruler. In the post-war world, military authoritarian states, those where authority rested with the army, became more frequent. Military juntas, as they are sometimes called, came to power through a *coup d'état*, or "putsch", and they stayed in power by establishing a popular base, which they then maintained through the use of force.

Military authoritarian regimes already existed in Europe, namely in Spain and Portugal. In the immediate post-war years they became prevalent in Latin America and the Middle East, where civilian leaders were perceived as weak, corrupt, and dependent on colonial powers. The military offered the people pride and patriotism, authority and political stability, as well as social and economic reforms. They appeared to be close to ordinary people and promised them a better future.

In the Middle East external factors also brought forth these changes. It was a region that had been traditionally controlled and humiliated by the imperial powers of Britain and France. This had left countries like Egypt with a political legacy of weak successive leaders and an economic legacy of an impoverished and dependent economy. In the aftermath of the war, nationalist movements began to challenge this status quo.

To further this humiliation, the Second World War also precipitated the events in Palestine, where two communities, the local Palestinians and the Jewish settlers, competed with one another over their right to the land. In 1948 the Arab League countries entered into a conflict with the new state of Israel. This war ended with the defeat of the Arab nations in 1949. In Egypt this defeat was blamed on the King and his incompetent government and it triggered a wave of discontent, which culminated in the military coup of 1952. The military regime that emerged in 1952 remained in power until the popular revolts of 2011.

Timeline

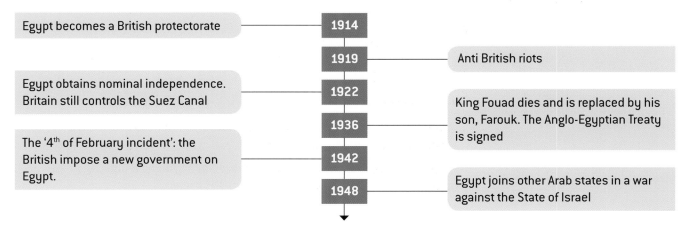

Egypt becomes a British protectorate	**1914**	
	1919	Anti British riots
Egypt obtains nominal independence. Britain still controls the Suez Canal	**1922**	
	1936	King Fouad dies and is replaced by his son, Farouk. The Anglo-Egyptian Treaty is signed
The '4th of February incident': the British impose a new government on Egypt.	**1942**	
	1948	Egypt joins other Arab states in a war against the State of Israel

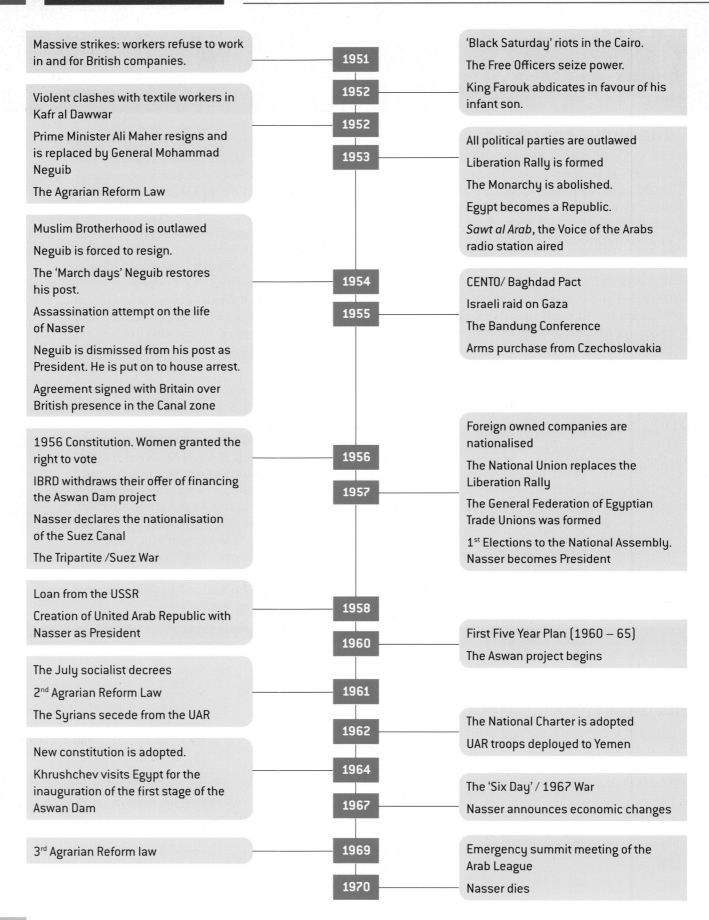

Massive strikes: workers refuse to work in and for British companies.	**1951** — 'Black Saturday' riots in the Cairo.
	The Free Officers seize power.
	1952 — King Farouk abdicates in favour of his infant son.
Violent clashes with textile workers in Kafr al Dawwar	**1952**
Prime Minister Ali Maher resigns and is replaced by General Mohammad Neguib	**1953** — All political parties are outlawed
	Liberation Rally is formed
The Agrarian Reform Law	The Monarchy is abolished.
	Egypt becomes a Republic.
	Sawt al Arab, the Voice of the Arabs radio station aired
Muslim Brotherhood is outlawed	
Neguib is forced to resign.	
The 'March days' Neguib restores his post.	**1954** — CENTO/ Baghdad Pact
Assassination attempt on the life of Nasser	**1955** — Israeli raid on Gaza
	The Bandung Conference
Neguib is dismissed from his post as President. He is put on to house arrest.	Arms purchase from Czechoslovakia
Agreement signed with Britain over British presence in the Canal zone	
	Foreign owned companies are nationalised
1956 Constitution. Women granted the right to vote	**1956**
IBRD withdraws their offer of financing the Aswan Dam project	**1957** — The National Union replaces the Liberation Rally
Nasser declares the nationalisation of the Suez Canal	The General Federation of Egyptian Trade Unions was formed
The Tripartite /Suez War	1st Elections to the National Assembly. Nasser becomes President
Loan from the USSR	
Creation of United Arab Republic with Nasser as President	**1958**
	1960 — First Five Year Plan (1960 – 65)
	The Aswan project begins
The July socialist decrees	
2nd Agrarian Reform Law	**1961**
The Syrians secede from the UAR	
	1962 — The National Charter is adopted
	UAR troops deployed to Yemen
New constitution is adopted.	**1964**
Khrushchev visits Egypt for the inauguration of the first stage of the Aswan Dam	**1967** — The 'Six Day' / 1967 War
	Nasser announces economic changes
3rd Agrarian Reform law	**1969** — Emergency summit meeting of the Arab League
	1970 — Nasser dies

1.1 The emergence of Nasser's Egypt, 1914–1952

The *coup d'état* of 1952

At 07.30 on the morning of 23 July 1952, the Egyptian people woke up to the voice of a young officer called Anwar Sadat who in a short speech on the radio announced Egypt's new political trajectory. Egypt had been "blessed with a revolution". The new leaders of Egypt called themselves the Free Officers. They justified their act because Egypt, they claimed, was poorly led and corrupt. This, they believed, had caused their country's humiliation.

In the words of Gamal Abdel Nasser, the emerging leader of this movement, in a book published in 1954 entitled *The Philosophy of the Revolution*, 23 July was "(...) represented the realization of a long-cherished hope – a hope entertained by the Egyptian people in modern times to achieve self-government and to have the last word in determining their own destiny". King Farouk abdicated in favour of his infant son Ahmad Fouad and on 26 July left Egypt for Italy on board his yacht, *al Mahrusa*. He lived there in exile until his death in 1965.

Conditions in Egypt before 1952

Egypt had obtained nominal independence from Britain in 1922. It was nominal because the terms of the agreement left British troops in total control of the Suez Canal. Since the opening of the Suez Canal in 1869, in the words of Laila Amin Morsy, "Egypt had served as highway of trade and a passage of conquest". As early as 1914, with the outbreak of the First World War, the strategic importance of Egypt and the Suez Canal had placed the country under tighter foreign control; the elected Assembly was abolished and Egypt became a British **protectorate**.

protectorate
A protectorate is distinct from a colony because it is an independent sovereign state. However, its autonomy is limited because it depends greatly on the administrative, military and economic support of a stronger state. In the Arab world, Aden in Yemen, Egypt and some of the Gulf states – Bahrain, Kuwait, Qatar and the Emirates – were all protectorates.

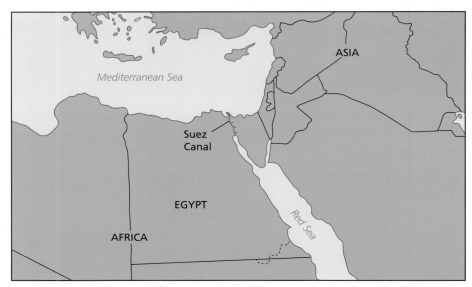

▲ "Fate had so willed that we should be on the crossroads of the world" Gamal Abdel-Nasser, *The Philosophy of the Revolution*

During the war Egypt was used as a base or, in the words of Peter Woodward, "a vast transit camp" for the operation of the Allied forces against the Central Powers. The Egyptian Expeditionary Force, formed in 1916, landed thousands of soldiers in the country and Egyptian farmers, the *Fellahin,* were compelled to surrender animals and crops to feed these soldiers. The persistent presence of British troops was a major source of controversy and discontent and it paved the way for numerous nationalist reactions in Egypt.

The First World War had demonstrated the importance of independence to the Egyptian nationalists. Saad Zaghlul, a member of the deposed Assembly and later the leader of the Wafd Party, demanded representation at the Paris peace talks: given that Egypt had participated in the war and had helped the Allies win the war, why should they not be represented at the peace conference? The British refused to agree to Zaghlul's demands and – to punish him for daring to challenge British authority – they exiled him to Malta. This only enraged the Egyptians more. In 1919, riots took place, in which 29 British soldiers and more than 800 Egyptians were killed. Tension continued until 1922 when finally the British government was forced to agree to terminate the protectorate and give Egypt its "independence".

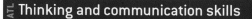

Thinking and communication skills

Below is the text of the Declaration to Egypt by His Britannic Majesty's Government (28 February 1922):

Whereas His Majesty's Government, in accordance with their declared intentions, desire forthwith to recognize Egypt as an independent sovereign State; and whereas the relations between His Majesty's Government and Egypt are of vital interest to the British Empire;

The following principles are hereby declared:

1 *The British Protectorate over Egypt is terminated, and Egypt is declared to be an independent sovereign State.*

2 *So soon as the Government of His Highness shall pass an Act of Indemnity with application to all inhabitants of Egypt, martial law as proclaimed on 2 November 1914 shall be withdrawn.*

3 *The following matters are absolutely reserved to the discretion of His Majesty's Government until such time as it may be possible by free discussion and friendly accommodation on both sides to conclude agreements in regard thereto between His Majesty's Government and the Government of Egypt:*

a *The security of the communications of the British Empire in Egypt;*

b *The defence of Egypt against all foreign aggression or interference, direct or indirect;*

c *The protection of foreign interests in Egypt and the protection of minorities;*

d *The Soudan.*

Pending the conclusion of such agreements, status quo in all these matters shall remain intact.

Choose to represent either the British government or the Egyptian government.

Discuss the terms of the 1922 Declaration of Independence above with a representative from the other government, and explain why you consider the terms of the Declaration to be fair or unfair.

At first, Egypt's journey towards independence was exemplary. The nationalists had led the way, showing courage in the face of a powerful enemy, and obtained their objective. It was the next phase of the journey, the governing of Egypt, that would prove to be a great deal harder. The 1923 constitution retained the powers of the king. In 1924 the first legislative elections were held; the Wafd Party secured 90 per cent of the seats in the Assembly and Zaghlul became Prime Minister. In spite of his excellent record as leader of the opposition, in office Zaghlul showed intolerance towards his opponents. He revived the restrictive press laws and clamped down on opposition newspapers. His untimely death in 1927 was also a setback for parliamentary rule because it deprived Egypt of an experienced politician. Besides, as already stated, the 1922 Declaration had paved the way for only a nominal British departure.

In 1936 the terms of the Declaration were reviewed. The Anglo-Egyptian Treaty of 1936 loosened Britain's grip a little, but maintained British troops in the country. Article 8 of the new Treaty stated: "In view of the fact that the Suez Canal ... is ... an essential means of communication between the different parts of the British Empire, His Majesty the King of Egypt ... authorizes His Majesty the King and Emperor to station forces in Egyptian territory in the vicinity of the Canal ..." A garrison of 10 000 soldiers and 400 pilots as well as the necessary ancillary personnel were stationed in the Canal Zone. Needless to say, the 1936 Treaty left the Egyptians extremely dissatisfied and resentful of the heavy-handed manner in which the British had treated them.

Unrest and disillusionment

The Second World War spread to the coast of North Africa. In November 1940 Italian forces attacked Egypt, in spite of its neutrality, and, once again, Egypt became involved in a war not of its making. Consequently the British increased their military presence and on 4 February 1942 they forced King Farouk to appoint the Wafd Party as the government that would bend to British demands. The incident, known as "The 4 February Incident" was a major turning point in modern Egyptian history: it humiliated both the King and the Wafd Party because they had both allowed Britain to interfere with the country's right to self-determination.

It took one last war, however, for King Farouk to finally lose his crown. In May 1948 the Egyptian army crossed the Sinai Desert with the intention of defeating the Israelis and returning the land to the Palestinians. The division, under the command of Colonel Mahmoud Seyed Taha, met its Israeli counterpart in the Faluja Pocket about 30 kilometres north-east of Gaza. In spite of the superiority of their adversary in the battle that followed, the Egyptians held their ground for almost 10 months before they accepted a truce, and in March 1949 an armistice was signed. For many of the officers who fought in that battle, this defeat was as much due to their own country's incapacities as the enemy's capabilities. King Farouk had, in their eyes, abandoned them. There were even rumours that the arms distributed to the soldiers had been defective.

The lesson the officers learned from this defeat was, ironically, an optimistic one: they were the ones who had to remedy Egypt's weakness. One of Colonel Taha's aides was none other than Gamal Abdel Nasser, who on his return would be crucial in forming the Free Officers Movement within the army. The objective of this movement was to overthrow the monarchy through a military *coup d'état*. It was in the trenches of Faluja that, as Nasser recalled later, "We sat in total oblivion of the siege (...), completely absorbed in how to fulfil the sacred duty of saving the motherland. (...) What is happening to us here is happening there, only more so. The mother country is also confronted with problems and besieged by enemies. It has also been duped in its turn – pushed into a battle without preparation. Ambitions, intrigues, and greed are toying with its destiny. It is also under fire, unarmed".

The outcome of the Arab–Israeli War, with the defeat of the Arab side, added to the existing unease in the country. Since 1944 Egypt had seen a succession of unpopular minority governments and two prime ministers had been assassinated. Neither the King nor his prime ministers were able to curb the anger of the people. In January 1950, a brief moment of optimism returned when the Egyptians once again voted in a Wafd government. There was hope that the new prime minister, the 70-year-old Mustafa al Nahhas, might put matters right.

This proved to be an illusion. In October 1951 the government boldly put an end to the Anglo-Egyptian Treaty of 1936, but it was a unilateral act that the British did not agree to, and British troops continued to occupy the Canal Zone.

The new government was unsuccessful at controlling the streets and never gained the confidence of the people. The politicians appeared more interested in retaining power than remedying Egypt's problems. The majority of them belonged to the aristocracy or were from prosperous families; many were high-ranking **pashas** with little sympathy or understanding for the underprivileged. Consequently they had few socio-economic reforms on their agenda. Far from redistributing the country's wealth, many saw their office as a means to further amass personal wealth. The failure of the 1950 Wafd government was also the failure of liberal parliamentarianism in Egypt. Egyptians were losing faith in voting and some were becoming more receptive to authoritarian ideas.

> **pasha**
> Pasha was an honorific title issued by the Sultan; it could be hereditary or non-hereditary. Holders of the title Pasha were often referred to as "Your Excellency". One of the first measures that the Free Officers carried out was the abolition of such honorific titles.

Violence and revolt

In the months that followed, violence erupted. A "popular struggle" encompassing workers, students, and militants with various ideologies broke out. The struggle targeted the British: workers refused to work in British companies and guerrilla bands calling themselves *Fedayeens* attacked British soldiers. The government looked the other way. When, on 25 January 1952, news reached Cairo of the bloody encounter between British troops and the Egyptian police in Ismailia, the garrison town in the Canal Zone, riots broke out in Cairo. The following day saw angry crowds on the streets of Cairo looting and burning more than 750 buildings.

The rioters targeted buildings that somehow symbolized the presence of the foreigners in Egypt; these included the opera house, casinos, dance clubs, cinemas, bars, and banks. The day, known as "Black Saturday", in which 26 people died and more than 500 were injured, signalled the end of an era in Egypt. The King tried in vain to appoint politicians capable of stabilizing the situation. Instead, cabinets came and went and no one emerged as a clear contender for this task until 23 July.

▲ The Rivoli cinema, Cairo, January 25th , 1952

> The presence of the army in the streets of Cairo is for the purpose of foiling the conspiracies of traitors who seek destruction and devastation. We will not accept a blow against the people. We will not fire one bullet against the people or arrest sincere nationalists …

> Everyone must understand that we are with the people now and for ever, and will answer only the call of the nation … The nation is in danger. Take note of the conspiracies that surround it. Rally around the Free Officers! Victory will come to you and to the people, of which you are an indivisible part!

Source: Quoted in Joel Gordon, *Nasser's Blessed Movement: Egypt's Free Officers and the July Revolution*, New York, Oxford: Oxford University Press, 1992, page 51.

The Black Saturday riots had not only shown that the people of Egypt were angry but also highlighted the weakness of the ruling elite. Both of these facts prompted the Free Officers to act fast: this was an opportunity not to be missed. In July, news reached the Free Officers that the King was about to go on the offensive by arresting them for disloyalty. They were left with no choice but to pre-empt the King. On the night of 22 July, units loyal to the Free Officers occupied key posts such as the airport, the telephone exchange, and the radio station. These actions, according to P.J. Vatikiotis, involved about 3000 troops and some 200 officers. Once royalist senior officers were arrested, the Free Officers were able to proceed and to announce their victory on the radio to the Egyptian people.

It is dificult to isolate one single factor that was responsible for the emergence of the Free Officers in 1952. Numerous factors had caused the humiliation of the people of Egypt: it was as much the weakness and passivity of the Egyptian leadership as the overtly dominant and unsympathetic presence of the British. In the words of Mehran Kamrava, King Farouk belonged to "an era whose time had passed". The political elite that worked alongside the King also lacked legitimacy within Egyptian society, thus undermining a liberal parliamentary regime. The ordinary people of Egypt felt neglected by its rulers, so when the opportunity arose for a group of "ordinary" officers to promise to put an end to the "the mischief-making elements", they rallied in their support.

The Free Officers and their methods

The *coup d'état* was a relatively bloodless event because, indeed, there had been little resistance. According to Joel Gordon, only two soldiers outside the Ras al Tin Palace were killed in scattered gunfire on 26 July. Many people in Egypt were, like the young officers, angry and fed up about their country's instability, the weakness of their King, and the politicians that had so far been running the country. They wanted to "clean" their country of this past. Anwar Sadat's short speech on 23 July 1952 explained the significance of their act, even though it did not offer a detailed plan of what was to come.

ATL Self-management and communication skills

Read the following text of the speech broadcast by Anwar Sadat on the radio on 23 July 1952. Extract from it the reasons he gives for why the Free Officers staged their *coup d'état*. List them in a column. In a second column, list what Sadat promises the Free Officers will do. In your opinion, is the speech aggressive or not?

Don't forget to back up your statements with evidence from the document.

Egypt has passed through a critical period in her recent history characterized by bribery, corruption, and the absence of governmental stability. All of these were factors that had a large influence on the army. Those who accepted bribes and were thus influenced caused our defeat in the Palestine War. As for the period following the war, the mischief-making elements have been assisting one another, and traitors have been commanding the army.

They appointed a commander who is either ignorant or corrupt. Egypt has reached the point, therefore, of having no army to defend it. Accordingly, we have undertaken to clean ourselves up and have appointed to command us men from within the army whom we trust in their ability, their character, and their patriotism. It is certain that all Egypt will meet this news with enthusiasm and will welcome it. As for those whose arrest we saw fit from among men formerly associated with the army, we will not deal harshly with them, but will release them at the appropriate time.

I assure the Egyptian people (army) that the entire army today has become capable of operating in the national interest and under the rule of the constitution apart from any interests of its own. I take this opportunity to request that the people never permit any traitors to take refuge in deeds of destruction or violence because these are not in the interest of Egypt. Should anyone behave in such ways, he will be dealt with forcefully in a manner such as has not been seen before and his deeds will meet immediately the reward for treason. The army will take charge with the assistance of the police. I assure our foreign brothers that their interests, their personal safety, "their souls", and their property are safe, and that the army considers itself responsible for them. God is the guardian of success.

Source: Steven A. Cook, *The Struggle for Egypt: from Nasser to Tahrir Square*, Oxford: Oxford University Press, 2012, page 11—12.

The movement barely needed to persuade or coerce people into supporting the putsch. Most Egyptians welcomed the change. After the Second World War there had been a revival of Arab nationalism. The nationalists were young men and women who protested against the continued presence and domination of the foreign powers in their countries. They were also angered by the establishment of a Jewish state in the territory they knew as Palestine and, last but not least, by the weakness and incompetence of their leaders.

Ideologically, this opposition remained diverse:

- Some chose a revivalist Islamic road; large number of students and army officers favoured the organization known as the Muslim Brotherhood, established in 1928. Its leader Hassan al Banna used Islam as a guiding principle to re-establish dignity, pride, and independence.

- Others opted for ideas closer to communism. The supporters of the Democratic Movement for National Liberation were mainly industrial workers, but the movement also had a significant number of followers among students and younger army officers. This movement, established in 1947 and led by Henri Curiel, emphasized the need for major socio-economic reforms as a means to restore Egypt's autonomy and spread social justice.

- Finally there were those who believed in achieving change through a reformed parliamentary system. The Wafd Party, which had come into existence in the turbulent days after the First World War, and its leader Saad Zaghlul represented those ideals. Though many were disillusioned by the party's politicians who had accepted the system, after 1945 there was a revival when younger Wafdists joined ranks with other nationalists to free Egypt from western domination.

Egypt in the post-war period had seemingly no shortage of ideas; what it needed was an institution that would bring those ideas to fruition. The one institution that presented itself capable of carrying out such a task was the armed forces.

The Free Officers were a secret group of nine young officers who had, for the most part, come of age during the turbulent years of Egypt's history. Gamal Abdel Nasser, born in 1918, was 18 years old when the Anglo-Egyptian Treaty was signed, 24 when the British had forced a change of government on King Farouk, and 31 when his division, in the face of a superior Israeli army, was forced to retreat from the Faluja Pocket. As soldiers, they were particularly sensitive to the loss of their country's pride, both diplomatically and on the battlefield. For the majority of these young officers, the 1948 war against Israel was their first experience of warfare. The defeat, which they blamed on the corrupt army hierarchy and the politicians, had come as a major personal setback: they had, to use Nasser's own terms, been "duped – pushed into a battle for which we were unprepared". Ideologically, the Free Officers did not represent one single set of principles but where they were unanimous was over the need to reform Egypt politically and economically – and the absolute necessity for the British to leave.

The army: a legitimate institution to lead?

Similar models of opposition within the ranks of the armed forces had appeared in another Arab country, Syria. There, in 1949, a group of officers had staged a *coup d'état* and overthrown the government.

What made the army a legitimate institution to lead this opposition? The fact that the army was a "modern" institution – through its familiarity with the modern technology of warfare, it was attuned to the modern world – put it in a position to be able to lead the country towards change. An army is organized, disciplined and can exert its authority: soldiers obey orders. This meant that they could get things done. The political instability of recent years and the King's apparent absence of authority made this feature particularly attractive. The army was conscripted and as such represented the nation as a whole; its soldiers came from different regions of the country and every sector of society. This built a bridge between soldiers and the rest of society, which made them very popular – unlike the political elite and the King, who distanced themselves from ordinary people through their wealth and social status.

At a time when Egypt was suffering shame and humiliation, the army was the institution that gave hope and promised a better future. Soldiers are courageous and love their country; they are the pride of a nation. In the words of Nasser himself, "[the army is] the only force capable of action [because it provides] a force concentrated within a framework separating its members to a certain extent from the continual conflict between individuals and classes, a force drawn from the very heart of the people, whose members trusted one another and had full confidence in themselves, a force equipped and capable of swift decisive action".

Nasser, the emerging leader

Of the nine core members of the Free Officers, Gamal Abdel Nasser stood out as the leader of the group. The son of a postal clerk, Nasser was born in Bakos, a neighbourhood of Alexandria, and had entered the Military Academy in Cairo in 1937. He was among the first cadets to benefit from the law passed by the Wafd Party in 1936 that opened the Military Academy to all social classes. Attending the Military Academy had allowed him to leave his home town and had offered him a career beyond his expectations. Living in the capital had also given him the opportunity to widen his experience socially and politically.

Cairo in the late 1930s was an eye-opener for the young Nasser. He recalled this time as "the days of great excitement and enthusiasm" when they "marched in demonstrations" and "joined delegations of students" calling on the leaders to "unite to safeguard the security of the mother country". The Great Depression of 1929 had brought about major economic and social problems, causing political unrest. Not only had the British renegotiated a treaty in 1936 reconfirming their military presence in the Canal Zone, but politicians were fighting one another to gain power instead of working together for the good of their country. King Farouk, who had acceded to the throne in 1936, was only 16 years old. The streets of Cairo were therefore overflowing with political agitation.

The young Nasser, witnessing this instability, was outraged – as much by the British military presence as by the internal rivalry of the politicians. Looking for a solution, he was attracted both by Mustafa Kamil's nationalism as well as Mohammad Abduh's Islamic reformism. Both proposed an "Egypt for Egyptians" as opposed to an Egypt that was constantly serving the interests of an external power. As Nasser's career in the army progressed, his political views also matured. He became more conspiratorial, more pragmatic and more opportunistic. He came to see the importance of strong leadership in a country that suffered from weak and hesitant leaders.

Conspiracy to rule

Contrary to the tradition of parliamentary opposition in Egypt, the methods used by the Free Officers were conspiratorial. As a small and secret cell of junior officers inside the army, they worked clandestinely to rally the support of like-minded officers. Their message was passed on either by word of mouth or through the distribution of pamphlets and leaflets. Given the secretive nature of their activities, there was little use of propaganda in these early days of the movement.

Their objective was to reach beyond the army to the "new middle class": young workers, professional classes, and government officials, as well as junior officers. This new middle class made up the section of the Egyptian population that felt disenfranchised by the older generation of politicians, who, in their eyes, were corrupt and too closely attached to the palace and the foreign powers. The Free Officers formed a coordinating committee in 1949 and gradually, but extremely cautiously, spread their message for change within the ranks of the army. They stayed underground to avoid arrest because, as soldiers, they ran the risk of being court-martialled.

A pragmatic approach to politics

The Free Officers recruited General Mohammad Neghib, a more senior officer and a hero of the 1948 war. This boosted their credibility because his was a name the public trusted. In 1952 they presented General Neghib as their candidate to the Committee of the Officers' Club. This was a bold move because, by contending for such a prestigious club, they were challenging the traditional elite of the army and the King himself. This was also the first time they made their existence public. Neghib won a landslide victory, and this indirectly triggered the 23 July coup: the palace realized that the Free Officers were a potential danger and started an investigation into the organization.

Neghib's role among the Free Officers, although of the utmost importance, proved in the long run to be fragile and temporary.

He was a means to an end. Although he appeared to be the leading figure in the July coup, the younger officers of the movement, in particular Gamal Abdel Nasser, proved to be the true deciders of Egypt's destiny. Indeed, the appointment of Neghib confirmed the movement's pragmatism.

As for opportunism, the Free Officers did not confine themselves to any single ideology. Realizing that their strength was in numbers, they kept contact with all three tendencies within the opposition – the Muslim Brothers, the Left, and the Parliamentary reformists – and made each feel as though they were promoting their brand of politics. This allowed them to broaden their ideological position and maintain a wide range of support. Furthermore, through their contacts with all the different opposition groups, they both appropriated their ideas and recruited supporters for themselves. Once in power, however, it became clear that the Free Officers and the armed forces were the sole initiators of policy. In this way they proved to be truly authoritarian.

The methods used by the Free Officers were neither coercive nor violent. There was, in fact, little need for the use of force or propaganda. The Free Officers had seemingly stepped upon a platform that had already been constructed by nationalists and ideologues before them. The "seeds of revolution" as Nasser recalled in his book "were inborn – a suppressed aspiration left as a legacy to us by a former generation". Given the absence of a clear programme, it was only in the days that followed the *coup d'état* that Egypt started to have a clearer idea of its new trajectory. It was in the years to come that history would be rewritten and the military coup of a handful of young military officers would be remembered as a popular revolution, the "July Revolution".

▲ Mohammad Neguib (left) and Gamal Abdel Nasser (right)

1.2 Nasser's consolidation of power, 1952–1954

Conceptual understanding

Key questions

→ How and why did the 23 July *coup d'état* become the July Revolution?

→ Which groups opposed the Free Officers and how did the Officers tackle them?

→ What were the consequences for Egypt of the manner in which the Free Officers tackled their opposition?

→ How did Nasser maintain his popularity in the first few years following their seizure of power?

Key concepts

→ Significance

→ Consequences

Maintaining leadership

The "popular struggle" that had started in January 1952 underlined the apparent disintegration of party politics. Between January and July, three prime ministers were given the task of restoring order. None succeeded. Public opinion shifted further and further away from entrusting party politicians and more towards purification (*al tahrir*) of the entire system. The situation, some started to believe, needed a "**just tyrant**" (*al-musta'bid al adil*), "a strongman who could stabilize and reform the political order without facing the constraints of party politics and parliamentary democracy". When news reached the people that a group of young officers controlled the city, many thought that they had found their "just tyrant".

However easy the first stage of this operation may have been, the Free Officers were soon to realize that consolidation and maintenance of power were more complicated. In spite of the apparent weaknesses and incompetence of the ruling class, Egypt had a developed infrastructure of political parties, trade unions, an extremely active press, artists, student activists, writers, and poets, not to mention a feminist movement dating back to the 1920s. Civil society existed and had high political expectations: civil rights, an uncensored press, and freedom of expression. There were also economic expectations: a better distribution of wealth, more autonomy from foreign capital, and a redistribution of land through agrarian reforms. Among those who welcomed change were the poor *Fellahin* who had supported the Free Officers because of their proximity to ordinary people and their ability to empathize with them. Finally, there were societal expectations: elimination of corruption and privileges that had barred the route towards social mobility and gender equality. All in all, the Free Officers had a lot on their plate, if they were to satisfy everyone.

just tyrant
A tyrant is another word for a dictator or an authoritarian ruler. A "just tyrant", also called a benevolent dictator, is a type of authoritarian ruler who claims to "benefit" the people by ending chaos and establishing order.

ATL Thinking and social skills

"Egypt was the cradle of the Arab media and press ... By 1882, it was the main platform on which political and ideological movements propagated their views ... The first indigenous Cairene papers were *Jurnal al Khedivu* (*The Khedive's Journal*) of 1827 and *al Waqa'ii al Misriyya* (*The Egyptian Events*) in 1828."

Ilan Pappé, *The Modern Middle East*, London: Routledge, 2005, pp. 186–7

What does such a long tradition of free and independent press say about a country?

Research and communication skills

Huda Shar'arwi (1879–1947) is considered Egypt's first feminist. In 1910 she opened schools for girls and in 1919 she organized the largest women's anti-British demonstrations. In that year she was also elected president of the Wafdist Women's Central Committee but later resigned after becoming disappointed in Wafdist politics, especially as they related to women. In 1923 she founded the Egyptian Feminist Union and published the feminist magazine *L'Egyptienne*.

The feminist tradition continued into the early Nasserist era: when the Party Reorganization Law was passed in 1952, of the 22 political parties that registered to participate in the new society to come, three were feminist parties.

Research Huda Shar'awi and the feminist movement in Egypt. Are you surprised to see pioneers such as Shar'awi in 1920's Egypt? Why do you think you are surprised?

Furthermore, in the expression "a just tyrant", was the emphasis on "just" or "tyrant"? Was the tyrant's job over once "justice" was restored? Had the military come to stay or, once the reforms were carried out, would they return to barracks? Were they the vanguard or the new rulers of the country? Was this merely a *coup d'état* or a fully fledged revolution?

Thinking and research skills

1 Research the two terms *"coup d'état"* and "revolution".

2 What do you think is the main difference between the two?

3 Why do you think Nasser preferred to use the expression the "July Revolution"?

Nasser's own version of events, as presented in his book *The Philosophy of the Revolution,* is characteristic of the official story: "I had imagined our role to be a commando advance-guard lasting only a few hours, after which the Holy March of the whole nation (...) would follow (...) But the reality I faced after July 23rd took me by surprise.(...) The masses did come. But they came struggling in scattered groups(...) It was only then that I realized, with an embittered heart, that the vanguard's mission had not ended at that hour but had just begun". Whether or not we accept this version as true, the fact is that the Officers did aim to consolidate their power over the following two years.

To consolidate their position, the Free Officers had to use a mixture of methods – force and propaganda as well as legal means. They had two extremely difficult tasks ahead of them:

1 They needed to satisfy the political groups – the Left, the Liberal reformists and the Muslim Brothers – who had supported change and participated in the demonstrations. However, since these groups had not been part of the Free Officers' movement, they needed to keep tight control of them and be prepared to act ruthlessly if they felt threatened by them.

2 They had to remain popular and appear in the eyes of the masses capable of changing their lives and offering them a better future. Since the nominal independence of 1922, many promises had been made but few had been kept. The breaking of these promises had been one of the reasons so many governments had, in the past, failed to survive.

"I knew full well from the beginning that our mission would not be an easy one, and that it would cost much of our popularity. (...) Our predecessors used to offer people nothing but dreams, and utter only what people liked to hear."

After the coup: the first few months

For the first few months after the coup the political changes were not too abrupt. Although the armed forces had successfully staged a military coup, Egyptians were told that government would remain in the hands of a civilian. Ali Maher, a conservative politician, a member of the aristocracy and a lawyer who had served in previous governments, became the Prime Minister. In full conformity with the law, Maher asked King Farouk to abdicate in favour of his son. Egypt remained a monarchy and a three-member Regency Council was formed to "rule" in the place of the infant King. Within the first week of the coup, the new government abolished the civil titles of pasha and bey, suggested income, profit, and inheritance tax reforms, and called on political parties and ministries to "purge" their ranks of the representatives of the old regime. Egypt was on its road to renewal.

Most accounts of these early months agree on the absence of a long-term project. The Free Officers seemed, as Nasser's account stated, to have come "as pioneers" to bring stability to Egypt and to clean the political arena of its corrupt elements. Appearances can, however, be deceptive. The Free Officers' Executive Committee, referring to itself as the Revolutionary Command Council (RCC), remained behind the scenes and indicated the way forward to the civilian government. Gordon referred to this command council as "the hidden hand" and stated: "Those who dealt directly with the officers found that hand often clenched in a fist".

▲ The Revolutionary Command Council. Sitting behind the desk, is Mohammad Neguib (the Chairman) and to his right, is Nasser (the Vice Chairman)

The elimination of rivals

The absence of resistance to the Officers' *coup d'état* could be explained in two ways. Those who were politically active chose to support it because they, too, wanted to end the status quo. Those who were part of the status quo remained passive because they apparently did not feel threatened. Ironically, in the course of the next two years, Nasser and the Free Officers chose to practically ignore those that had run the country previously (with the exception of the King and a few of the most prominent politicians), yet would use every means at their disposal to eliminate their previous supporters. Those who had supported the change had high expectations. Those who had protested alongside the Officers wanted to participate in the future of their country. However, the nature of authoritarian rule forces it to reject this type of pluralism.

Of the three potential political rivals, the Left, the Liberal reformists and the Muslims, the new government's first confrontation was with the Left. In August 1952 a strike led by textile workers turned bloody in Kafr al Dawwar, a major industrial centre and municipality on the Nile Delta in northern Egypt. The workers, who had supported the July coup, expected a favourable response to their demands. Instead, they found themselves in a pitched battle with the army. In the confrontation, four workers were killed and hundreds injured. Once the strike was ended, the army set up a special military court and tried the arrested workers. Two of the alleged leaders were convicted for high treason and executed. Many more received prison sentences. This was followed by the arrest of 30 people accused of belonging to an outlawed communist party. "We decided that the only way to deal with the situation was to make an example of those who had started a riot", wrote Neghib.

The Democratic Movement for National Liberation (DMNL), a party of the Left that had supported the Free Officers, consequently denounced the new government as a military dictatorship. Furthermore, when

Al Misri, a leading newspaper, reported the incident, the army surrounded the newspaper offices with armoured vehicles and threatened to shut it down. The relationship between the Left and the Free Officers would never recover. Given the context of the Cold War, the Left in Egypt started to accuse the Officers of colluding with the United States. The Officers, who prided themselves on being free from foreign influence, reacted ruthlessly. Their credibility as nationalists was being questioned. In the course of Nasser's rule, those suspected of communist sympathies were severely repressed.

On 7 September 1952 Ali Maher resigned in opposition to the proposed Agrarian Reform Laws. That night the Free Officers ordered the arrest of 64 prominent politicians and former palace men. The following day General Neghib of the Free Officers replaced Maher, in what still constituted a civilian government. For Steven Cook, "Ali Maher's departure indicated that ... governments under the new regime were not supposed to be an independent policymaking body; but rather the implementer of the Free Officers' desired initiatives".

The next potential challenge came from the Liberal reformists, namely the Wafd Party. As soon as the Neghib government took office, it decreed two extremely important laws: the Agrarian Reform Laws and the Party Reorganization Law. Whereas the first helped to increase the Officers' popularity with the rural population, the second helped curb opposition under the guise of a "cleansing campaign". This move was partly to rid the parties of their older-generation leaders and replace them with younger politicians, who were more likely to be favourable to the Free Officers. In the pursuit of this second objective, the new government set an example by launching a "cleansing campaign" of its own; hundreds of people were arrested. According to Neghib, these included "800 bureaucrats and 100 army, navy, air force, and police officers". He described their fate in the following way: "the least guilty were allowed to resign ... the guiltier were discharged ... the guiltiest were later tried before the Tribunal of the Revolution". The "cleansing campaign" was a way to show the need for renewal at every level of society.

In December a "corruption tribunal" was set up to try those who had allegedly abused public funds. The Party Reorganization Law forced the political parties to first dissolve and then to apply for recertification from the Ministry of the Interior. The process required each party to submit its political platforms, its finances and a list of their leaders. The law authorized the Ministry of the Interior to suppress any party whose objectives were "not in the public interest" or whose officers included anyone accused of corrupt practices or other crimes and misdemeanours. The purpose of the law, according to Neghib, was "to protect the people from political charlatanism".

The leader of the Wafd Party, Al Nahhas, refused to obey the new law. Furthermore, the party took the matter up with the State Council, the highest administrative court, thus challenging the law's legality. Instead of waiting for the court's ruling, the Free Officers outlawed all political parties. The old order was thus abolished and the blame for this was put on the political parties that had resisted voluntary purification. "It has become clear to us that personal and party interests ... seek to reassert themselves in these dangerous times in our nation's history", announced the government. A month later, in February, Nasser declared that reforming the parliamentary system had become a "minor objective compared to the wider aims of our revolution".

The banning of the parties was accompanied by the announcement of a three-year transition period and the launching of a new political movement directly attached to the Free Officers, the Liberation Rally (*Hai'at al-Tahrir*), which would mobilize the people and rally their support for the government. Nasser became the Liberation Rally Secretary General.

The Liberation Rally planned to open branches on campuses and in factories. Its aim was to create a civilian base for the RCC. With these new developments, it became apparent that the Officers' mission was not going to end after a series of socio-political and socio-economic reforms; they seemingly planned to stay in power more permanently.

The Liberation Rally's 11 articles

The Liberation Rally presented Egyptians with an 11-point programme of objectives:

1 complete and unconditional withdrawal of foreign troops from the Nile Valley

2 self-determination for the Sudan

3 a new constitution expressing the fundamental aspirations of the Egyptian people

4 a social system in which all citizens shall be entitled to protection against the ravages of unemployment, illness, and old age – i.e. a welfare state

5 an economic system designed to encourage a fair distribution of wealth, full exploitation of natural and human resources, and the maximum investment of new capital

6 a political system in which all citizens shall be equal before the law and in which freedom of speech, assembly, press and religion shall be guaranteed within the limits of the law

7 an educational system designed to develop a sense of social responsibility by impressing youth with its duties as well as its rights and with the overriding need to increase production in order to raise Egypt's standard of living

▲ The Liberation Rally *Hai'at al Tahrir* Cairo, January 1953

8 friendly relations with all Arab states

9 a regional pact designed to increase the influence of the Arab League

10 friendly relations with all friendly powers

11 firm adherence to the principles of the United Nations, with special emphasis on their application to subject peoples.

The July coup was on its way to becoming the "July Revolution". Nasser even presented his "Philosophy of the Revolution": "All people on earth go through two revolutions: a political revolution to recover their right to self-government from the hands of a despot (...) a social revolution – a class conflict that ultimately ends in realizing social justice (...) Unity, solidarity and co-operation (...) are fundamental factors for the success of a political revolution (...) dissension and discord among classes as well as individuals (...) form the foundation of a social upheaval. (...) One revolution [the political] demanded that we should stand united and forget the past. And another revolution [the social] demanded that we should restore the lost dignity of moral values, and not forget the past. There was no alternative to carrying out the two revolutions together." The original "duty" of the Officers, which had been to carry out a coup, had been transformed into a much larger and more ambitious long-term project. Soon, "Nasserism" would be coined as an ideological model that could be exported to other states.

Rewriting the constitution

In the February, a committee of 50 prominent figures was put in charge of rewriting the constitution. The new constitution would give the new regime a legal framework. By June the constitutional declaration was ready: Egypt abolished its monarchy, deposed the infant King and became a republic. "The world's oldest kingdom became for the time being, the world's youngest republic", wrote General Neghib, Egypt's first president. Five prominent Free Officers became ministers in the new government. Nasser became the Minister of the Interior as well as the Deputy Prime Minister. In November a new Ministry of National Guidance was created whose task was to promote the new government. Throughout November and December a successful publicity campaign was started and representatives of the Free Officers travelled in the Delta and Upper Egypt to drum up popular support. It was also an opportunity for the people to see the members of this still little-known group.

In spite of all these measures, there still remained a potential political rival: the Muslim Brothers, who still enjoyed a great deal of loyalty and support throughout the country. The relationship between the Muslim Brothers and the Free Officers was never very clear. Most of the Officers had been close to the Muslim Brothers in the years preceding the July coup, when there was a great deal of collusion between the two groups, and a member of the Muslim Brothers had been in the government. However, as the Free Officers started to move further towards authoritarian rule and political uniformity, the popularity of the Muslim Brothers started to pose problems. When in January 1954 ceremonies commemorating those killed in the Canal Zone turned violent, the government arrested 450 Muslim Brothers and banned their organization. The banning of the party, however, did not end support for the organization. On the contrary; in the months to come, the Free Officers faced a great deal of opposition from a large spectrum of society for their heavy-handed authoritarian rule. To survive as they did, the Officers resorted to the use of force as well as a dramatic use of propaganda. In this process, Nasser outmanoeuvred his rivals and emerged as the sole leader of the movement.

Nasser triumphant

Following the decision to ban the Muslim Brothers, dissent started to appear within the ranks of the army, starting with General Neghib, The "reluctant dictator", as the foreign press had called him, criticized the authoritarian measures that Nasser had taken and called for the reopening of Parliament. On 23 February Nasser forced Neghib to resign and placed him under house arrest. In a communiqué, the RCC accused Neghib of undermining the views of others and seeking total control. The announcement of the resignation led to an outcry both among the public and, more importantly, within the ranks of the army. The reaction was so severe that Nasser stood back and allowed Neghib to resume his post as President. Nasser took over the premiership. On resuming office, Neghib announced: "I have returned as President on the understanding that ours shall be a parliamentary republic". Neghib's victory was, however, short-lived.

Nasser's retreat had been tactical. While Neghib was enjoying his apparent victory, Nasser and those loyal to him were conspiring to stir up the political environment. Hundreds were arrested on charges of counter-revolutionary activities: they were accused of having exploited the division between Neghib and Nasser with the aim of restoring the old regime.

In March, in what appeared like yet another setback for Nasser, Neghib was given back his post as Prime Minister, but appearances were once again deceptive. In a move to outmanoeuvre his rival, Nasser put forward a resolution in the RCC calling for immediate elections. The resolution was passed. The resolution called on the RCC to surrender its powers and thus "proclaim the end of the Egyptian Revolution". It announced that all political parties could resume their activities and free elections were called for on 23 July 1954. The announcement of this resolution caused panic. Choosing Neghib over Nasser was choosing chaos over order. It was choosing the old party political system over the revolution.

As protest movements for and against the elections spread in Cairo, the Free Officers were able to step in once again as the saviours of the ordinary people. Newspapers were put under strict censorship. Universities were brought under tight surveillance. A number of officers accused of incitement to mutiny were tried and given long prison sentences. On 29 March the RCC announced that the elections were cancelled. Support for Neghib started to wane as the public saw him as regressive, as the one who wanted to return Egypt to the way it was. On 17 April Neghib resigned as Prime Minister but remained President until November, when he was dismissed, accused of treason, and put under house arrest.

With Neghib out of the way, Nasser could now turn to the elimination of the Muslim Brothers. In October 1954 Nasser was speaking at a rally in Alexandria when a gunman fired at him. He missed his target and Nasser, unscathed, managed to finish his speech: "Let them kill Nasser. He is one among many and, whether he lives or dies, the revolution will go on". It soon became apparent that the gunman, Mahmood Abdel Latif, belonged to the Muslim Brothers. The assassination attempt was followed by mass arrests and the execution of three Muslim Brother leaders. Nasser's last potential rival had been eliminated.

The cult of the leader

Great importance was given to the role of the leader within the Free Officers' movement. This was partly because, as soldiers, they were used to discipline and obedience and partly because of the clandestine circumstances of the movement's early existence. The original members, who had elected Nasser as president, credited him as the driving force and uncontested leader of the movement. He inspired devotion among his fellow officers. Once the Officers had taken over the reins of power, they fully understood the advantages of developing a cult of personality around Nasser. When and if Nasser was elevated to the role of the infallible leader, he and the Free Officers would remain in absolute control. Nasser responded well to this role: he was, indeed, a charismatic leader who enticed his listeners and reached out to ordinary people: "He spoke like a rural *saidi* of Upper Egypt, and was full of well-known references to daily rural life. Nasser was not just an Egyptian, he was an ordinary Egyptian ...".

Much has been written about whether this movement intended from the start to become so authoritarian or whether the Officers were simply a vehicle for change. Had the 23 July coup become the July Revolution because the Free Officers, as Nasser insisted, were on their own, or was it a preconceived plot on their part to obtain total authority? In this equation two hypotheses can be put forward. The first would rest entirely on Nasser, whereas the second concerned the ideological basis of the Free Officers.

Within two years of the coup, Nasser's confidence had grown; by October 1954 he had successfully eliminated not only his personal rival, the senior-ranking and popular war hero Mohammad Neghib, but also political parties such as the Wafd – whose historical status as the nationalist party that had stood up to the British was insurmountable – as well as the ideological movements of the Left and the Muslim Brotherhood, which also enjoyed a wide following – a far greater one among students and factory workers than the Liberation Rally. Step by step, he had outmanoeuvred them all, leaving the Egyptians with little choice but him for their leader. In the words of Peter Woodward, in this process "the secret of the revolution was slowly being revealed, not the least to the RCC itself: Nasser was its leader and all the world increasingly realized it".

As for the second hypothesis, it rests upon the absence of a guiding ideology for the Free Officers, whose main platform was their patriotism and nationalism. Unlike the other opposition groups, they lacked a strong ideological grounding. This meant that they were unable to compromise over policy, which made them less amenable to power sharing and certainly less tolerant of dissent. When opponents such as the Left or the Muslim Brothers challenged them on their loyalty to the nation, they had no choice but to react ruthlessly.

ـ انت مش كنت عايز تشوف الحرية .. أهيه يا سيدى قدامك
أزمة الديمقراطيه (١٩٥٤)

▲ Three military officers, including Nasser, show an Egyptian citizen an angel trapped in a storefront window. The angel is labeled "Freedom". A smiling general says, "Didn't you say you wanted to see freedom? Here she is, sir, right in front of you."

Finally, in order to understand the success of Nasser – this young officer with very little prior experience in governing a country – one can also turn to the failure of opposition forces to pre-empt Nasser's moves: they all fell into the traps he laid for them. Even Neghib, the biggest challenger of Nasser's authority, admitted in his memoirs that he had been "outmanoeuvred by Abd el Nasser and [his] junior colleagues".

The consequences for Egypt of Nasser's treatment of the opposition were a society that would be led by the whims of an authoritarian ruler and a government whose source of strength remained the use of force. As members of the armed forces, the Free Officers maintained their monopoly on the use of force and they ruthlessly repressed opposition and challenges to their authority. In the words of Woodward, "the coup of July 1952 had been essentially a takeover not so much *by* the army as *of* the army …". In the years to come, leaders would come and go but the authoritarian rule of the institution of the army would remain.

1.3 Nasser's policies, 1952–1970

Key questions

→ How successful were Nasser's domestic policies from the point of view of different sectors of Egyptian society: the poor peasants, the rural middle class, the feudal aristocracy, the industrialist and private entrepreneurs, and the state bureaucracy?

→ To what extent did Nasser change Egypt? Why did certain problems persist?

→ How successful were Nasser's foreign policies - as seen from the global perspective, the Arab perspective, and the Egyptian perspective?

→ What were the short- and long-term consequences of Nasser's foreign policies?

Key concepts

→ Consequences

→ Significance

→ Continuity

→ Perspectives

Nasser's development strategy

By 1954 Nasser had undisputed control over Egypt. He had emerged from the quasi-obscurity of the ranks of the armed forces to the centre of the political stage. The failed assassination attempt on his life had offered Egyptians a hero, a champion, a benefactor. He would free Egypt from the grip of the imperialists and release the *Fellahin* from the suffocating control of the wealthy landed aristocrats. Nasser and those loyal to him were now free to build their regime and fulfill these promises. All obstacles had been removed and so they could now put into effect the "national revolution", which, in the words of Nasser himself, would offer Egyptians "a better life, free from the chains of exploitation and underdevelopment in all their material and moral forms".

The new regime was committed to bringing about social and economic changes in order to solidify its support, tackle Egypt's underdevelopment and strengthen the power of the state apparatus. We refer to these policies as Nasser's "development strategy". The economist Riad el-Ghonemy breaks up Nasser's development strategy into two distinct phases:

- Phase one, from 1952 to 1956, was characterized by what he called "private enterprise economy".

- Phase two, from 1956 to 1970, saw a move towards greater state intervention and justified the expression "**state capitalism**".

state capitalism
State capitalism is when the state subsidizes capitalists. The system remains capitalist; there is a maximization of profit but production is "owned" by the state. In the case of Egypt, after 1957 the state started to take over companies belonging to individuals. Later, the state invested in major projects.

In Egypt the year 1956 witnessed a major shift in both its foreign and domestic policies. This was the year in which a new constitution was drafted, offering Egypt one single party, the National Union, which replaced the Liberation Rally and maintained Nasser as its president. Elections for the National Assembly were held a year later, with women voting for the first time in Egyptian history. The National Executive Committee of the Union, a government-selected body, screened the candidates, disqualifying a large number of them.

In the same year Egypt began to move away from the Western camp. Nasser announced the nationalization of the Suez Canal in 1956, which brought about a tripartite war involving the Israelis, the British, and the French. The assumed Egyptian victory in this Suez Canal War propelled Nasser into a leadership role throughout the region and led to the emergence of the United Arab Republic (UAR) in 1958. The establishment of the UAR meant that a new constitution was needed. The 1956 constitution was abolished and replaced with a provisional constitution that brought the larger region, Syria and Egypt, under its jurisdiction.

The year 1956 also saw a move towards greater state intervention in the economy and a greater concentration of power in the hands of the leader and the **state bureaucracy**. This trend accelerated during the 1960s: the July decrees of 1961 pushed Egypt further down the road to state capitalism as the state's share of the economy grew. In 1961 the secession of Syria from the UAR (see below) once again called for a new reorganization. This time, a congress was convened to discuss the 1962 Charter. Once this was adopted, elections followed in 1964 and Nasser was again nominated president.

The importance of cotton in Egyptian history

Alexandria's Cotton exchange first opened in 1865. It was where cotton merchants met and set the price of cotton, based on levels of demand and supply. Of the 35 registered cotton brokers in 1950, only two were Egyptian; the most influential cotton exporters were British. Nasser closed the Exchange in November 1952 and set a nominal price at which the government would buy cotton from the farmers. The purpose of this was to bring stability to the economy and give farmers a secure income.

Nasser reopened the Cotton Exchange in September 1955. Later, in the 1961 reforms, the Exchange was nationalized. Today a cotton museum traces its history: http://www.thecottonmuseum.com/en#b

Nasser's domestic policies

The problems facing the Egyptian economy were predominantly linked to Egypt's ties with the imperial power, namely Britain. Foreign investment had not only chosen *what* Egypt was to produce, it had made Egyptians totally dependent, passive and slow to move forward. The concentration on cotton production maintained Egypt as a predominantly backward rural economy that was vulnerable to the world market for cotton; Egypt's revenue fluctuated in relation to how much the world needed cotton. In addition, agriculture – primarily cotton production – was the biggest source of employment, so changes in the world price had an enormous effect on Egypt as a whole. This unhealthy situation caused economic instability.

state bureaucracy
State bureaucracy is a system of government where, instead of elected representatives, appointed state officials make decisions. For the sake of efficiency, every country needs a bureaucracy but in some countries, such as Egypt, the power of the state bureaucracy surpasses that of the elected representatives.

The changing price of cotton	
Years	Price of cotton per 50 kg (in Egyptian £)
1918–1927	7.8
1928–1947	3.1
1948–1952*	16
1952	12

*The effects of the Korean War

Source: Waterbury, J. *The Egypt of Nasser and Sadat: The Political Economy of Two Regimes*.

feddan
An Egyptian unit of area equivalent to
1.038 acres.

The slow economic development of the country had also kept the rural population, the *fellahin,* extremely poor and the gap between rich and poor relatively static. A tiny proportion (0.4 per cent) of the landowners held about a third of all cultivable land, while the remaining landowners controlled five **feddans** or less. At the bottom of the scale came the millions who owned no land at all but had to rent land in order to make a living. Owning land was therefore high on the wish list of most of the rural population. "Land hunger", as Waterbury calls it, raised the rents; sometimes the *fellahin* had to pay about 60 per cent of their income in rent to the landowner.

The solution to this problem was twofold:

- Firstly, it would be necessary to distribute land from the rich to the poor.

- Secondly, it was necessary to diversify and move the Egyptian economy away from being purely a rural one.

Agrarian reforms

The agrarian reform laws aimed to redistribute land by taking land away from large landowners and giving it to small ones. The former royal family's lands were entirely expropriated, and the law aimed to set a ceiling on the amount of land anyone could own. The idea, though not a new one, was met with opposition from Prime Minister Maher, who did not want to take such a drastic step against the landowning classes, but in September 1952 the problem was "resolved" when Maher was replaced by General Neguib. As soon as the government changed hands, Prime Minister Neguib passed the First Agrarian Reform Law (Law 178) on 9 September 1952. This was justified morally as well as politically. To quote Neguib, "A landless peasant is a demoralized man and defenceless person. A landed peasant is a man of spirits who will defend his land". Over the next 17 years Egypt would pass two more agrarian reform laws, in 1961 and 1969.

The first law limited land ownership to 200 feddans. A landowner was permitted to dispose of another 100 feddans as a donation to his wife and children, thus raising the ceiling to 300 feddans per family. The rest would be taken from them in return for government bonds and redistributed, in parcels of two to five feddans, to those who owned five feddans or less. The state retained ownership, so all farmers receiving land were under an obligation to pay back the loan to the state in instalments within 30 years. Those owning less than five feddans were obliged to join a land cooperative. The 1952 law also fixed a minimum wage and it became illegal to pay labourers less than 18 piasters a day (equivalent to 52 cents). Before the July Revolution the average wage for a labourer had been 8.5 piasters when, to keep them alive, a farmer needed 8 piasters per day for a donkey, 12 for a mule and 28 for a water buffalo. The second law (Law 127), passed in 1961, reduced the ceiling to 100 feddans per family. In 1963 foreign landowners had their land expropriated. Finally, in 1969, a third law (Law 50) was passed where the ceiling was halved to 50 feddans per owner, while maintaining 100 feddans for a family.

According to the figures provided by John Waterbury, which do not include 1969, the main beneficiaries of Nasser's reforms were the poorest *fellahin*. In 1952 those owning five feddans or less were in

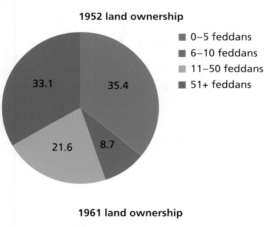

1952 land ownership

■ 0–5 feddans
■ 6–10 feddans
■ 11–50 feddans
■ 51+ feddans

33.1　35.4
21.6　8.7

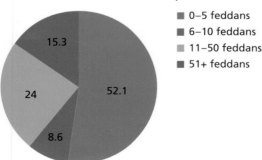

1961 land ownership

■ 0–5 feddans
■ 6–10 feddans
■ 11–50 feddans
■ 51+ feddans

15.3
24　52.1
8.6

▲ Percentage of land ownership in Egypt

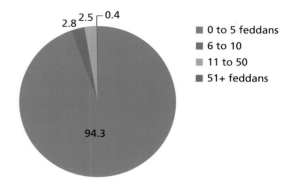

possession of 35.4 per cent of the total cultivable land; in 1961 this
figure rose to 52.1 per cent. At the other end of the scale, the richest
landowners started to control less land: those who owned 50 feddans
or more controlled 33.1 per cent of the land in 1952 but only 15.3 per cent
in 1961. The amount owned by the groups in the middle – the rural
middle class (6–50 feddans) – remained extremely stable.

The net takeover of land was 930,299 feddans and 318,000 families
benefited from this redistribution. The cultivable land in Egypt was,
however, 6 million feddans, so only a small percentage of the cultivable
land underwent reform. "The laws ... redistributed 13 per cent of
the total agricultural land among small tenants, in family units of
two feddans, on average representing only 10 per cent of the total
agricultural households".

The policies increased the number of small landholders. Land was
taken from the very wealthy and given to the poor, but the number of
poor farmers remained high. In 1952 those who owned five feddans
or less constituted 94.3 per cent of all landowners and by 1965 the
percentage had risen to 95.1. Consequently there were more very small
landholders but the numbers of those who owned more land remained
relatively stable. Society was thus transformed modestly; those who had
previously owned enormous plots of more than 200 feddans no longer
existed. The laws reduced the grave inequalities in land distribution and
the absolute poverty of those who now owned land for the first time.
However, the reforms did not succeed in giving land to everyone; in
1972 half the rural population was still landless. It can also be argued
that, by increasing the number of smallholdings, the economy as a
whole did not benefit and the poor remained poor.

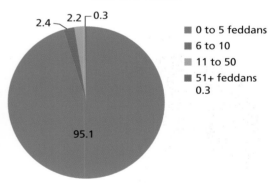

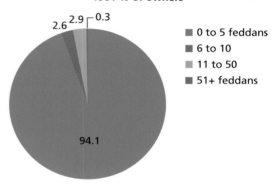

▲ Nasser handing documents to an Egyptian fellah in a land distribution ceremony in Minya in 1954

▲ Percentage of land owners in Egypt

Another feature of the reforms was the imposition of a rent freeze on land. Rents were fixed at seven times the tax on land and, despite the fact that the price of other commodities rose, land rents remained the same until 1976. Consequently, tenants had little incentive to move and landlords had even less of an incentive to make land improvements (Oweiss). This rigidity brought stagnation, which would explain the sharp drop in yield growth after 1963. According to Bent Hansen, "Probably the most serious allocation effect of the fixed rents is that there is no longer any mechanism (aside from the black market) to ensure that the most competent people cultivate the land".

These measures had as much a political and social objective as an economic one. They aimed to transform Egyptian society from a **feudal system** to a system managed directly by the state. Therefore there was a power shift in society. The 'rural middle class' came to replace the old feudal lords as the 'richest landlords'. Those *Fellahin* that gained mostly from the government's agrarian reforms were the new rural middle class. Recognizing the new revolutionary state apparatus as their "benefactor", they became the local overseers of the state in the countryside and in return the state was ready to turn a blind eye and allow them to benefit from the reforms. The very poor continued to be dependent and exploited. Inequalities, especially in income, persisted. "[The Revolution] wanted to liberate the *fellah* by abolishing large landownership ... but it handed over the political, economic, social and cultural leadership of the Egyptian countryside, not to the *fellahin* but to the state bureaucracy and to the class of small big landowners or big small landowners" (Louis Awad, an Egyptian intellectual and writer).

One channel through which the state bureaucracy "controlled" the rural districts politically was the cooperatives. These had started in 1952 with a membership of around 500 000. By 1970 around 5000 cooperatives existed with a membership of over 3 million. The cooperatives came under the supervision of the Ministry of Agriculture and were locally run by an elected council. Through the cooperatives, the government assisted the farmers in improving production: they offered them credit at very low interest rates, provided seeds, fertilizers, animals, machinery, transportation and storage facilities, and sent them agronomists. These "experts" were, however, often viewed as "the heavy hand of the government" because they followed government policies. These policies left many farmers unhappy. Mohammed Neguib alluded to this when he wrote: "Another criticism of our land reform is that we have given too much power to the Government-controlled cooperatives. Our cooperative programme is said to smack of authoritarianism". Although Neguib defended the policies, it is nonetheless interesting that he saw fit to raise that concern in his book. The richer farmers (the rural middle class) had more means to evade these measures than the smaller and poorer farmers. They took advantage of the cooperatives' offer of credit but avoided their more rigid dictates, such as prescriptive crop rotation.

When the 1969 reforms were announced, the enthusiasm of the early 1950s had clearly waned. Although the ceiling fell to its lowest, at 50 feddans, the amount of acreage allocated to redistribution was small. For Waterbury this explains why the Ministry of Agriculture never published its statistics of 1969. With this last law, the process of redistribution in Egypt came to an end.

feudal system

A feudal system is a way of structuring society so that economic and political power is in the hands of large landowners. In Egypt, the feudal lords became the symbol of the corrupt old regime.

The move towards industrialization

While recognizing the importance of agriculture for the Egyptian economy, the new regime was also fully aware of the need to industrialize. Without its own indigenous industry, the country would always remain dependent on the industrial nations. The regime also understood that the state would need to assume the bulk of this work because it was unlikely that the private sector would want to invest in such major projects. This did not, however, mean that the regime discouraged private investment.

The first phase, 1952–1956

In the first phase of industrialization – the phase referred to above as "private enterprise economy" – the policies of the new government aimed simultaneously at encouraging private investors and starting to build the public sector through state investment. In pursuit of the first objective, industrialists and private investors were offered a number of incentives. Law 26 in 1954 facilitated repatriation of earnings and allowed foreign investors to own up to 51 per cent of the shares in an Egyptian company. A new law also permitted foreign investors to have access to Egypt's underground resources; this was with a view to enticing petroleum companies to Egypt. Laws 430 in 1953 and 25 in 1954 offered tax exemptions to those investing in Egypt. A law was passed that lowered the import duties for raw materials and machinery. These measures reflect the pragmatic nature of Nasser's regime in the early years and bring into question the image of the hot-headed, anti-western socialist that would be associated with him in the years to come.

Unfortunately these incentives were not very successful. Between 1953 and 1961 foreign investment amounted to only £E8 million. Private investment, which was around £E30 million a year in the 1950s, had stagnated by the 1960s. The 1950s were not the most welcoming period for investors, in particular European investors. Neighbouring countries such as Tunisia, Morocco, and Algeria were in the middle of anti-colonial conflicts, thus rendering investment a little risky. Other Middle Eastern countries had also witnessed political disturbances, which again reduced the viability of investment. The Free Officers' land reform programme, infringing private property, had also provoked the mistrust of private investors. The absence of private investment rendered the task of developing the public sector that much more urgent.

In October 1952 (a month after the first Agrarian Reform Law) the Permanent Council for the Development of National Production was established. In this council civilian experts as well as army technicians met to discuss plans for long-term national development. The experts were fully aware of the need to put Egypt on the classic path of import substitution industrialization (ISI). In other words, they needed to produce what they would otherwise have imported. They also sought to promote regional development, reduce unemployment, and see that consumers' needs were met. Given the importance of agriculture as Egypt's main source of income, the industrial projects were aimed at boosting the agricultural sector. These included a project to construct a high dam at the site of the old Aswan Dam, built in 1902. This project would ensure a steady supply of water. Other projects included a fertilizer plant in Aswan, an iron and steel complex in Helwan, and desert reclamation in Tahrir Province.

These projects needed funding. In August 1954 the government requested $100 million in military and economic assistance from the US government. Washington, under pressure from the British, hesitated.

The second phase, 1956–1970

In the absence of funding from private investment or the United States, the government shifted towards a more coercive and authoritarian posture with regard to private ownership. Through **nationalization** and **sequestration**, Nasser's regime came to extend its control of the economy and the pattern of development moved further and further away from private entrepreneurship.

A large number of Egyptian entrepreneurs lost their assets and suffered at the hands of the regime's new economic policies during this second phase, but the most startling act of sequestration was announced on 26 July 1956, only a week after the United States withdrew its offer of credit. On that day, speaking from the balcony of the Alexandria Cotton Exchange (see page 29), the symbol of British economic domination, Nasser announced the nationalization of the Suez Canal.

The news came as a shock to the entire world. From nationalist anti-British rhetoric to the act of actually dispossessing Great Britain of its vital asset in Egypt, Nasser had taken a defiant step. "Today, citizens," he announced, "the Suez Canal has been nationalized and this decree has in fact been published in the Official Gazette and has become law. Today, citizens, we declare that our property has been returned to us … Our canal … How could it be otherwise when it was dug at the cost of 120 000 Egyptian lives?"

This was the beginning of a series of heavy-handed sequestrations. In the same month the Ministry of Industry was established, thus underlining the state's intention to replace the private sector as primary investor. The seizure of the Canal triggered a tripartite war (see below), at the end of which all French and British assets were taken over by the Egyptian government. In January 1957 all commercial banks, insurance companies, and commercial agencies for foreign trade were taken out of non-Egyptian hands. As the pace of sequestration grew, the state formed public holding companies (the Economic, the Misr, and the Nasr companies) to administer the newly acquired assets. At first these holding companies kept their managerial staff and competed with one another with the aim of increasing their efficiency and productivity.

In the same year the government presented Egypt's first industrial plan. The plan's objective of public investment was reached within three years, but private investors were once again not as forthcoming as the state had hoped. The state had invested £E90 million in state-run projects. This was done with a substantial loan from the USSR, signed in January 1958. The Ministry of Industry was gradually becoming the powerhouse of the regime and those in charge gained tremendous influence. All new industrial plants required a licence from the Ministry. In 1959 the government passed a law limiting profit distribution to stockholders and obliging stock companies to invest in state bonds.

nationalization
The process of taking a private industry or private assets into public ownership by a national government.

sequestration
The process of taking legal possession of assets.

The Suez Canal

The Suez Canal was a French company with headquarters in Paris, but Great Britain had acquired the majority of its shares. The company's assets were about £E95 million in 1956. Egypt's revenues in royalties had been £E2.3 million in 1955, rising to £E42 million in 1958 and £E77 million in 1962.

Class discussion

Who was the rightful owner of the Suez Canal?

The facts:

- Britain and France had built the Canal.
- Britain had purchased France's shares of the Canal.
- The Canal is situated in Egypt.

The first Five-Year Plan

In 1960 the first Five-Year Plan was launched. Its objective was to expand the consumer goods sector, promote industries with export potential and achieve an equitable regional distribution of industry. Its slogan, "From the needle to the rocket", set an ambitious objective for Egypt: become totally self-reliant within five years.

In July 1961 a series of socialist decrees further nationalized a considerable proportion of the non-agricultural sector. These included banks, shipping and insurance companies as well as firms in heavy and basic industry. The three existing holding companies were replaced by 39 state organizations grouping 438 companies. In October that year Nasser's policies became more vindictive. The state dispossessed and withdrew the political rights of a large number of "reactionary capitalists". A number were even arrested. The country's wealth was being concentrated into the hands of the public sector and private entrepreneurs were being discarded.

Nasser explained that these socialist decrees had become necessary because "an exploitative private sector seemed bent on milking the public sector and that if allowed it would be the major beneficiary of the Five Year Plan and not the masses". "The socialist solution", he wrote in the National Charter (see page 38), "was a historical inevitability imposed by reality". Waterbury explains this move by describing Nasser's tactic as a "zero sum game"; it was to be either "them" or the state. What was taken from the private sector would directly benefit the state. Where Nasser was probably mistaken was that the equation was not as simple as that; enlarging the public sector did not automatically increase its productive capacity. In the absence of competition and therefore incentive, the public sector under mediocre management could become a large and inefficient bureaucratic machine that could lead to economic stagnation.

By 1962 it was becoming apparent that the Plan was not functioning as efficiently as had been wished. Although the rate of annual growth remained high, per capita productivity did not rise. To make matters worse, imports did not go down; nor did exports go up. The country started to register serious balance of payment deficits. The public sector had grown too large. It was over-staffed and over-protected. This was the year Nasser presented the Charter, in which – instead of addressing the problems and offering a change of direction – for ideological reasons, he dug further into his model of "Arab socialism". He was indeed becoming a prisoner of his own discourse.

This realization would not become public until 1967, when it was clear that something had to be done. After a significant reshuffling of a number of highly positioned managerial staff, Nasser spoke at the opening of the Congress of Production on 18 March 1967. What he said to the attendees was summed up by Waterbury in the following way:

1   Management is a science whose rules do not change under socialism and capitalism.

2   Wages must be linked to production.

3   The ASU (Arab Socialist Union) should no longer interfere in the production process.

At this point Nasser's struggle to alter the economic system came to an end. The dismantling of the state capitalist system was to be left to his successor, Anwar Sadat.

Silencing the opposition

Although by 1954 political parties had been banned and replaced by the Liberation Rally, civil society was not yet completely suppressed. Autonomous forums that could potentially voice opposition, such as trade unions, universities, or the mosques, still existed. These "alternative centres of power" were, however, unacceptable to an authoritarian political system: "A basic feature of authoritarian political systems is the unwillingness ... to countenance the existence of alternative centres of power".

The regime had a harder time suppressing these groups because they had supported the Free Officers' coup. Nasser was also aware of the importance of having their backing. In the March crisis of 1954, when Nasser's authority was being challenged by Neguib and those who wanted a return to liberal democracy, mass demonstrations of workers demanding the continuation of military rule confirmed Nasser's leadership.

Nasser therefore had to tread carefully. His tactic was appeasement and repression at the same time. Concessions were given to appease, but repressive measures were available in case of opposition. Ultimately Nasser's regime acted as authoritarian regimes always do: it silenced any potential form of opposition by restricting civil rights; it curtailed the autonomy of "the centres of power", such as workers and student unions, by incorporating their members through containment and control; and it stifled all remaining opposition by ruthlessly suppressing it.

Controlling the unions

The trade unions had already, in August 1952, posed the first major challenge to the new government with their strike at Kafr al Dawwar, but their action had been brutally suppressed and those who stood accused were ostracized as "communists" and "traitors". In the words of one trade union veteran, "the executions were a regime stand against the communists and not the workers". A year later another strike of textile workers in Imbaba, a neighbourhood of Giza, met with a similar degree of repression. The army was sent in and around 3000 arrests were made. Militant trade unionists got the message; they would think twice about organizing another strike.

It was now time for the government to switch to "appeasement". As a counterbalance to the repressive measures, workers were offered a series of benefits: with the Law of Individual Contracts (December 1953) workers received an increase in severance pay, extended annual vacations, and free transportation and health care. Prior to this law the government had increased job security by making it harder for employers to make their workers redundant. These benefits, however, came at a cost: strikes were no longer permitted. The unspoken agreement was "no strike in exchange for no dismissal without cause".

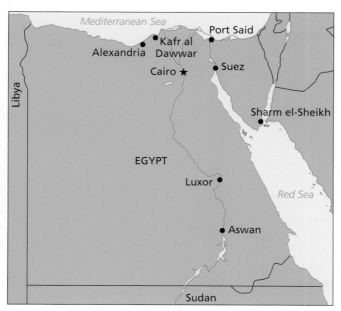
▲ Location of Kafr al Dawwar

Trade unions were not banned; on the contrary, Nasser wanted to prevent "a concentration of union power" and so he allowed their proliferation. The number of trade unions doubled and their membership tripled in the first six years of Nasser's rule. In 1957, with the aim of tightening control over the workers, the General Federation of Egyptian Trade Unions was born. This body, whose executive board was wholly appointed by the government, came to represent the workers throughout Nasser's regime.

Nasser had succeeded in incorporating the workers and thus eliminating their existence as an "alternative centre of power". He had also changed the workers' social status and given them positions in parliament and company boards. These kinds of privileges had been non-existent in Egypt before 1952.

Controlling the universities

The students proved to be a harder forum to silence. They, too, had pledged support for the Free Officers, but once the suppression of civil rights – such as the right to hold elections or the right to belong to a political party – was announced, the activists among them joined the ranks of the opposition. In March 1954 the students demonstrated in support of change and put up great resistance to the Revolutionary Command Council (RCC). To counter this, Liberation Rally offices, mainly consisting of government representatives rather than students, were established on university campuses to recruit supporters and intimidate opponents. After the establishment of the Arab Socialist Union in 1962 (see below), these offices were replaced by socialist youth organizations. The Ministry of the Interior employed "university guards" and informants to control student activities. The Ministry of Higher Education kept close surveillance on the recruitment of professors and controlled those who enrolled as students. They also offered incentives such as government posts to those who agreed to be incorporated.

The silencing of the student opposition, however, cannot only be explained by repression. Nasser's popularity in the country affected the student body as much as other sectors of society. Many students genuinely supported the regime and were proud of Nasser's achievements. Furthermore, the promise of a better future and better job opportunities, not to mention free education, were no doubt incentives that mattered to many students.

Controlling the mosques

The biggest challenge to Nasser's authority came from the mosques and in particular the Muslim Brothers. Nasser's stand on religion was ambivalent. In all his writings and speeches he proclaimed his strong adherence to religion. In the last pages of *The Philosophy of the Revolution*, he spoke of the "third circle" that bound Egyptians to the outside world, "the circle of our brethren-in-Islam" and he advocated the need to strengthen "the Islamic tie". However, in 1952, through the creation of the Ministry of Religious Endowments, *Awqaf*, the Free Officers had taken away the mosque's financial autonomy and in 1954, following the assassination attempt, they had banned the Muslim Brothers, executed some of its members, and arrested many more. Furthermore, Nasser's "Arab socialism", while not openly hostile to Islam, had a secular overtone. So in the 1960s, as the regime tightened its grip on all forms of potential opposition, Nasser once again found himself face to face with the Muslim Brothers.

▲ Al-Azhar University, *Jāmi'at al-Azhar*, founded in 970, is one of the most important centres of Islamic learning. In 1961 Nasser brought it under state control.

▲ Seyed Gutb, one of the leaders of the Muslim Brothers was accused of plotting to assassinate Nasser was hanged in 1966

In the summer of 1961, in the euphoria of the socialist decrees, Law 103 brought Al Azhar University, the world-renowned centre of Islamic learning in Cairo, under state control. Nasser appointed non-clerics to the university board and added scientific subjects to the curriculum. With the Muslim Brotherhood disbanded and through extending its control over Al Azhar, the regime was confident that it would be able to incorporate Islam into the system and thus silence it as a potential "centre of power". This confidence was seemingly premature. When a number of Muslim Brothers were released from prison in the late 1950s, they set about reconstructing their movement. They chose Seyed Qutb as their new spiritual leader and, under Qutb's leadership, the party grew in size and conviction. There was no doubt that its message clashed with Nasser's message and challenged the society that Nasser was constructing.

In the mid-1960s, discovering the revival of the Muslim Brothers, the state went on the offensive. Possessing Seyed Qutb's writings became a crime. A military tribunal court tried a number of the movement's leaders; they were accused of having once again plotted to assassinate Nasser. In August 1966, a number of leaders, including Seyed Qutb, were hanged. The execution of Qutb brought the threat of opposition to a temporary end. Nasser himself would not be challenged by this organization, but the movement would continue to proliferate and grow in the years to come.

The National Charter

After the secession of Syria from the United Arab Republic (see below) in September 1961, a new constitution was needed. Nasser planned to use the occasion to introduce some important changes. On 21 May 1962, he submitted a document called "The National Charter" to the inaugural session of the National Congress of the Forces of the People, which approved it on 30 June. With the Charter Nasser outlined the ideological foundation of Arab socialism and offered Egypt "a blueprint for the future". The Charter's slogan was "Freedom, Socialism and Unity". It addressed not just Egyptians but the "Arab Nation". This was fully in line with Nasser's foreign policy that aimed to unite the Arab Nation under his leadership.

The Charter also announced the creation of one single all-encompassing party, the Arab Socialist Union (ASU), *al-Ittiād al-Ištirākī al-'Arabī*. This political party would replace the National Union. Workplaces, factories, cooperatives, and businesses had each to form their individual branches of the ASU and, as a way to respect social parity, the new party insisted on fixed representation by occupation: at least 50 per cent of its membership had to be either workers or farmers. The aims and objectives of the Revolution could be attained only through a united voice, hence liberal, pluralist democracy was set aside as superfluous. The path offered to the Arabs was revolution. The text of the Charter dedicated a whole section to the "necessity of the revolution": "The revolutionary path is the only bridge, which the Arab Nation can cross to reach the future it aspires to". Nasser, however, distinguished his methods from others; the Arab Revolution followed a new approach and did not "blindly copy" existing revolutionary models.

The Charter's chapter entitled "True Democracy" gives us an insight into Nasser's aims and the rationale behind those aims. In this chapter he exposed the "appalling fraudulence" of the system of government that called itself "democratic" prior to the revolution and outlined six principles that he believed constituted "true democracy". In the light of these principles, we can have a better grasp of why some of the policies were introduced. The table on the next page is a summary of the principles and policies.

	Principles	Policies
1	*Political democracy cannot be separated from social democracy; in order to be "free to vote", a citizen needs to be free from exploitation, enjoy a fair share of the nation's wealth and be free from anxiety.*	This would explain policies of sequestration and nationalization; through public ownership, citizens would share the nation's wealth and be free from exploitation and anxiety.
2	*Political democracy cannot exist under the domination of any one class ... it is indispensable to liquidate the forces of reaction, deprive them of their weapons and prevent them from making any attempt to come back to power.*	This would explain the banning of political parties.
3	*The values of true democracy can only be guarded through national unity.*	This would explain the setting up of a single party, the Arab Socialist Union.
4	*Popular organizations, especially cooperatives and trade unions, can play an effective and influential role in promoting sound democracy.*	This would explain the importance given to these institutions.
5	*Criticism and self-criticism are among the most important guarantees of freedom. The most dangerous obstacle in the way of free criticism ... is the infiltration of reactionary elements.*	This would explain the banning of the opposition press, as they were regarded as the means through which 'reactionary elements' 'infiltrated.
6	*The new revolutionary concepts of true democracy must impose themselves [through] education ... the educational curricula in all subjects must be reconsidered according to the Principles of the Revolution.*	This would explain the tight control of the state over education.

▲ Summary of the principles and policies of the National Charter

In March 1964 elections for a National Assembly were held and a provisional constitution based on the Charter was put into effect. This constitution gave the president an exceptionally strong role. As head of state, he was in charge of the executive; he appointed and dismissed all the members of the cabinet as well as his vice president; he had the power to initiate, propose, approve, or disapprove laws. An interesting innovation came in the form of voting: the country was divided into 175 constituencies, each sending two representatives to the legislature. Both representatives had to be members of the ASU, literate and over the age of 30, but one of the two *had* to be either a worker or a farmer. This occupational representation reflected the importance that the Charter allocated to those two groups in its aim of restoring social justice and achieving "true democracy". Of the 360 representatives forming Egypt's second legislature since the revolution, half were workers and farmers, eight were women and ten were directly appointed by the president.

Evaluating Nasser's domestic policies

The agrarian reforms helped cement popular support for the RCC in the early years when its power was easily challenged by some of the more senior politicians such as those in the Wafd party. Through the redistribution of land, Nasser aimed to achieve "sufficiency and justice", which he claimed were the two supports of his brand of socialism. In the domain of agriculture, "the Arab application of socialism" did not entail transferring land to public ownership. On the contrary, he believed that land reform necessitated "the existence of individual ownership of land and the expansion of this ownership by extending the right to own to the largest number of wage earners".

However, Nasser's agrarian reforms could be criticized for having tried too hard to reorganize traditional agriculture. They introduced compulsory crop rotation, they forced farmers to consolidate fragmented holdings and, last but not least, they introduced cooperatives, which in the long run became the symbol of the growth of the state bureaucracy's power and control. Also, as poverty persisted, the farmers used the survival strategy that they knew best: they had more children. This in turn placed major obstacles in the way of Egypt's economic prospects. "No matter how determined the state, its investment efforts would be wiped out as long as the population grew in excess of 2.5 per cent in annum". Egypt's population growth remained higher than 2.5 per cent throughout this period. Nasser addressed the issue in the Charter, but he believed that a rise in production would counterbalance the problem: "The doubling of national income every ten years allows for a rate of economic development which greatly exceeds the rate of increase in the population". However, since national income did not rise as fast as he had hoped, the rate of population growth became a serious problem. In 1966 the Higher Council for Family Planning, *al-majlis al-ala li-tanzim al-usra*, was established and the Egyptian General Family Planning Association, supported by the Ministry of Social Affairs, was formed. On 6 August that year, the newspaper *Al Ahram* announced that 2,850 family planning clinics had opened throughout the country. However, it was not until 1972 that the birth rate started to fall, so the high population growth still hampered the economic reforms.

As for the expansion of the public sector, although there was a rational basis for all the projects, they were not always adequately studied and the RCC became irrational in the pursuit of its objectives. The land reclamation project in Tahrir Province is a good illustration of this. The project aimed to increase the land available for agriculture – hence the expression "horizontal expansion" – in order to increase the country's revenue. The idea was a perfectly viable one and its aims were totally rational: Egypt used only 4 per cent of its total surface area productively. In the pursuit of its objectives, however, its promoters became a little unrealistic. A new model of society was to be introduced, with large, mechanized state-owned farms. Villages were to be self-contained, with schools, clinics, and recreational facilities. They would ideally attract many people and relieve the overcrowded urban areas.

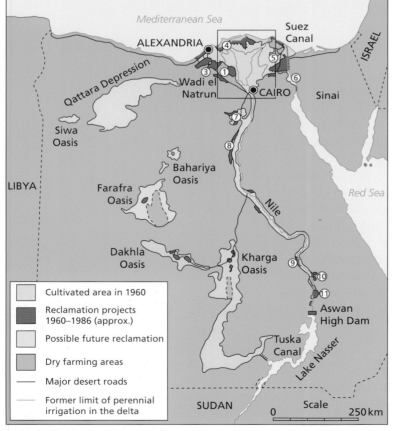

▢	Cultivated area in 1960
▣	Reclamation projects 1960–1986 (approx.)
▢	Possible future reclamation
▨	Dry farming areas
—	Major desert roads
⋯	Former limit of perennial irrigation in the delta

▲ Tahrir irrigation project

The Tahrir project was overambitious to start with, but it was also gravely mismanaged. It was not until 1964 that the soil was tested and it was found to be of poor quality; some of the irrigation grids that had been installed were unsuitable for the soil; there was no drainage system. More and more money went into the project at the expense of traditional farming. By 1970 only a third of the area was producing anything.

Between 1960 and 1970 £E483 million was invested in new projects, but only £E192 million was spent on improving and increasing existing yields from traditional agriculture. On 23 July 1969 Nasser publicly acknowledged the failure of the land reclamation programme. The Tahrir project illustrated the dangers of an overzealous bureaucracy whose objectives had become very personal: while attempting to "reinvent" the Egyptian farmer, the bureaucrats were neglecting the basic needs of the existing Egyptian farmer.

Nasser justified these authoritarian measures in the economic field by promoting the idea of nationalism: he was placing Egypt's economy beyond the reach of western economic interference, which he strongly believed (probably rightly) did not have Egypt's interests at heart. The anticipated private investors' contribution had not materialized and this inflated the power of the state. In the long run, however, this form of state capitalism did not offer Egypt a sound economic infrastructure to face external challenges. Too much was in the hands of the public sector, which had become a massive state bureaucracy, too large to manage. In the opinion of Robert Mabro, "Nationalization is ultimately a political action related to Nasser's persistent drive for hegemony". The public sector was the ultimate authoritarian tool – the platform through which the state controlled the people. Maintaining it served a political purpose rather than an economic one.

Nasser's rejection of democracy and the establishment of a single party – as "defended" in the Charter – served a similar authoritarian purpose. The Charter made valid criticisms of the previous system of government, as a system that had served the purpose of a landed aristocracy. By concentrating power within the framework of one large institution, the state, and giving it the ultimate power of decision-making, Nasser's regime had created a new "aristocracy" of its own. While not born into its ranks, the new aristocrats/elites, the rich middle classes, and the state bureaucracy used every means possible to maintain their newly gained privileges through nepotism and corruption.

Egyptian society had changed. There had been a shift in the elites. The poor remained poor and exploited. The new elites brought with them a new discourse; they also had a different set of priorities. They remained closer to the people culturally and linguistically, but maintained the gap in terms of rights and privileges.

Nasser's foreign policy aims

Nasser's first and foremost ambition was to "free" Egypt from imperialism and consequently offer Egypt a more active role in world politics. This, therefore, defined the main traits of Egypt's foreign policy in the Nasser era. In the pursuit of these objectives, he was passionate and at times extremely emotional. He used tactics that appeared rash and risky. Some of the risks

ATL Thinking and research skills

Over the 16 years of Nasser's presidency, *Time* magazine chose him for its cover page six times. Research these cover pages and discuss the message they each offer the reader. How do you think public opinion would have been affected by the way in which Nasser is portrayed?

he took paid off; others did not. His decisions forced Egyptians to the battlefront, brought about many deaths and finally caused his own. Without a doubt, in the course of Nasser's rule Egypt did come to play a more active role in world politics: the world's attention became fixed on Egypt.

Egypt's move away from the western camp

To understand and evaluate this shift, it is important to remember the original platform of the Free Officers, which was "Egypt for Egyptians". They had promised to "rid Egypt" of the imperialist stranglehold that had since the 1880s suffocated and stalled Egypt's development.

First on the agenda was therefore Egypt's relationship with Great Britain. The charter of the Liberation Rally had called for the unconditional British withdrawal from the Nile valley. Their ultimate ambition was to eliminate British power from both Egypt and the Arab world. On 19 October 1954 the RCC signed an agreement with Britain over the Canal Zone. After long and complicated discussions, they finally reached the following compromise: for the next seven years the British would continue to man the Canal Zone but as "technicians" rather than uniformed soldiers. British troops would have 20 months to evacuate the site, but would be permitted to return if the region – Egypt, any other Arab country, or Turkey – came under attack. The agreement was not a great victory for the RCC; clearly the British would continue to wield a great deal of power.

As a counterweight to the British, the RCC sought military aid from Washington – aid that the United States would have been favourable to had it not been for pressure from Britain. Winston Churchill, the British Prime Minister, argued that aid should come from *both* the British and the Americans. Once again, Nasser felt the British stranglehold.

The Cold War was very quickly dividing up the world into two adversarial zones, with each side trying to extend the size of its zone. In the Middle East, the proposal to group a number of countries into the western camp came in 1955 in the form of CENTO, the Central Treaty Organization, also known as the Baghdad Pact. The proposal suggested a military alliance bringing together Iran, Pakistan, Turkey, and Iraq, with Great Britain. The objective was to form a military bloc against the USSR, but Nasser interpreted it as an attempt by the British to isolate Cairo. This is why, when the opportunity arose to attend the non-aligned conference three months later, not surprisingly, Nasser jumped at the opportunity. In April 1955 he attended the conference in Bandung, Indonesia, and lobbied for a large number of resolutions condemning the colonial powers in Africa. On his return, Nasser declared Egypt's **"positive neutralism"**.

In Bandung he had rubbed shoulders with world leaders such as Nehru, Sukarno, and Tito and had emerged on to the world scene. This boosted his confidence and made him extremely popular, which angered the British even more.

Removing Britain's influence was, however, not for Nasser synonymous with discarding the United States. On the contrary, it would appear that in the early years Nasser tried to build, in spite of British interference, an independent relationship with the USA. In early 1956 Nasser turned to Washington and the International Bank for Reconstruction and Development (IBRD) for a loan of $200 million towards financing a high

positive neutralism
This expression was used during the Cold War by countries that actively and consciously sought not to adhere to either side. These countries presented themselves as the third force and tried to recruit countries to their cause. They were also known as "non-aligned nations".

dam in Aswan. The Bank agreed. A few months later, however, following Nasser's recognition of the People's Republic of China as well as his attendance at Bandung – both considered hostile moves against the West – Washington decided that Egypt had positioned itself in the opposing camp and the bank reversed its decision. This news reached Nasser on 19 July; seven days later he announced the nationalization of the Suez Canal. The British troops would be asked to leave the Zone. The agreement signed with the British in 1954 was annulled and the revenue from the canal would now be used to finance the construction of the High Dam at Aswan.

The Suez (Tripartite) War

The nationalization of the Canal was a major blow to the British. Similarly, the French also had a historical connection to the Canal, and their hostility to Nasser was aggravated by Nasser's support for the Algerian National Liberation Front. Israel also had a stake in this story: Nasser was their enemy and his popularity in the Arab world only strengthened the Palestinian cause. Furthermore, he had since 1955 closed the Tiran Straits, thereby blocking Israel's access to the Red Sea. Representatives from the three countries therefore met and put together a plan to overthrow Nasser's regime.

▲ Nasser being interviewed by American journalist Edward R. Murrow in November 1956

On 29 October 1956, the Israeli army attacked Sinai and advanced towards the Canal. The following day the British and the French issued an ultimatum to both Egypt and Israel. It demanded the immediate withdrawal of their troops ten miles east and west of the Canal in order to ensure freedom of navigation along the Canal. The Israelis complied, as had been decided. Egypt refused, as had been expected. On 31 October France and Britain attacked Egypt. On 5 November French and British paratroopers landed in Port Said, which introduced the Soviet Union into the story; the USSR threatened to enter the conflict in support of Egypt. Within a few days the region found itself on the verge of a world war.

President Eisenhower was furious. Two of his NATO allies, France and Britain, had acted without even consulting him. They were endangering world peace merely to maintain their imperial positions in Africa, a position that in the eyes of Eisenhower was impossible to defend. He took the matter to the UN General Assembly where he secured a resolution demanding immediate withdrawal of foreign forces from Egyptian soil. American pressure worked. The Anglo–French forces withdrew their troops by December. Israeli soldiers remained until March the following year. The UN despatched an emergency peacekeeping force (UNEF) to Sinai. UNEF would ensure that the Straits of Tiran would remain open.

This short war had cost the lives of approximately 3000 Egyptian soldiers and was not a military victory. However, since it ended the British presence in the Canal Zone, it was pronounced a major political victory for Egypt. It greatly increased Nasser's popularity both at home and in the Arab world. Indeed, Suez was proclaimed as an "Arab" victory.

Egypt's move towards the Soviet camp

The relationship between Egypt and the USSR was one of convenience for both sides. Although Nasser's policies underlined the need for social justice and on more than one occasion he spoke vindictively of capitalism and capitalists, his brand of socialism was never based on the Soviet model. In fact, his regime had had numerous clashes with trade unionists and his prisons were constantly filled with communists. He accused communists of serving the interest of another country and therefore questioned their loyalty to Arab nationalism. In 1955, however, he had purchased arms from a communist country, Czechoslovakia. Due to the arms embargo imposed after the 1948 war, no other country was prepared to supply arms to Egypt.

In 1958 he turned to the Soviet Union for a loan because he needed the money for the Aswan Dam project, which was of crucial importance to the future of Egypt. Nikita Khrushchev, the Soviet leader, agreed to offer Egypt the loan because the USSR needed to extend its sphere of influence in the Middle East and the Mediterranean, a region that was predominantly in the western sphere of influence. Khrushchev's statement to the 21st Congress of the Communist Party in February 1959 revealed the pragmatic nature of this relationship: "… differences in ideological views must not interfere with the development of friendly relations between our countries".

Consequently, both Khrushchev and Nasser trod cautiously and maintained a working relationship. In October 1958 the Soviets agreed to offer Egypt technical assistance in addition to the loan. The Aswan project started in January 1960 and Khrushchev was the guest of honour at the inauguration of its first phase in May 1964. This relationship caused the United States great concern and it had far-reaching consequences for the entire region. Nasser was portrayed as the ideological "enemy" of the West and the West's allies. This created a division within the Arab countries and created enemies for Nasser. It also solidified the western countries' relationship with Israel because, from a Cold War perspective, it was their only reliable ally in the region.

The United Arab Republic (UAR)

In the final section of his book *The Philosophy of the Revolution,* Nasser dwelt on the concept of "place". He wondered what "positive role" Egypt should play in this "troubled world" and in which region or place it should play that role. This was, of course, a rhetorical question and the answer simply underlined Nasser's plans for Egypt. Egypt belonged to the Arab Circle, the African Circle and the Muslim Circle and, as a consequence of its geographical location, it had to shoulder grave responsibilities. While in his foreign policy Nasser pursued all three to some extent, it is within the first circle that he left his greatest imprint. As he said himself, "There is no doubt that the Arab Circle is the most important of all these circles and the circle most closely connected with us".

The 1956 Suez War had propelled Nasser into the role of infallible leader, but, instead of enjoying this role as an Egyptian and savouring it with his compatriots, Nasser chose this moment to be an Arab. He insisted that Egyptians were "Arabs of Egypt" and that the victory was an Arab victory. Although the leaders of the neighbouring Arab states were not enchanted with these words and, indeed, started to view him as a threat to their authority, a less defined entity appreciated this "Arabism". "Arabism," wrote Haykal, a journalist close to Nasser, "took him for its hero and lifted him out of Egypt into an inter-Arab international role".

▲ Monument of the Arab-Soviet Friendship, commemorating the completion of Aswan High Dam

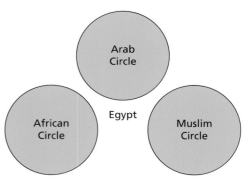

Arabism or pan-Arabism, an ideology that sees Arabs as one nation with no state boundaries, came about during the 1940s through Michel Aflaq and Salah Bitar, the founders of the Baath (Renaissance) party. Nasser advocated similar views, not as a follower of the Baath movement but as a result of his outrage at the way Arabs had been subdued by non-Arabs in history. To convince his readers of the "need for unity" in *The Philosophy of the Revolution*, he outlined the Arab nations' sources of strength. These were:

- their geographical closeness to one another

- their location on the globe giving them access to three continents

- the oil that existed in abundance under the ground of their nations.

By the time he presented the Charter in 1962, he not only spoke of Arab unity but also defined the form this unity would take: socialism.

These ideas indeed materialized in a somewhat unexpected manner. Among the Arab states, Syria was the most unstable. Shaken by a number of military coups, it was governed by a broad front that included members of the Baath and the National parties as well as communists. Fearing the growing influence of the communists, a delegation came to visit Nasser in January 1958, seeking union with Egypt. Although Nasser imposed stringent preconditions for this unity, the Syrians agreed and the United Arab Republic, *al-Jumhūriyyah al-ʾArabiyyah al-Muttahidah*, was born in February 1958. In a somewhat hasty manner, they put a constitution together, held elections and Nasser became the president of the UAR.

The Syrio–Egyptian project proved, however, to be short-lived. Within two years the Syrians had realized that union for Nasser was incorporation into Egypt and in September 1961 Syria seceded from the Union. Nasser submitted to the Syrian wish, but nonetheless kept the idea of a United Arab Republic alive, in case at a later date other Arabs chose to enter into such a union. In 1963 there was a second attempt at unity, this time bringing three Arab countries together: Iraq, Egypt, and Syria. In April a formal agreement was signed, but the project never came to fruition; ideological differences between them became a heavy counterweight to the ethnic and cultural affinity that "Arabism" proposed.

The failure of the Syrio–Egyptian experiment was mainly due to the differences between the two countries; whereas Egypt was a stable country with a popular ruler and a planned economy that was seemingly well managed, Syria was an unstable country, suffering from divisions within the ranks of its leadership. The Egyptians therefore (wrongly) believed that the Syrians were looking for their brand of social, political and economic "stability" and that, once the union was established, they could simply export their policies into Syria. This clearly was not how the Syrians had seen the union.

The idea and, later, the collapse of the UAR had important repercussions in the region. It was a warning to the existing heads of state to keep a tighter control of their opposition. It was also a warning to the West, which consequently increased its presence in the Arab countries. British troops were sent to Jordan and American troops to Lebanon. Within Egypt, Syria's secession became an excuse to plunge Egypt further into the socialist path – and it was in the following year that Nasser presented the National Charter.

▲ The Arab Nation: this diagram shows the location of the Arabic-speaking countries

The failure of the union was a major blow to Nasser personally. However, by maintaining the UAR as a possibility, he retained his ideas about the unity of the Arab Nation and refused to admit that he had been wrong. Was the UAR experiment an illustration of Nasser's obsession with power? Maybe. One has to remember, however, that it was not Nasser who had initiated the idea of union, but Syria. The UAR idea probably better illustrates Nasser's conviction that he was right. In other words, if he imposed economic, social and political changes on Syria, it was because these reforms were *the only way to proceed.* Derek Hopwood addresses this point and quotes extracts from Nasser's speech given on 16 October from the Presidential Palace to the people of Egypt after the dissolution of the union with Syria. In the four lines that Hopwood chooses, the words "I" or "my" recur eight times: "I have chosen to spend the past days thinking ... I thought about our people everywhere ... I wanted my choice to be theirs, and my attitude to be an expression of theirs ... I say to you now that I have chosen ... and my choice was that the road of revolution should be our road". It is this conviction that best underlines the authoritarian character of Nasser's regime.

The Yemen episode

Another attempt at Arab unity came with North Yemen, an Islamic theocracy in the southern part of the Arabian Peninsula. This episode, however, was further proof of "Arab disunity". In 1962, following a military coup aiming to overthrow the leader/imam of Yemen and establish a republic, civil war broke out. The loyalist forces sought assistance from Saudi Arabia and Jordan, whereas the military went to Nasser for help. Egyptian soldiers, officially referred to as UAR soldiers, were sent and they fought until 1967 to help the republicans. This war, which Nasser justified as part of his "Arab unity" project, was a major drain on Egypt's finances. The much-needed economic reforms suffered enormously because money was being poured into this war. Furthermore, Egyptian *fellahs* were taken off the land and sent to fight a war whose purpose remained unclear to them. The war lasted five years and involved 60–70 000 soldiers at its height, of whom approximately 26 000 never returned. This episode slowly started to affect Nasser's popularity.

The Yemeni civil war ended in victory for the republican forces. Although this result may to some extent be attributed to Nasser's decision to send troops there, it nonetheless remained a decision that he regretted. He had landed himself in an embarrassing situation, fighting Arabs while he preached Arab unity and spending money on war rather than on much-needed industrialization.

Confrontation with the State of Israel

Nasser's "Arab consciousness" had started, according to his personal account, when as a student he had demonstrated against the Balfour Declaration, the document that promised "a national home for the Jewish people in Palestine". This "consciousness", in other words his pro-Palestinian posture, was present throughout his rule. It raised tensions with Egypt's newly settled neighbour, Israel, and put Egyptian soldiers on the battlefront twice.

Clashes with Israel started in 1955 when the Israelis retaliated against Palestinian border incursions by attacking and destroying the Egyptian headquarters in Gaza, killing 38 people. Although, compared with the wars to come, this raid was a minor incident, it nonetheless had a far-reaching impact on Nasser's foreign policy as a whole. Following this event, Egypt decided to defy the arms embargo that had been put into effect after the 1948 war. Czechoslovakia was the country that responded to their request for arms but, by signing the agreement with them in August 1955, Nasser inadvertently offered the Soviet camp a trump card.

After the Suez Crisis of 1956, the position of Egypt towards Israel hardened considerably. The Israelis clearly viewed Nasser's rising popularity and his belligerent discourse as a major threat. However, after the US/UN intervention and the presence of UNEF in Sinai, the two countries pursued only a propaganda war.

The "War over Water"

In January 1964 a summit meeting of the Arab League was convened in Cairo. One of the points on the agenda was the plan to divert the Jordan River. This "War over Water" would be one of the long-term causes of the 1967 War. As a result of the armistice lines drawn up in 1949, Israel, Jordan and Syria had to share the waters of the Rivers Jordan and Yarmuk. In 1955 the Jordan Valley Unified Water Plan, allocating a water quota for each country, was drawn up. Although the plan was rejected by the Arab League nations, Israel went ahead and, with the completion of its National Water Carrier project in 1964, started siphoning water from the Sea of Galilee. The January meeting in Cairo viewed Israel's action as threatening and issued a statement menacing Israel with "collective Arab military preparations". They also decided to put into effect a plan that would divert the water in such a way as to reduce Israel's water supply by 35 per cent. Israel responded by stating that such a project would infringe Israel's sovereign rights. Other than clashes on the Syrio–Israeli border, nothing concrete came of the threat issued by the Arab League, but the issue remained unresolved.

The 1967 War (The Six Day War)

The 1967 War started with a pre-emptive air strike by the Israelis on 5 June. The circumstances that led the Israelis to carry out this action are complex and, as is often the case, each side has its own narrative. According to Steven Cook, two factors pushed Nasser to raise the stakes in the months prior to this event:

1. Between April and May clashes along the Syrio–Israeli border had escalated; in April the Israeli air force shot down six Syrian MiG-21s and in May Nasser received a Soviet report that Israeli forces were moving towards the Syrian border. Both of these incidents put pressure on Nasser, the acclaimed leader of the Arab world, to react.

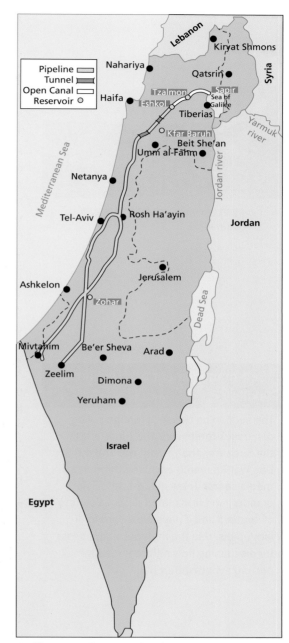

▲ The route of the Israeli National Water Carrier

▲ Egyptian prisoners are held during the Six Day War

Self-management and research skills

The section on Nasser's foreign policy discusses three wars: the Triparticle or the Suez War, the Yemeni war and the Six Day War Research each one through a media search (newspapers, television, or radio) and find material from a variety of sources and if possible a variety of languages. Use the material as the basis for discussing how different media portray events differently.

2   Since UNEF had been placed in Sinai, Arab leaders hostile to Nasser accused him of "hiding behind the UN". This left Nasser with a dilemma: should he ignore them and tarnish his reputation as leader of the Arab world, or act? Nasser chose the second option.

Nasser's decision was the ultimate example of his risk-taking and his unsound foreign policy. The Egyptian army was already involved in the Yemeni war and clearly not ready to participate in a war against Israel.

First, Egypt issued a statement asking for the withdrawal of UNEF; taking "peacekeeping" forces out could be interpreted as an intention to attack. Then Nasser announced the closure of the Tiran Straits, a matter that Israel had made clear in 1956 that they regarded as *casus belli*: they would go to war if the Straits were closed to Israeli shipping. In response, on 5 June Israel attacked.

The Six Day War, as it is commonly known, was a massive defeat for Egypt: 300 aircraft, 900 tanks, 500 artillery pieces, and 10000 vehicles were either captured or destroyed. Between 10000 and 15000 soldiers were killed in action and 500 were captured. About 250000 Egyptians became refugees. On 9 June a ceasefire was announced.

Evaluating Nasser's foreign policies

Nasser's "foreign adventures" clearly gave Egypt regional as well as global stature. Although the end of his rule, with Egypt's defeat in the 1967 War, was not glorious, in the course of his leadership there were moments of glory, which may have been intentional or unintentional.

From a global perspective, Nasser's policies left none of the actors indifferent:

* To the British, Nasser was an undisputed demon who forced them out of Egypt in a somewhat humiliating fashion. In the words of one historian, Britain left the Middle East "not with a roar, but with a whimper".

* For the United States, Nasser offered at first a potential pro-western client state. The decision to place Egypt in the opposing camp and therefore eventually demonize Nasser was to a large extent circumstantial and Britain had an important role to play in that choice.

* The Soviet Union considered Egypt a useful tool. Their relationship satisfied both their aims, even though it proved to be a costly one for Nasser.

* The Israelis regarded Nasser as a real threat to the state of Israel's existence; Egypt was the biggest of its Arab neighbours with the largest army and, with Nasser as its leader, it now had the most vocal pro-Palestinian/anti-Israeli discourse, potentially capable of arousing Arab sentiments in other Arab countries too.

* From the Arab perspective, Nasser's rule was disturbing. His policy of disregarding state boundaries and uniting the Arab Nation brought into question the legitimacy of existing rulers. His rapprochement with the USSR increased the West's vigilance in the region, which

took away the autonomy of some of the Arab rulers. The idea of Arab unity, attractive as it may have seemed, was in practice unworkable: the existing Arab states were unwilling to give up their rights. It was therefore a dream that for a while occupied the Arab people and promised them a more powerful existence. But in the end the dream was, as dreams often are, unreal.

The Egyptian people were the ones who suffered most as a result of Nasser's rash foreign policy decisions. They were the ones who paid with their lives when unprepared and unnecessary wars were declared. They also paid with their meagre savings because their economies financed the wars. They were, however, also the ones who enjoyed the euphoria of the moment when Nasser was subjecting the world to his views.

Culture and Nasser's use of the media

"Throughout their struggle against imperialism ... [the Egyptian] people [are] determined to establish new social relations, based on new values to be expressed in a new national culture". Forging new values and a new national culture also becomes a useful way for an authoritarian ruler to increase his support. The media and culture were excellent tools of persuasion in forging "the new national culture" and Nasser was fully aware of this. Even though educational opportunities had greatly expanded and the percentage of children receiving primary education rose from 50 to 90 per cent in towns and 75 per cent in the rural districts. Egypt remained primarily a country with a low literacy rate and a strong oral tradition in which images and sounds were far more accessible than the written word. Furthermore, given that the Arab world shares the same language, Nasser's message travelled beyond Egypt's frontiers. Two important tools that spread the message were the cinema and the radio.

The cinema

The first full-length feature film in Egypt had been produced in 1927 and since the 1930s Egypt had been known as the "Hollywood of the Orient". In 1952 Nasser therefore found not only a well-established film industry producing up to 50 films a year, but also an audience eager to fill the cinema halls. Putting the two together, he had a ready-made platform to influence the masses. Joel Gordon, in an account of Abd el Halim Hafiz, a popular singer and a film star in the Nasserist era, describes a meeting between the two men. In November 1952, the star had been summoned to the headquarters of the military junta, where Nasser spoke to him of the "importance of art in building a new society and anointed him as the voice of the new era". Abd el Halim Hafiz was, in the words of Nasser, a national treasure, *tharwa quawmiyya*.

Abd el Halim's movies were melodramatic and celebrated middle- and lower-middle-class virtues. He often played the romantic hero falling desperately in love with a lady much wealthier than him. Depending on whether the setting was pre-revolutionary or not, the young man would overcome the class boundaries, or not. The movies were critical of the past and painted an optimist picture of the Nasserist reforms.

▲ Abd el Halim Hafiz, photographed in the 1960s

In 1961 the film industry was nationalized. Egyptian movies were highly popular in the rest of the Arab-speaking world. Thus Nasser's message travelled beyond Egyptian borders.

The radio

Another means through which Egyptian views were exported was the radio. The Free Officers were fully aware of its importance, both inside and outside the country. The radio was a particularly useful propaganda tool: it was cheap, entertaining, and accessible in remote areas, especially in regions where people could not read. *Sawt al Arab* (Voice of the Arabs) was aired for the first time on 4 July 1953 as a half-hour radio programme. By the end of its lifetime in 1967 it was being broadcast for 15 hours a day and had become one of the most influential media tools in the Arab world, being compared today to Al Jazeera. At the height of its popularity, the station claimed to have received 3000 letters from its listeners every day. Ahmad Said, its chief announcer, became a recognizable voice throughout the Arab world.

Voice of the Arabs was based in Cairo and it came directly under the tutelage of the Ministry of National Guidance. Nasser once described the radio as his way of "reaching his power base". The programmes were mainly news, commentary, press reviews, interviews, and, most importantly, music. Patriotic songs known as *wataniyyat*, sung by popular singers such as Umm Kulsum and Abd el Halim Hafiz, were the most attractive feature of the station. Their songs became part of Egypt's cultural heritage: through the radio broadcasts they were heard and re-sung throughout the Arab world. The commentaries served as a tool to promote Nasser's views, especially in relation to his arch-enemies: imperialists, Zionists and Arab reactionary leaders.

Anas Alahmed analysed two of the programmes that illustrated how the radio served as propaganda. The first was called *Truth and Lies*, in which the announcer would read out anti-Nasserist articles, dismiss them as lies and then state "the truth". The other, called *Do not forget*, reminded its listeners of all the wrongs that had been done to the Arab world.

The language used for broadcasting was colloquial Arabic, *ammiyya*, as distinct from the literary Arabic used by officials. This brought it closer to its public. The use of "we" when referring to the Arab world was also an interesting way of reaching out to the Arab people as one entity and forging this identity. It served Nasser's idea of "Arab unity".

The radio station's popularity came to an abrupt end when the "truths" turned out to be lies. When the 1967 War broke out, Ahmad Said continued to announce to his listeners that the Egyptian forces were winning, when it had become clear that the defeat was massive. The radio had by 1967 outlived its purpose.

The "post-1967" Nasser

On 9 June 1967 Nasser appeared on Egyptian television a broken man. He accepted responsibility for Egypt's setback (*al naqsab*) and announced his decision to resign. He said he planned to "return to the ranks of the citizenry" and do his duty as "any other citizen". Millions poured out on to the streets in protest. In response to the public outcry, Nasser took back his resignation and promised to stay "until a time that we can rid ourselves of enemy aggression".

In the ensuing months, accusations, arrests, and trials of "those responsible" for the defeat followed. There was a purge of high-ranking officers from the army and the air force. Commander-in-Chief Amer was also accused of conspiracy against Nasser; he committed suicide in his cell in August that year.

Nasser also used the occasion to re-evaluate some of his polices. In the economic sector, where productivity had seen a sharp plunge, he toned down his socialist discourse and reduced the interference of the ASU. In March 1968 he announced a "mandate for change" and demanded that certain "centres of power" be cleansed. Similar modifications were heard in relation to the other Arab leaders. He now needed the support of wealthy countries such as Saudi Arabia. With regards to Israel, however, the tone remained the same. In March 1969 he started a war of attrition, attacking Israeli soldiers in Sinai. This resulted in bloody reprisals, but it was also a prelude to greater superpower interest in the region, which is precisely what his successor Anwar Sadat would achieve.

As a leader who underlined the absolute need for Arab unity, Nasser's last act was extremely fitting. In September 1970 an emergency Arab Summit meeting was convened in Cairo, to address the Jordanian–Palestinian crisis known as "Black September". Nasser succeeded in getting both King Hussein of Jordan and Yasser Arafat, the chairman of the Palestinian Liberation Organization, to talk. The summit concluded its work on 28 September, hours before Nasser died of a heart attack. He was 52 years old.

> ## TOK discussion
>
> This chapter on Nasser has made extensive use of his book *The Philosophy of the Revolution Falsafat al Thawra*, published in 1954.
>
> a) Evaluate the strengths and weaknesses of this book as a source.
>
> b) Do you think Nasser's version of events may have left certain things out? Why?
>
> c) Why do you think it was included in this narrative?

▲ Nasser mediating between Arafat and King Hussein at the emergency Arab League summit in Cairo on 27 September 1970

<table>
</table>

ATL **Research and communication skills**

The shaping of collective memory is sometimes prescribed, but it is often "hand picked" by the community itself. Look for an example of collective memory.

a) How is this event remembered in your country, in your town and by your family?

b) In the example of your choice, was the "memory" prescribed or selected?

c) Are there other "narratives" of the same story? If so, why? Consider what goes into the process of writing history?

collective memory
How a whole community selects its memory collectively; what a community chooses to remember.

Nasser's legacy

In the last section of *The Philosophy of the Revolution*, Nasser writes about a play called *Six Characters in Search of an Author* written by the Italian dramatist Luigi Pirandello (1867–1936) in 1921. The play is about a theatre company rehearsing, when suddenly six unfinished characters arrive on the scene looking for an author. Nasser considered himself to be one such actor and he wrote: "I don't know why I always imagine that in this region there is a role wandering aimlessly about in search of an actor to play it. And I do not know why this role, tired of roaming about in this vast region, should at last settle down, exhausted and weary, on our frontiers beckoning us to assume it as nobody else can".

Nasser's relatively short rule over Egypt has left long-lasting marks both on Egypt and the region as a whole. Whether the "author" of Egypt's contemporary history was looking for an "actor" or whether Nasser's personal ambition and opportunism forged the role to fit him, no one will ever know. What we do know is that between 1952 and 1970 Nasser imposed himself on his country and – in the pursuit of his world view – obliterated all obstacles to his rule.

With Nasser gone, his successor, Anwar Sadat – while maintaining the armed forces' monopoly of political power – liberalized the economy, signed peace with Israel and forfeited Egypt's dominant role in the Arab world. The Egyptians had seemingly turned the page. In 1996, however, a film entitled *Nasser 56* came out. The popularity of the film reopened the Nasserite debate, showing that nostalgia surrounding the Nasser era had survived in the **collective memory**.

The critics remembered Nasser's "inclination to solitary decision-making" and claimed that his rash and compulsive policies had endangered Egypt's independence and finally led to the loss of territory. Nasserites emphasized social justice and his stand against imperialists. Where the two sides did not differ was on the question of democracy and political freedom. Nasser had established authoritarian rule, where pluralism was restricted, the press was censored and all forms of opposition were repressed.

Source skills

Nasser: some verdicts

With reference to their origins and purpose, assess the value and limitations of the four extracts below.

Source A

He pushed Egypt ahead, but soon let his fantasy take over, leading to the disaster of 5 June 1967 … From a zaim [Arabic for the courageous one] he turned into a prophet whom no one could criticize. He was all in one. In him were embodied all the national gains of Egypt ever since the country had a recorded history. Suez was the turning point. It led him to believe that revolutionary Egypt vanquished imperialism and that had it not been for Nasser this would not have happened. Victory was his victory, protected by Providence. Everyone forgot Egypt was not victorious in 1956!

Hussein Dhu'I Fiqar Sabri in *Rose –el Youssef* (an independent Egyptian weekly newspaper), 18 July 1975.

Source B

He signalled to the nation and it awoke; he signalled to the army and it moved; he signalled to the king and he departed; he berated imperialism and it exited from the country, feudalism and it was smashed, political parties and they were dissolved.

M. Rabi' in his book *Shakhsiyyat Abdel Nasir (the Personality of Abdel Nasser)*, 1966, quoted in PJ Vatikiotis, *Nasser and his Generation*.

Source C

Nasser's charisma may well have anaesthetized the Egyptians. The fact remains that his autocracy founded little that is politically lasting, even though it may have provided the outlines of social and economic change in the future.

PJ Vatikiotis, *Nasser and his Generation*.

Source D

He overwhelmed us with his magic … and the hopes, dreams and promises which underlay the victories of the revolution which he repeatedly announced to us … with their pipes and drums, anthems, songs and films, which made us see ourselves as a great industrial state, leaders of the developing world… and the strongest military power in the Middle East.

Tawfig al Hakim, Egyptian author; his play in 1960, *El Sultan El Haer (The Perplexed Sultan)*, which explored the legitimacy of power, could be regarded as a mild critique of Nasser. Quoted in PJ Vatikiotis, *Nasser and his Generation*.

53

Exam-style questions

1 To what extent was Nasser's rise to power due to popular support.

2 Examine the role of the media in spreading Nasser's message inside and outside Egypt.

3 How successful was Nasser in dealing with his opposition?

4 "In domestic politics, Nasser knew the language of the people." To what extent is this statement valid?

5 To what extent did Egyptian society change as a result of Nasser's rule in Egypt?

6 How successful was Nasser's policy in relation to the State of Israel?

7 To what extent did the nationalization of the Suez Canal benefit Egypt?

8 To what extent was Nasser's objective, "Egypt for Egyptians", met?

Answering exam questions

Question

To what extent was Nasser's rise to power due to popular support?

Analysis

The first thing to do *before* writing the introductory paragraph is to understand the question. You can break the question down into two parts in order to understand what the requirements of the question are. The introductory paragraph must show that you have understood the question.

1. The "rise to power" part of the question requires knowledge of the circumstances that allowed Nasser and the Free Officers to gain popularity and the methods they used to challenge/overthrow the previous regime.

   A 'rise to power' essay <u>should not</u> cover the period *after* the 'rise to power'.

   However, Nasser, like many other authoritarian rulers came to power in stages: in the first stage, the Free Officers and Nasser 'rose to power' when they overthrew the King. In the second stage, Nasser overcame his main rival, General Neghib, and 'rose' to power, as an unchallenged ruler of Egypt.

2. The command term, "to what extent" part of the question calls for an *evaluation* of the arguments and needs to end with a relevant and coherent conclusion. You are therefore being asked:

   a) First to gather the evidence of the factors that helped the Free Officers/Nasser to come to power.

   b) Then to evaluate each piece of evidence to see whether they prove 'popular support' or not.

   You are also being asked to provide evidence that would back an argument and a counter-argument:

   a) the argument – the evidence proving that Nasser's rise *was* due to popular support

   b) the counter-argument – evidence proving that Nasser's rise was *not* due to popular support.

Based on the evidence you have found and provided in your essay, you will conclude whether 'Nasser's rise to power' was due to popular support or not.

Finally, as a large number of factors led to Nasser's rise to power, you need to be selective. You need also to choose the order in which you want to present these. They can be broken down into long-term, medium-term and immediate factors; they can also be divided into foreign and domestic factors. They can be classified by their degree of importance or they can follow a straight forward chronological order. In all cases, *all* the factors you choose to include need to be relevant to the question and be supported by appropriate evidence.

Sample answer

On July 23rd 1952 a group of officers overthrew King Faruq of Egypt in a bloodless coup. Amongst the officers, Gamal Abdel Nasser would emerge as leader and remain in office until his death in 1970. The Free Officers' rise to power was due to a combination of internal and external factors that had rendered their adversaries unpopular in 1952 and allowed the military coup to be a success. In the two years that followed, through a number of tactical manoeuvres Nasser was able to rid himself of his opponents and form a favourable popular base amongst the people, thus becoming the undisputed ruler. His success was partly due to his adversaries' incapacity to rule and partly due to his personal capacity to turn the events to his favour through a well-organised propaganda machine. This essay will evaluate the various elements that helped Nasser in his quest for total power and determine to what extent they were due to popular support.

Examiner comments

The introductory paragraph should:

- contextualise the subject
- address the question
- present an outline of what is to come
- offer a clear line of argument and counter-argument.

In this example of an introductory paragraph, the student has:

1. established the context
2. addressed the question
3. set the time limits by showing awareness that it is a 'rise to power' question
4. distinguished between the two stages of 'coming to power'
5. shown awareness for the need to evaluate each side of the argument.

2 CUBA – CASTRO

The global context

Cuba, a small Caribbean island situated about 145 kilometres (90 miles) off the coast of Florida, was a Spanish colony for several centuries until 1898, when, with the help of the US, the Cubans forced the Spanish to relinquish control of the island and remove all their troops and officials. Cuba's fate was always closely intertwined with that of its powerful neighbour, and even as early as the 1820s, US politicians had sought to add Cuba to the United States, viewing the island as a resource to be exploited.

Despite officially gaining its independence from Spain in 1902, Cuba took almost another 60 years to become a truly self-governing state. After the revolution of 1959, when Fidel Castro gained power from the puppet government of Batista, the USA saw Cuba as a dangerous enemy that needed to be crushed by economic and, at times, military means. Its Latin American neighbours viewed Cuba both as a threat to their pro-American governments and as a source of hope for the left-wing nationalist movements that resisted them. After 1959 the Soviet Union saw Cuba as a potential nuisance for the USA, then as a valuable ally (from 1961 to 1962) and then, after the Cuban Missile Crisis of 1962, as a dangerous and uncontrollable maverick.

Timeline

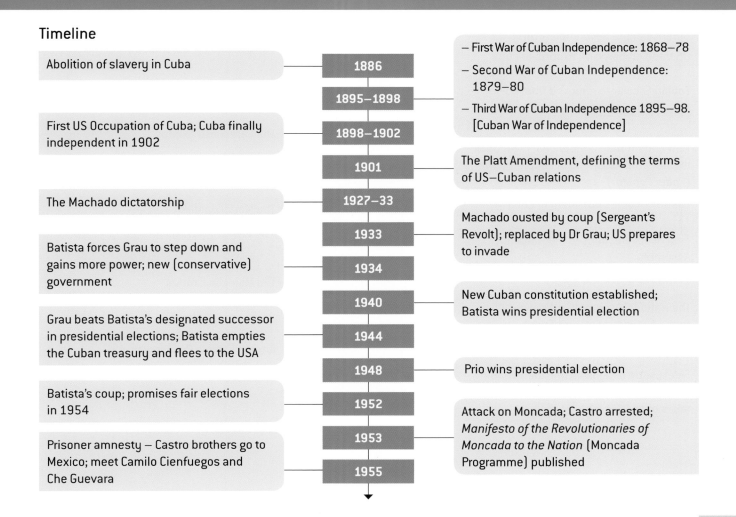

Abolition of slavery in Cuba	1886	– First War of Cuban Independence: 1868–78
	1895–1898	– Second War of Cuban Independence: 1879–80
First US Occupation of Cuba; Cuba finally independent in 1902	1898–1902	– Third War of Cuban Independence 1895–98. [Cuban War of Independence]
	1901	The Platt Amendment, defining the terms of US–Cuban relations
The Machado dictatorship	1927–33	
	1933	Machado ousted by coup (Sergeant's Revolt); replaced by Dr Grau; US prepares to invade
Batista forces Grau to step down and gains more power; new (conservative) government	1934	
	1940	New Cuban constitution established; Batista wins presidential election
Grau beats Batista's designated successor in presidential elections; Batista empties the Cuban treasury and flees to the USA	1944	
	1948	Prio wins presidential election
Batista's coup; promises fair elections in 1954	1952	
	1953	Attack on Moncada; Castro arrested; *Manifesto of the Revolutionaries of Moncada to the Nation* (Moncada Programme) published
Prisoner amnesty – Castro brothers go to Mexico; meet Camilo Cienfuegos and Che Guevara	1955	

	1956	*Movimiento 26 de Julio* (M-26-7) created Granma expedition; defeat for Castro; guerrilla war in Sierra Maestra
M-26-7 organizes unsuccessful general strike; Batista convinced he can still win Failure of Operation *Verano* Batista resigns and flees to Dominican Republic	**1958**	
	1959	Castro enters Havana Elections suspended "temporarily"; Manuel Urrutia becomes president
US bans some trade with Cuba; USSR signs trade deal with Cuba US-owned oil refineries in Cuba refuse to refine Soviet crude oil US-owned oil refineries nationalized by Cuba US increases trade bans on Cuba; Cuban sugar exports to USA cut; USSR buys surplus to save Cuban economy Cuba nationalizes some US-owned businesses Castro at UN General Assembly; Castro delivers his First Declaration of Havana speech; close friendship with Khrushchev; all US businesses in Cuba nationalized; establishment of Committees for the Defence of the Revolution (CDRs) US trade embargo on exports to Cuba	**1960**	INRA established; Agrarian Reform Act passed Urrutia resigns as president; Osvaldo Dorticós takes over as new president Huber Matos arrested for being anti-communist
	1961	Cuban Literacy Campaign launched CIA launches unsuccessful invasion (the Bay of Pigs); Castro announces Cuban Revolution as socialist Political parties in Cuba dissolved; left-wing anti-Batista groups merge to form the Integrated Revolutionary Organizations (ORI) – which becomes the Communist Party of Cuba (PCC) in 1965
Fabián Escalante removed from power Cuban Missile Crisis	**1962**	
	1965	The Camarioca Exodus
New constitution announced; creation of the National Assembly of People's Power (*Poder Popular*) Castro becomes president of Cuba	**1976**	
	1980	The Mariel Boatlift
First direct elections to the National Assembly	**1993**	
	1994	The Malecón Exodus
The National Assembly makes socialist form of government permanent	**2002**	
	2003	Arrest of Varela Project activists
Fidel Castro resigns as president, ending 49 years in power; his brother Raúl Castro takes over	**2008**	

Conceptual understanding

Key questions

→ What were the main social, economic, and political factors that created the situation in which Castro could come to power?

→ To what extent was Castro's rise to power due to his own traits and actions (as opposed to pre-existing socio-economic or sociopolitical factors)?

Key concepts

→ Continuity

→ Change

▲ Cuba in the early 20th century, showing the six provinces and major cities

How did Castro take control of Cuba?

The actions and words of Fidel Castro have helped to shape Cuba and the world for more than 50 years. To understand how this charismatic lawyer-turned-revolutionary-turned-leader was able to take control of Cuba in 1959, within only six years of his initial, failed attempt to do so, we need to examine the context within which he was operating.

During the 19th century, the country's economy was almost entirely dependent on slave-produced goods and trade with the USA. US corporations owned many Cuban plantations. European immigration had been primarily to the western part of the island while the eastern provinces, separated by the heavily wooded Sierra Maestra mountain range, was a more lawless, politically neglected and economically undeveloped frontier land. This geographical divide was exacerbated by the ocean currents, which meant that Cuba's main trading ports were also in the west of the island. Escaped slaves found refuge in the east and, by the late 19th century, there was a marked ethnic division in Cuba, too, with most black Cubans living in the east and those of mainly Spanish descent in the west, where they were far more likely to enjoy socio-economic advantages. Oriente, the easternmost province, was the poorest and most rebellious of the island's six provinces, witnessing many slave revolts.

In 1886 the Spanish government finally abolished slavery in Cuba, partly in an effort to stave off the calls for independence, but the former slaves and their descendants were relegated to lives of crippling poverty and political impotence in the eastern provinces. This is why José Martí chose, in 1895, to begin his war against the Spanish rulers by stirring up a revolt in Oriente province.

This social divide continued to influence Cuban politics in the 20th century, engendering mass support for Fulgencio Batista in the 1930s and 1940s. By the 1950s, in spite of the limited social improvements implemented by Batista in the 1940s, Oriente province still had the lowest literacy rates in Cuba and accounted for almost 30 per cent of Cuba's unemployed. With all these factors leading to severe political dissatisfaction, it is hardly surprising that Fidel Castro chose, in July 1953, to emulate José Martí and start his revolution in Oriente province.

Cuban independence from Spain

From 1868 to 1898, the Cuban independence movement fought three wars to force the Spanish to relinquish their hold on the island. The third and final war was inspired by José Martí (1853–1895), the man who would become celebrated as Cuba's greatest national hero – "the Apostle of Cuban independence". Despite not being a military man, Martí was killed in action and his martyrdom inspired his followers to accept nothing less than the complete removal of the Spanish. When (by April 1898) the Cuban nationalists had gained the upper hand in their struggle, the USA – what Martí had referred to as "The Colossus to the North" – joined the war on their side. The Spanish finally relinquished their hold on Cuba in December 1898, but their troops were immediately replaced by US troops, heralding the First US occupation.

Source skills

▲ Cartoon from *Puck Magazine*, April 1901

This American cartoon was published a month after the Platt Amendment of March 1901. The caption reads: "Good governance vs revolution… an easy choice."

1   What can you see? Who or what does each character represent? What is happening in the image?

2   What does it mean? What message is the artist trying to convey?

3   Compare this source to the statement made by US President John F Kennedy, quoted later in this chapter. Identify the similarities and differences between the two views of US–Cuban relations in the 20th century.

4   With reference to its origin and purpose, assess the value of this source to an historian studying US–Cuban relations in the 20th century.

Cuba and the USA

During the 1880s, three major factors combined with the political desire for an empire to drive US public opinion towards intervention in Cuba:

1   the increasing intensity of the Cuban revolts against Spanish rule

2   pressure from American corporations and businessmen with investments in Cuba

3   the increased efforts of Cuban nationalists like José Martí.

US businesses had been closely involved with Cuba since the early 19th century. By 1895, US corporations had invested vast amounts of money in Cuba and worried about what would happen if the Cuban nationalists won their independence from Spain. They exerted pressure on the American government to protect their interests. Activists from both Cuba and America used anti-Spanish propaganda to sway public opinion towards supporting an American military intervention. The American public grew more supportive of military action after February 1898, when an American warship (the *USS Maine*) mysteriously blew up during a visit to Cuba. Blaming the Spanish for its destruction, the

US government declared war in April 1898. By August, the Spanish forces had been defeated and the USA occupied Cuba.

In 1902 the USA formally gave Cuba its independence, but the 1901 Platt Amendment gave the USA the right to intervene militarily in Cuba whenever it wanted. Elections were rigged in favour of candidates who would follow pro-US policies. US corporations and trade with the USA dominated the Cuban economy, creating a wide gap between the extremely wealthy minority and the increasingly impoverished and exploited majority. As a further reminder of their place within the US economic system, Cubans had the evidence of the US occupations (1898–1902 and 1906–1909) and the so-called "Sugar Intervention" of 1917–1922 – all of which saw US troops stationed in Cuba.

Politicians who did not support the US economic policies found themselves unable to gain power or were removed within a very brief period. The only Cuban governments that survived were noticeably corrupt. Naturally, this fostered the anti-Americanism already present in Cuba and set the stage for the Cuban political movements of the 20th century, which were based on the idea that the only way to achieve socio-economic change was to use force to enact political change.

The Cuban Revolution (1933–1934) and the puppet presidents (1934–1940)

The corrupt and brutal dictatorship of Gerardo Machado of the 1920s was eventually overthrown in 1933. Student protests had been met with Machado's habitual police brutality, but the impact of the Great Depression (after the 1929 Wall Street Crash) on the Cuban economy ensured wide support for the students, with strikes and protests by workers. The turning point, however, was the "Sergeant's Revolt" of September 1933, when a group of army NCOs (non-commissioned officers) decided to support the students and arrested their own officers. They were led by a mixed-race army stenographer from an impoverished background who went on to become the most politically influential man in Cuba: Sergeant Fulgencio Batista y Zaldívar.

With encouragement from the US government, Machado resigned and was replaced by a provisional government headed by Dr Ramón Grau San Martín, a university professor. A "new Cuba" was promised, with a democratic government, an end to social inequities, higher wages, lower prices, and voting rights for women. Furthermore, the new government declared the Platt Amendment null and void.

These proposed changes worried the corporations and the US government threatened military action. The provisional government began to fall apart under this pressure, Grau and his fellow leaders struggling to achieve a commonality of purpose about how to best serve Cuba's needs while placating the USA. The policies of the more left-wing elements, such as Eduardo Chibás Ribas, would not be palatable to the USA, so Batista (now Chief of the Armed Forces and with the rank of colonel) chose to support the more right-wing Colonel Carlos Mendieta y Montefur. The USA quickly recognized this new provisional government and the promise of social and economic reforms died. Renewed student protests and workers' strikes were again met with

police and army brutality, martial law was imposed and the governments of the 1930s (often referred to as the "puppet presidents") found that the real power lay with Batista and the armed forces.

In an effort to reduce the violence, the government bribed some of the armed gangs that controlled the University of Havana with positions of power (such as the post of Chief of Police in Havana), but this plan simply increased the levels of corruption within Cuban society and politics. This played into Batista's hands by continuing to show the weaknesses of the "puppet presidents", thus paving the way for his own electoral success in 1940.

Significant individuals during Castro's rise to power

José Martí (1853–1895)

A key figure in the Cuban independence movement; killed in battle by the Spanish. Politicians during the Republic of Cuba (1902–1959) regularly attempted to position themselves in the public consciousness as the ideological heir of Martí.

Gerardo Machado (1871–1939)

A general during the Cuban War of Independence (1895–1898); President of Cuba (1925–1933); pressured by the US to resign during the Cuban Revolution of 1933.

Àngel Castro y Argiz (1875–1956)

Spanish immigrant to Cuba; self-made Cuban planter; father of Fidel Castro.

Dr Ramón Grau San Martín (1881–1969)

A popular university lecturer who led the Revolutionary Directorate (1933–1934); leader of the Partido Auténtico; President of Cuba 1933–1934 and 1944–1948.

Fulgencio Batista y Zaldívar (1901–1973)

A mixed-race, working class army sergeant; helped lead the Sergeants' Revolt (1933–1934); became Chief of Staff, then President of Cuba 1940–1944 and 1952–1959; fostered links between Cuba and US Mafia; noted for his regime's brutality and corruption in the 1950s; fled to Dominican Republic in 1958 and died in Spain.

Eduardo René Chibás Ribas (1907–1951)

Cuban radio presenter and politician; set up the socialist Partido Ortodoxo in 1947; by late 1940s became strongly opposed to communism; expected to win election of 1952 but Batista launched his coup before votes were cast; killed himself live on air.

Ernesto "Che" Guevara (1928–1967)

Argentine doctor; anti-imperialist; Marxist (although the extent of this is disputed); rebel leader during Sierra Maestra campaign; declared "one of the 100 most influential people of the 20th century" by *Time* magazine.

Francisco "Frank" Paìs (1934–1957)

A schoolteacher who joined M-26-7 after Castro's "History will absolve me" speech; organized urban resistance to Batista's regime; led Santiago uprising of November 1956; his arrest and murder by police led to biggest spontaneous display of public hostility to Batista since the coup in 1952.

Batista's presidency, 1940–1944

Batista was able to gain support from a wide cross-section of Cuban society. His humble origins certainly helped: he came from an impoverished peasant background, only learning to read and write after he joined the army. As Cuba's first non-white ruler, he was able to draw on the support of the non-white population, which formed the majority of the disenfranchised working classes. His control of the military enabled him to improve the pay and conditions – and the promotion prospects – of non-white soldiers, which won him their support. This popular support was enhanced by Batista's efforts to bribe journalists, clergymen, and union leaders. The result was that he was convinced that the Cubans genuinely loved him.

Batista's presidency saw him remain true to his pro-American, pro-capitalism ideologies while placating his communist supporters by introducing labour laws and social reforms intended to redress the economic imbalance of Cuban society. Batista's Cuba began to resemble "a modern corporate state", where the most economically powerful members (the cattle barons, plantation owners, industrialists, and mill owners) maintained their monopolies and profits by bargaining through government ministries. The communists and labour unions denounced his detractors and opponents (especially Grau) as fascists.

The Second World War (1939–1945) proved a blessing for Batista's government as demands for Cuba's exports (especially sugar) skyrocketed, thus boosting the economy. Although the majority of the profits went to foreign corporations, there was still a tangible benefit for the average Cuban citizen. This economic bonanza began to wane after the war ended and demand returned to pre-war levels, but by that time Batista was no longer in power.

The Auténtico presidencies, 1944–1948 and 1948–1952

In 1944 Batista was constitutionally obliged to step down as president. When it became apparent that his chosen successor would lose the election to Grau and his Auténticos, Batista emigrated to the USA with a large portion of the Cuban treasury. The intention (as identified by US diplomatic cables of the time) was to leave Grau's presidency financially handicapped before it had even begun. Batista continued to be involved in Cuban politics, being elected to the Cuban Senate *in absentia* in 1948 and getting Grau's grudging approval to stand as a presidential candidate in the 1952 election. By this time the Cuban political landscape had changed, with Eddy Chibás's Partido Ortodoxo, founded in 1947, seen as an alternative to the communists, who had been tainted by their association with Batista's government. The Ortodoxos had attracted the talents of a charismatic young law student who would go on to change Cuba and the world: Fidel Alejandro Castro Ruz.

The traditional Cuban political methods of corruption, violence, intimidation, and bribery continued. One of the first acts of Grau's presidency was to reward his supporters from the violent political gangs in Havana with appointments such as chief of police or state director of sports. In return, they provided the Auténticos (whose leadership and support base were drawn from the professional middle class) with a private army that acted as bodyguards and, at times, as a police force. On a superficial level, they resembled the *Sturm Abteilung* that had played a similar role for Hitler's National Socialist party in Germany during the 1920s and 1930s. Violence and bribery was used against Grau's opponents or, when that failed, murder. Fidel Castro, at that time still a student in Havana, was therefore not alone in having to survive at least one assassination attempt during his time at university. The left-wing parties also used force and there was a resurgence of the violence that had waned during the economic boom years of 1940–1945.

Grau had abandoned socio-economic reforms in favour of ensuring the support of wealthy businessmen, plantation owners, and US corporations. His successor, the Auténtico president Carlos Prío Socarrás, continued in the same vein. This administration became "the most polarized, corrupt, violent and undemocratic" since 1901. The 1952 elections were fiercely contested, with support for the Auténticos and Chibás's Ortodoxos pushing Batista into a distant third place.

▲ Fulgencio Batista during the 1950s. Despite resorting to increasingly dictatorial methods, Batista was still convinced that he enjoyed the same popularity with the average Cuban people as he had during his first presidency of 1940–1944.

Batista's coup, March 1952

As the election drew closer, the US Mafia sought (unsuccessfully) to protect their investments by offering President Carlos Prío Socarrás a bribe of $250 000 to stand down in favour of Batista. In August 1951, during his weekly radio show, Eddy Chibás announced his suspicions of a coup by Batista, then shot himself live on air. (Unfortunately for Chibás, his shockingly dramatic act occurred during a commercial break and was not broadcast live as he had intended.) Seven months later, on 10 March 1952, he was proved correct when Batista used the army (whose loyalty he had commanded since the 1930s) to stage a coup. The coup met little resistance from the main political parties, for the following reasons:

1   Batista claimed (falsely) that Prio had been plotting a coup of his own.

2   Batista promised to hold fair and free elections in 1954.

3   The Cuban public was weary of the corruption of the Auténticos and (by extension) all politicians.

4   Batista enjoyed the support of the military, the police, and the secret police (the **BRAC**).

> **BRAC**
> The Cuban secret police, the Bureau for the Repression of Communist Activities (the BRAC), focused on preventing communist influences in Cuba.

Batista was also helped by the emerging Cold War between the USA and the USSR because his pro-business rhetoric of the 1930s and 1940s helped guarantee that the US government would not thwart his seizure of power. Some Cubans, however, wanted to take direct action to counter the coup. These Cubans (mostly young, white, and middle class) came from different parts of the political spectrum but were united in their frustration at the lack of resistance by the political parties.

Castro's early life

Fidel Castro was the son of a Spanish immigrant who had worked his way up from labouring to eventually becoming a wealthy planter himself. Fidel Alejandro Castro Ruz was born in August 1926 (although Coltman claims that he was born in 1927 and his father lied about his age to get him into school) and he grew up among the children of the labourers on his father's plantations. Castro would later claim that this exposure to the plight of the poor families in and around his father's estate played a formative role in shaping his later political views.

His father's wealth and connections helped the young Fidel to access the prestigious, Jesuit-run Belén college in Havana. He was not an ideal student, preferring sport to academia, but Castro went on to study Law at the University of Havana in 1945. At university, he quickly became involved in the student activist movements that formed a major part of university life.

The emergence of Fidel Castro

A consistent impression of Castro is that he was a populist leader with an ability to inspire his audiences (especially young, politically charged students) through a combination of dramatic oratorical skills and a somewhat simplistic message of heroism and action. He had been drawn to the Ortodoxos by their ideology of social reform and justice, not their strategy of following the parliamentary process.

The strongest indicators of Castro's social conscience and belief in socio-economic justice are his actions prior to 1953. After denouncing the corruption of the government and its links to the armed gangs in 1949, Castro had (wisely) fled to the US for several months. On his return to

Cuba in 1950, he completed his law studies. His wife's wealthy family offered to arrange a well-paid job in a prosperous firm in Havana but Castro and his friends, Jorge Azpiazu and Rafael Resende, chose instead to set up a legal practice in an impoverished area of Old Havana. From 1950 to 1952 they barely made enough money to cover their meagre rent as they defended the "victimized workers, slum-dwellers, detained students and poor clients in general".

Throughout this time, Castro remained a vocal critic of the seemingly endemic corruption and the Auténtico government of President Prío in particular. Despite his misgivings about the parliamentary route for enacting social change, he also grew more involved in the Ortodoxo campaign for the 1952 elections and was nominated as a congressional candidate by two poor districts. However, he saw electoral success as a means to an end – stating years later that his intention, had he been elected to congress, would have been to prepare the way for a revolutionary movement that would enact the much-needed social and economic changes. As he later declared, he "was convinced then that [change] could only be realized by revolutionary means".

By 1954 the US government was using the **CIA** to install US-friendly dictatorships throughout Latin America and the Caribbean. To avoid accusations of being "too socialist" and thereby inviting CIA intervention in Cuba, Batista reversed or withheld the long-awaited reforms to working conditions. He used the corrupt judiciary and politicians to maintain his grip on power while using the BRAC to brutally crush any opponents (or potential opposition) that the courts could not dissuade or block. The more Batista relied upon violence to quell opposition, the more he entrenched himself in the eyes of Cubans as just another link in a long chain of imperialist oppressors.

While the Ortodoxo leadership advocated passive resistance and civil disobedience, the student and youth movements argued for more direct action and they rallied around young leaders such as Fidel Castro, who used militant rhetoric that harked back to the romantic Cuban nationalist myths of a glorious, violent struggle for freedom. Castro launched a legal challenge to Batista's undemocratic seizure of power, but he was foiled by the corrupt court system. Realizing that he had declared himself unequivocally an "enemy of the state" and therefore a target for arrest or assassination by the BRAC, Castro went into hiding and began planning the armed revolution that he felt was now essential to liberate his country.

Castro's attack on the Moncada Barracks, 26 July 1953

In 1953 Fidel Castro and his brother Raúl planned an uprising against the Batista regime. With approximately 160 young rebels, mostly drawn from the Ortodoxo youth movement, Castro attacked the Moncada Barracks near Santiago de Cuba, the capital city of the impoverished and turbulent Oriente province. The plan was to quickly capture the barracks, issue a rousing call to the people, and rely on the boldness of their actions to inspire a spontaneous uprising in the province. The rebels would then use the captured military weapons and supplies to equip the masses, thus spreading the revolution to all of Cuba. Bloodshed was to be avoided if at all possible.

CIA
President Harry S. Truman created the American spy agency, the Central Intelligence Agency (CIA) in 1947. The CIA had the role of intelligence service to support the actions of the US military and to counter the Soviet spy agency, the KGB. By 1953, the CIA's remit had expanded to include the role of influencing governments.

ATL Research and thinking skills

Before the attack on the Moncada Barracks, Castro made this speech:

> "In a few hours you will be victorious or defeated, but regardless of the outcome – listen well, friends – this movement will triumph. If you win tomorrow, the aspirations of Martí will be fulfilled sooner. If we fail, our action will nevertheless set an example for the Cuban people, and from the people will arise fresh young men willing to die for Cuba. They will pick up our banner and move forward … The people will back us in Oriente and in the whole island. As in '68 and '92, here in Oriente we will give the first cry of Liberty or Death!"

Coltman, L. 2003. *The Real Fidel Castro*. New Haven. Yale University Press.

Research the speeches of at least two political leaders. Compare the ways in which they choose words and phrases to accentuate their main arguments. If possible, watch video footage of them delivering the speeches. Compare the body language and gestures employed. Use this to help you decide the extent to which major events are shaped by the actions and personalities of leaders.

The plan failed dismally, with 19 dead soldiers and policemen, and 27 wounded. In contrast, six attackers were killed and a further 15 wounded during the fighting. The garrison's commanding officer, Colonel Alberto del Río Chaviano, told his soldiers to capture the remaining attackers, torture and kill them. According to Castro, 56 of the attackers were tortured to death after their capture. Castro survived thanks to a black lieutenant, Pedro Sarría, who ignored these instructions and prevented his men from torturing or executing their prisoners. The ethnicity of this officer is relevant since, at that time, black and mixed-race Cubans were mainly supportive of Batista, Cuba's first non-white ruler. Castro and his guerrillas were all of Spanish descent and resembled the white ruling elite that had disenfranchised the non-white Cubans for centuries. Despite having no sympathy for Castro's cause, the lieutenant decided to take Castro to the town prison instead of to the barracks, thus saving his life and altering the course of history.

▲ July 1953: Castro (seated, right) being interrogated by Colonel Alberto del Río Chaviano (seated, left) and accompanied by Lieutenant Pedro Sarría (standing, right), the officer who arrested Castro and prevented his men from torturing or killing him. Also present is Police Chief Jose Izquierdo Rodriguez (standing, left). Colonel Chaviano was later promoted to general and given control of the campaign against Castro's guerrillas in the Sierra Maestra. Lieutenant Sarría was never promoted.

The simplicity of Castro's plan has been described as naive, "reckless" and "somewhat over-ambitious" – both the attack itself and, by extension, Castro's entire revolutionary escapade. The failure of the attack could well have been the end of Castro's revolution if it had not been for some fortuitous events.

Castro's trial and the Moncada Programme, October 1953

The evidence of soldiers torturing captured rebels to death created a scandal that forced Batista to bring the surviving rebels (including the Castro brothers, Fidel and Raúl) to trial. During the trial, Castro openly admitted his role in the attack and justified it by pointing out the illegal nature of Batista's coup and regime. The trial gave Castro a national platform to deliver his manifesto – the famous "History will absolve me" speech – in which he said:

"When we speak of the people, we do not mean the comfortable and conservative sectors of the nation, who welcome any regime of oppression, any dictatorship, any despotism, prostrating themselves before the master of the moment until they grind their foreheads into the ground. We understand by people, when we are speaking of struggle, to mean the vast unredeemed masses, to whom all make promises and who are deceived and betrayed by all; who yearn for a better, more dignified and more just nation; who are moved by ancestral aspirations of justice, having suffered injustice and mockery generation after generation; and who long for significant and sound transformations in all aspects of life, and who, to attain them, are ready to give even the very last breath of their lives, when they believe in something or in someone, and above all when they believe sufficiently in themselves.

... As for me, I know that prison will be hard ... but I do not fear it, just as I do not fear the fury of the despicable tyrant that tore out the lives of seventy of my brothers. Condemn me. It does not matter. History will absolve me."

Research and thinking skills

Compare Hitler's Munich Putsch (November 1923) with Castro's attack on the Moncada Barracks (July 1953). Draw a table with two columns (one for each) and identify the similarities in terms of:

- why this happened
- what happened
- why this was significant in the short term
- why this was significant in the long term.

Repeat the process for the differences between the two events.

Similarities between Castro's trial in 1953 and Hitler's in 1924

There were similarities between the way in which Adolf Hitler and Fidel Castro used their respective trials to their advantage:

- Neither admitted regret for their attempts to seize power.
- Both were relatively unknown, relatively minor political activists prior to their trials.
- Both became household names (and gained international recognition) as a result of their trials.
- Both used their eloquent public speaking skills to deliver their manifesto to a wider audience.
- Both used their trials to publicly denounce their respective governments as illegitimate.
- Both gained many supporters as a result of their performance at their trials.
- Both (for different reasons) were treated relatively leniently when sentenced.
- Both commemorated the date of their failed attempts once they had power:
  - Castro named his revolutionary movement Movimiento 26 de *Julio* after the date of his attack on the Moncada Barracks
  - The NSDAP marked the 15th anniversary of the Munich Putsch with anti-Jewish riots (later known as *Kristallnacht*)

- Both claimed that history would judge them more fairly than the court:
  - Hitler claimed that "the goddess of the eternal court of History … finds us not guilty."
  - Castro used the phrase "History will absolve me."

Another crucial effect of the trial was that it gave Castro the chance to outline his vision for a new Cuba, in what became known as the **Moncada Programme**. His desire for a more open, fairer society and an end to the corruption that plagued Cuban politics struck a chord with the working classes. In short, his eloquence and courage at the trial won him many new supporters (including Frank Pais, a young teacher from Santiago de Cuba who would go on to play a crucial role in Castro's future success) and embarrassed Batista even further.

Many of his co-defendants at the trial were let off with relatively lenient sentences. Castro and his brother were sentenced to 15 and 13 years respectively, thus removing their threat to the regime. However, in the run-up to the presidential elections promised for 1954, Batista relaxed the censorship laws in Cuba and allowed rival political parties to campaign. This meant that Castro's supporters could also campaign for his freedom. With both internal and international pressure to appear more lenient, Batista granted all political prisoners (including the Castro brothers) an amnesty in May 1955.

As the only candidate, Batista had "won" the 1954 elections but this did not signal the end of his problems. His secret police force was kept busy dealing with the increasing numbers of opposition groups plotting against his regime. Castro's *Movimiento de 26 Julio* seemed a minor concern in comparison and, not for the first or last time in history, the regime dismissed as insignificant was the group that would eventually destroy them.

By 1955 Batista's regime was growing more unpopular and his responses to the increasing number of protests was growing more repressive. A cycle of violence ensued, with more protests and a series of bombings, leading to even more government repression.

Castro's exile in Mexico and return to Cuba, 1955–1956

Following his release from prison in May 1955, Fidel Castro attempted to re-enter the political arena but, within six weeks, he and his brother Raùl had fled to Mexico. Their growing popularity and unwillingness to repent for their revolutionary actions made them likely targets for re-arrest or assassination by BRAC agents. This served to strengthen Castro's belief that Cuba (and Latin America in general) could not achieve meaningful change through parliamentary methods.

Source skills

Quote from US President Kennedy from 24 October 1963:

"I believe that there is no country in the world, including any and all the countries under colonial domination, where economic colonization, humiliation and exploitation were worse than in Cuba, in part owing to my country's policies during the Batista regime. I approved the proclamation that

---

The Moncada Programme

This was Castro's programme for social reform, comprising five "Revolutionary Laws":

1 Return power to the people by reinstating the 1940 constitution

2 Land reform: giving rights to those living or squatting on small plots (less than 165 acres)

3 Profit sharing for industrial workers (30 per cent of the company's profits)

4 Profit sharing for sugar workers (55 per cent of the company's profits)

5 End corruption: those found guilty of fraud to have their property confiscated – this would then be used to pay for workers' pensions, schools, hospitals and charities

---

Movimiento de 26 Julio

Castro used the date of the failed attack on the Moncada Barracks as the name of his revolutionary group: *Movimiento 26 de Julio,* or M-26-7.

Fidel Castro made in the Sierra Maestra, when he justifiably called for justice and especially yearned to rid Cuba of corruption. I will even go further: to some extent it is as though Batista was the incarnation of a number of sins on the part of the United States. Now we shall have to pay for those sins. In the matter of the Batista regime, I am in agreement with the first Cuban revolutionaries."

Question

To what extent do you agree with the quote from Kennedy above?
Use the rest of this section to help you in your answer.

In Mexico in 1955, Castro organized the M-26-7 group in preparation for their return to Cuba. M-26-7 members in Cuba formed secret underground cells to help support Castro's return. Frank Pais established one such group in Santiago de Cuba. These secret groups began stockpiling weapons and ammunition as well as printing anti-regime newsletters and posters, spreading the promises of the Moncada Programme throughout the country and preparing the way for popular uprisings in support of Castro's cause.

During his time in Mexico, Castro met Camilo Cienfuegos, a young Cuban nationalist, and Ernesto "Che" Guevara, an idealistic young Argentinian doctor. Both of them, like Castro, were committed to the cause of ridding Latin America of American corporate imperialism. Castro was less committed to Marxist or communist ideals than Guevara and more interested in Cuban nationalism. In 1956, Castro flatly refuted Batista's claims that he was a communist, writing an article in which he denounced the Cuban dictator's former links to that party. In particular, he played upon the fact that Batista's 1940 election victory was due to the support of the communists (the PSP) and that "half a dozen of his present ministers and close collaborators were leading members of the Communist Party".

Although his condemnation of the PSP was obviously a political move designed to reassure his more conservative supporters, Castro had often been critical of the communists. In particular, he was wary of aligning himself too closely with them due to the level of control exercised by the USSR over their actions. Furthermore, the PSP at this time were calling for non-violent opposition to Batista and this was not what Castro wanted. Their earlier collaboration with Batista had made the PSP of the 1950s unpopular among Cuban workers.

By early 1956 Castro had enough support for his ideas and his M-26-7 movement to officially break away from the Ortodoxos. M-26-7 members in Cuba immediately began to increase their efforts to pave the way for Castro's return. In Oriente province, since the Moncada Barracks attack, Castro's movement had gained great popularity. Especially due to the work of Frank Pais and the other cells, recruitment increased, as did the essential work of gathering medical supplies and military equipment with which to support the rebels.

Meanwhile, in Mexico, Castro had secretly recruited, armed, and trained a fighting force of 82 volunteers who would sail with him on his mission to liberate Cuba. With funds from a variety of anti-Batista sources (including ex-President Prío), Castro had purchased an old yacht (the *Granma*). As he had promised, Fidel Castro would return to Cuba before the end of 1956.

The *Granma* expedition and Santiago uprising, November 1956

Castro's invasion force of 82 revolutionaries were secretly carried from Tuxpan in Mexico to the western tip of Oriente province, near the town of Manzanillo. The landing point was chosen partly because of its symbolic nature – it was 288 kilometres (180 miles) west of where José Martí had landed during his expedition in 1895.

The PSP failed to dissuade Castro from launching the expedition, arguing in vain for non-violent opposition to Batista. When it became clear that this would not work, they tried to get him to wait until after the cane harvest in January to coincide with planned strike activity. Furthermore, Frank Pais informed Castro that the Oriente M-26-7 cells were not yet ready to support the expedition. However, Castro was adamant that it would go ahead as planned, arguing that the longer they took to launch it, the greater their chances of being discovered. Castro had publicly declared that he would return to liberate Cuba before 1957 and he showed his awareness of the importance of public relations and propaganda by his determination not to renege on this promise.

Due to their lack of funds and the need to maintain secrecy, the rebels were ill equipped and the *Granma* was a leaky, ageing yacht in terrible condition. The 1988-kilometre (1235-mile) crossing was hazardous and uncomfortable due to bad weather and conditions in the overcrowded boat (designed for 25 passengers, not 82). Almost immediately, the *Granma* ran into a storm and nearly foundered, losing precious time and fuel as they rescued a man who fell overboard. Due to mechanical problems and their dwindling fuel reserves, they were forced to jettison precious supplies. As a result, the crossing took two days longer than planned.

The plan also called for a popular uprising in Santiago de Cuba and a simultaneous attack on the Moncada Barracks once the *Granma* expedition had landed. However, the delayed journey and poor communications meant that this attack was launched two days too early. Frank Pais's rebel cells engaged the army and police but, without Castro's support, they could not hope to win. After 30 hours of sporadic fighting, they withdrew, pursued by Batista's army and a number of planes.

One indication of how support for Castro's revolution had grown since 1953 is how, during this second attack on the Moncada Barracks, at least 67 soldiers refused to fight the rebels. Some policemen in Santiago joined the rebels and willingly gave them their weapons, while many citizens helped the rebels hide from the army. Those rebels who did not flee to the countryside removed their olive drab uniforms and black-and-red armbands, hid their weapons and merged back into their normal lives. They felt safe to do this, trusting the citizens of Oriente to not hand them over to the BRAC, police or army.

Journey to the Sierra Maestra, November 1956

Two days after the Santiago uprising, with the M-26-7 forces dispersed and defeated, the *Granma* eventually arrived. It ran aground off the designated landing point, forcing the sick, exhausted and hungry revolutionaries to carry their heavy equipment ashore through the shallows and the mudflats. Batista's air force soon spotted them and they were attacked by planes and warships, with the threat that the army would soon arrive, too.

Leaving their equipment, they pushed into the dense cover of the swamp but, within days, they walked into an ambush that all but destroyed them. They were forced to leave most of their weapons, ammunition, food, and medical supplies as they fled through what Castro later described as "that hellish swamp" and into the forests of the Sierra Maestra mountain range.

Only about 18 (the exact number is disputed) of the original 82 revolutionaries survived the trek into the Sierra Maestra and the army attacks that plagued them. Castro later claimed that the majority of his men who died were murdered after capture. Although this could be anti-regime propaganda, the actions of the government forces during the 1950s (especially after the Moncada attack) suggest that he was probably correct.

The Sierra Maestra campaign, 1956–1959

The survivors (including the Castro brothers, Che Guevara, Juan Almeida Bosque and Camilo Cienfuegos) eventually regrouped deep in the Sierra Maestra mountains to form the core of the guerrilla army. As planned, they would wage a hit-and-run campaign against Batista's forces in Oriente province. With help from the peasants and M-26-7 activists (such as Melba Hernández, Frank Paìs, Vilma Espín, Celia Sánchez and Haydèe Santamaría), the rebels began their campaign.

Even in the face of seemingly insurmountable odds, Castro remained (at least publicly) positive. According to one anecdote, shortly after the ambush that had dispersed and decimated the attack force, one bedraggled group of fighters finally joined up with Castro's equally bedraggled and demoralized group. When Castro saw Che Guevara and his handful of disease-ridden, mostly unarmed rebels trudging miserably towards their camp, he had jumped up and cheerfully exclaimed *"Ahora sí, Batista se jodió!"* (loosely translated as "Batista's had it now!"). In addition to Castro's morale-boosting leadership, the rebels were also helped by a number of other factors – most importantly support from the peasants.

Gaining the support of the peasants

The Fidelistas, as Castro's rebels were known, were instructed to treat the long-mistreated peasants of the region with kindness and respect, paying for whatever they needed. Castro and Guevara insisted that they should educate the peasants they encountered, whose illiteracy rate was more than 80 per cent. They also provided medical assistance wherever they went. For many of these peasants, Guevara was the first trained doctor that they had ever seen.

The Fidelistas also helped the peasants with physically demanding tasks such as gathering the harvest. They used this chance to listen to the grievances of the peasants while telling them what the M-26-7 movement promised to do. Abusive landlords and corrupt officials were tried and punished by Castro's men. Furthermore, any of Castro's own men caught mistreating the peasants could also expect to be severely and swiftly punished.

Through these methods, Castro managed to turn the peasant's passively sympathetic attitude into active support by mid-1957. However, possibly the strongest recruiter for the rebels was, ironically, Batista's own regime. In response to the rebels' hit-and-run attacks, Batista's army and police would often resort to brutal treatment of peasants suspected of helping the rebels.

▲ Fidel Castro with a hunting rifle, in the Sierra Maestra Mountains, 1957. Behind him stand Camilo Cienfuegos (right, with the Thompson submachine gun) and his brother Raul (left, with a hunting rifle). Their American weapons and military equipment are the same as the Cuban army would have had.

The army compounded the rebels' advantages by adopting a reactive strategy intended to contain Castro's forces. They did not engage the rebels with counter-insurgency tactics but relied on their main advantages (US-supplied military equipment, including tanks, aircraft and artillery) and remained within their heavily defended garrisons. This made them static targets for the rebels who were rapidly learning the importance of mobility and surprise in their attacks. The rebels often attacked army patrols to grab weapons and ammunition before disappearing back into the dense forests. The army's brutal methods of interrrogation played into Castro's hands by increasing still further the peasants' support for his rebels. It also led to an increasingly demoralized army.

In contrast, the Fidelistas were under strict instructions to avoid brutality with civilians or captured enemy soldiers. The torture or murder of prisoners was forbidden and, if the situation permitted, an enemy's wounds would be treated. However, if any person (Fidelista, civilian or soldier) was found guilty of crimes against the peasants he would be (after a brief trial) executed by the unit leader or the injured party. Most peasants saw this harsh but effective brand of revolutionary justice as far fairer than the corrupt police and legal system.

▲ Che Guevara (left) relaxing with friend and fellow *Fidelista* Camilo Cienfuegos during the last days of the Sierra Maestra campaign, c. 1958

The rural campaign

Castro had not intended to wage the war from a rural base, but the failure of the Santiago uprising and his own disastrous landing two days later meant that he had to adjust his plans. He abandoned the initial strategy (to inspire an urban-based campaign of sabotage, insurrection, and guerrilla activity) in favour of a rural guerrilla campaign, which soon developed into full-scale engagements with the army in the Sierra Maestra. This shows one of the factors that led to Castro's eventual success: his movement's flexibility and his willingness to adapt to the situation. This would not have been possible with a less motivated or resilient cadre of activists. Other anti-Batista organizations had also tried to use force against the regime but had failed to overcome the army and police. The wide array of his opponents – students in March 1957; the Ortodoxo ex-president Prío and his supporters in May 1957; some officers and sailors in Cienfuegos in September – all failed. This only helped to secure Castro's position in the public consciousness as the only opponent to Batista's regime who had a chance of success.

Comparison of Castro's Sierra campaign and Mao's Long March

There were similarities between Castro's Sierra campaign of 1956 and Mao Zedong's Long March of 1934–1936:

- Both were outnumbered by enemy forces.

- Both operations began badly, were heavily outgunned by their enemies and were nearly wiped out.

- Both lost much of their force to desertion as the situation looked increasingly bleak.

- Both faced difficulties in resupply.

- Both were leading forces of ideologically driven and committed troops against an enemy whose army mostly comprised conscripts and unmotivated soldiers.

- Both sides struggled to gain recruits at first; their seemingly impossible plight discouraged any but the most dedicated from joining them.

- Both initially began an urban campaign that then had to move to the countryside.

- Both ordered their troops to treat the peasants with kindness, help them, educate them and not abuse them.

- Both were facing an enemy who treated the peasants with disdain and brutality, thus helping the rebels even further.

- Both were successful at planting "revolutionary seeds" among the peasants and recruiting them, leading to their future success.

The role of the urban revolutionary movements

Often overlooked in descriptions of the Cuban Revolution is the invaluable role of the urban revolutionaries. The underground cells of the M-26-7 movement hiding in the cities embarked upon a determined campaign of sabotage and propaganda to support Castro's guerrilla campaign in the Sierra Maestra. They coordinated with middle-class professionals and Ortodoxos, organized strikes, anti-regime graffiti and the dissemination of information to counter the government's own propaganda. As Balfour states, "the war in the Sierra could not be described in any sense as a peasant war."

According to one calculation, over 30 000 acts of sabotage were committed during the two-year campaign. Carlos Franqui, a revolutionary who in 1960 fled Cuba in protest at Castro's alignment with the USSR, declared that Castro and his immediate followers were the heart and soul of the revolution – not the peasants, as the propaganda claimed:

> *"The Comandante and his Twelve Followers were the revolution, not the city, the clandestine war, the 26 July Movement, the strikes, the sabotage, the people's boycott of Batista's elections. The revolution was the hero not the people."*

While this verdict can be put down to the bitterness of a disillusioned former comrade, it cannot be entirely ignored. Was the Cuban revolution really about the people of Cuba, or about Castro and his followers imposing their view upon the nation? The level of popular support that the M-26-7 rebels enjoyed would suggest that a good proportion of Cuba's populace shared the revolutionary aims.

Frank Pais's resistance cells had been the hub for the M-26-7 organization in Oriente province and his murder by the police in July 1957 in Santiago sparked a strike that soon spread from Santiago to the provinces of Camagüey and Las Villas. Batista reacted by suspending constitutional rights, thus playing into the hands of those who labelled him an undemocratic dictator.

Castro's forces in the Sierra Maestra gained in strength during this time, launching more attacks against the increasingly demoralized government outposts and forcing Batista to withdraw his forces entirely from the area by spring 1958. In March 1958, the rebels called for a nationwide general strike as a show of solidarity with the M-26-7 movement. The strike was organized for 9 April and received strong support in eastern and central Cuba. However, it had little success in the west, where the majority of the labour force lived. Since the labour unions and the PSP still mostly supported Batista, Batista felt that he must still enjoy popular support, so he authorized his police force to employ brutal methods to quell the protests. Castro himself described the failure of the general strike as "a major setback". However, it was not enough to regain Batista the support he was losing from almost all sectors of Cuban society; nor did it reinvigorate his demoralized army.

Overall, the urban campaigns did not enjoy the same degree of success as the rural campaign and, by 1958, the resistance to Batista was centred around the liberated areas of the Sierra Maestra mountains and Oriente province.

Castro's use of propaganda

Castro was clearly aware of the power of political speeches and propaganda, which he had used to good effect in his student days. One aim of his Moncada plan had been to capture the radio at the base and use it to broadcast revolutionary messages to inspire the hoped-for uprising. Similarly, in 1957, one of the rebels' first acts was to establish *Radio Rebelde* (Rebel Radio) to broadcast their propaganda and to counteract the government propaganda.

As Batista's forces failed to crush the guerrilla movement, the radio broadcasts exaggerated its victories and continued to inform the Cuban public about the Moncada Programme and other M-26-7 promises. They also served to counter the government claims that Castro was dead.

Growing international awareness of the brutality of Batista's regime, contrasted with the seemingly noble and charismatic Fidelistas, helped convince the US government to withdraw their military support for the regime. With Castro's broadcasts constantly advertising his plans for rejuvenating the Cuban economy, business leaders began to give their support to the rebels.

Castro's propaganda also helped to convince Batista that, by 1958, the guerrilla army in the Sierra Maestra numbered between 1000 and 2000 experienced fighters. In reality, Castro had little more than 300 fighters until just before his final victory in 1959.

Batista's counter-attack: *Operation Verano*

In June 1958, convinced that the tide was turning in his favour, Batista launched *Operation Verano* (Operation Summer) with 12 000 government troops, backed by air support, tanks, and artillery. Despite their overwhelming superiority in numbers and equipment, the government forces were handicapped by a number of weaknesses:

1   More than half (approximately 7000) were conscripts with little training and even less incentive to fight.

Class discussion

Discuss the role played by propaganda in securing Castro's rise to power.

2   The operational command was divided between two rival generals: General Eulogio Cantillo and the inept, but politically connected, General Alberto del Rio Chaviano (the same officer who, as a colonel, had been responsible for the torture and execution of the Moncada attackers in 1953).

3   Castro's forces knew the ground well and were able to prepare for the offensive by planting minefields and planning ambushes.

4   By mid-1958 the local population was firmly supportive of Castro and his men, providing them with excellent intelligence about troop movements while doing the exact opposite for the government forces.

The first major engagements were a disaster for the army, which suffered heavy casualties. Castro's men often treated their enemies mercifully, sometimes even allowing them the choice to join the rebels. This encouraged the disheartened troops to seek out an opportunity to surrender rather than fight.

The one government "victory" of *Operation Verano*, the Battle of Las Mercedes (29 July to 8 August), was still a victory for the rebel forces in the long run. An ambush succeeded in trapping two rebel columns, killing 70 men. Total disaster was avoided because Guevara's column managed to cut off 1500 army reinforcements. This bought time for Castro to negotiate a ceasefire and suggest that he was willing to discuss an end to the war. During the six days of the negotiations, the rebel forces quietly slipped away so that when the negotiations eventually failed, the Cuban army resumed their assault but found no rebels left to fight.

ATL Thinking and communication skills

1   List the main reasons for the failure of Batista's counter-attack (*Operation Verano*).

2   Explain the significance of the failure of *Operation Verano* in terms of the final outcome of the Cuban Revolution.

Castro's victory

Following the failure of *Operation Verano*, Batista's forces were aware that the end was nigh. Castro immediately launched a counter-attack to capitalize on the situation. His forces now moved into central Cuba, their numbers swollen by peasants and army deserters. By December 1958 the Fidelistas numbered nearly 3000 – a remarkable growth from the original 18 survivors of the *Granma* expedition. Castro's supporters abroad helped him by smuggling in new weapons and ammunition by plane but most of the rebel weapons came from Batista's own forces, which had surrendered them or left them behind as they fled.

▲ Fidel Castro and his *Fidelistas* celebrate their victory in 1959.

After bitter fighting in the cities of Santiago and Santa Clara and the defeat of the army garrison at Yaguajay on 30 December 1958, Batista fled from Cuba to the Dominican Republic. Castro entered Havana in triumph on 2 January 1959.

Herbert L Matthews' interview with Castro, February 1957

One of the ways in which Castro used the media was by allowing *New York Times* journalist Herbert L Matthews into the Sierra Maestra for a candid interview. Embedded with the rebels, Matthews wrote about the potency and popularity of the guerrilla band and their enigmatic leader. Through careful stage-managing of his rag-tag band of rebels, Castro managed to give Matthews (and, thereby, the American and Cuban public) the impression that his force was not only much larger than it was but also that they controlled a wide area of the mountains. Thus the myth of Castro's invincibility was disseminated to a wider, previously sceptical audience. It was not long until more international journalists came to see for themselves.

Before Matthews' interview, the Cuban press had written mostly about the resort atmosphere of Havana, and the government did a fairly good job of controlling the stories that left the island. After Matthew's interview, *Reader's Guide* articles focused on rebel demands and interviews with Castro, which kept the revolution on the front pages of the US press.

Why did the Batista regime collapse?

According to Balfour, the main reason for the Batista regime's collapse was "because it was corrupt and barbarous". Additionally, Batista's failure to retain the support of any social elites meant that he relied on the communist-led trade unions and organized labour. The M-26-7 movement's promises of reducing corruption appealed to the working classes, especially the peasants in eastern and central Cuba. The escalating violence and the economic crisis caused by their revolution damaged Batista's support from the business elite (support that had already been weakened by the corruption of his regime). His failure to counter Castro's propaganda, combined with his police force's use of torture, led to public pressure on the US government to withdraw their support for Batista while simultaneously encouraging more international support for Castro. Even Batista's connections to the politically powerful US corporations and the Mafia could not hide his regime's corruption and brutality.

Batista believed that he could recreate the popularity that he had enjoyed during his 1940–1944 presidential term. However, the illegitimacy of his 1952 coup and his failure to address the issues of social inequity and corruption strengthened the arguments of his opponents. Relaxing press restrictions prior to the 1954 elections meant that his opponents could openly challenge the legitimacy of his regime.

In response to growing international awareness of Batista's brutal regime through pro-Castro articles (such as the Herbert L. Matthews interviews in the *New York Times*) the US government finally banned arms sales to both sides in Cuba. Although the ban had little material impact (Batista had stockpiles of US weaponry and ammunition and the rebels continued to be supplied by arms smugglers), it had the symbolic effect of showing that the US no longer fully supported the Cuban leader.

Class discussion

Draw and complete a summary table with the following headings to show how Castro's ideological stance changed over time:

- date
- evidence of communist/Marxist views
- evidence of nationalist views
- source.

Class discussion

Create a simple storyboard for Castro's rise to power, to establish the narrative clearly in your mind. Colour-code each frame to show which factor(s) played a significant role at each stage. Then choose one of these factors at random and discuss how this was significant in Castro's rise to power.

The Cuban plantation owners, industrialists and bankers whose business interests had already been negatively affected by recent US economic policies now saw the potential for further losses. Batista's slavish adherence to a pro-US economic policy seemed no longer viable and they attempted to curry favour with the young, charismatic, and increasingly successful rebel who promised an end to US corporate imperialism in Cuba. The fact that Castro had openly declared (on more than one occasion) that he was not a communist but a Cuban nationalist, helped secure their support.

It could also be argued that Batista was defeated by the ghost of José Martí, symbolically reincarnated in Fidel Castro. In keeping with what historians call the Great Man Theory (a compound of the views of the 19th-century historians Thomas Carlyle and Herbert Spencer), Castro's success was a result of his personal qualities as well as the social conditions of the time. In the public imagination Fidel Castro cut a dashing figure; a fitting heir to the revolutionary tradition of José Martí. This was partly due to his masterly use of the media and partly due to the failed policies of Batista. As he rode in triumph from Santiago to Havana in January 1959, Castro was greeted all along his route by cheering crowds who hailed him as the latest and the last in the line of Cuban nationalist heroes.

Class discussion

Look back at the Castro section so far. To what extent is it accurate to claim that the failure at Moncada in 1953 was the main reason for Castro's success in 1959?

Class discussion

To what extent can the Great Man theory be applied to Castro's rise to power in Cuba? Create a balanced response to this question by identifying the arguments for both sides.

ATL Self-management and communication skills

Create a series of revision cards to explain Castro's rise to power. Set yourself a question, for example, "To what extent was the use of force the main reason for Castro coming to power in Cuba?"

a   Make each card about 7.5cm by 12.5cm.

b   Use different-coloured cards for each main factor.

c   On one side write the date (month and year) and a brief comment about the event, for example, "November 1958: *Granma* expedition launched".

d   On the other side write bullet points about the event, selecting information carefully for relevance to the question.

Working with a partner, shuffle the cards and deal out six random cards each. Construct an essay plan using just those six. Verbally explain your essay plan to your partner.

Political parties in Cuba

Partido Revolucionario Cubano Auténtico (the Authentic Cuban Revolutionary Party; aka the Auténticos)

Conservative/nationalist party set up by Dr Ramón Grau San Martín during his exile in the USA (1934–1940); primarily middle class support base; opposed Batista's government; once in power (1944–1948) used armed political gangs to deal with opposition and had close ties to American Mafia organizations.

Partido Socialista Popular (the Popular Socialist Party; PSP)

Formed in 1925 as the Partido Comunista de Cuba (the Cuban Communist Party); renamed in 1944. Supported Batista in the 1930s against his wealthy middle-class opponents in Grau's Auténticos. In 1944 the PSP lost the election that brought Grau back to the presidency. Dissolved in 1961 before being resurrected (in 1965) as the Partido Comunista de Cuba once more.

Partido Ortodoxo (the Orthodox Party)

Socialist, nationalist, anti-imperialist/anti-US, populist party; founded in 1947 by Chibás in response to corruption, demands for social justice and lack of reforms of the Batista and Grau governments; adopted a strongly anti-communist outlook c. 1947–1948; Fidel Castro was a prominent member from 1947; looked likely to win the 1952 election before Batista's coup.

Partido Liberal de Cuba (the Liberal Party of Cuba)

Centre-right party founded in 1910; dissolved in 1959; allied with various parties against the Auténticos in the 1954 election with Batista as their presidential candidate; the Liberals came second.

Similarities and differences in the rise to power of Adolf Hitler (Germany), Fidel Castro (Cuba) and Hugo Chávez (Venezuela)

Key event	Hitler	Castro	Chávez
Failed attempt to seize power by force	Munich Putsch, November 1923	Attack on the Moncada Barracks, July 1953	Failed coup attempt – Operation *Zamora*, February 1992
Failed coup led to public popularity	The speech he gave at his trial ("The Goddess of History acquits me") and the book (*Mein Kampf*) he wrote while in prison	The speech he gave at his trial ("History will absolve me") and its subsequent publication as the Moncada Programme	His televised call for his soldiers to surrender/cease fighting after the coup failed and his subsequent trial
Time in prison	From November 1923 to December 1924; released after serving nine months of a lenient five-year prison term	From October 1953 to May 1955; released during a government amnesty as Batista attempted to appear less dictatorial in the wake of the widely condemned 1954 elections	From February 1992 to early 1994; released from prison after the impeachment of the president that he had tried to oust
Method of gaining political power	Changed tactics and achieved power through the democratic process; President Paul von Hindenburg used his emergency powers to make Hitler Chancellor of Germany in January 1933	Fought a guerrilla war from November 1956 to December 1958; achieved power through military victory; became de facto leader of Cuba in January 1959	Following his release from prison, he used his popularity from the coup to begin a political career; won the presidential elections in December 1998

Establishing the "new Cuba"

▲ Victorious Castro and his supporters enter Havana, January 1959 – It has been repeatedly stated that Castro's victorious rebels did not engage in any of the looting or violence that customarily accompanied a military victory like this.

After Batista fled Cuba in 1958 (and a brief attempt by some army officers to establish a US-supported junta), Fidel Castro and his supporters took power. The Cuban Revolution had achieved its primary aim and it now had to create the "new Cuba" that Castro had promised in his Moncada Programme back in 1954. The new state had been born out of violent political revolution but to survive it would need very quickly to achieve the legitimacy of a parliamentary democracy.

Castro knew he needed to consolidate his position fast in order to secure the future of the Cuban Revolution. The fact that the CIA had arranged a coup in Guatemala in 1954 at the behest of US corporations showed the lengths the US government would go to to protect the profits of their most powerful companies. This forced Castro to move cautiously with his programme of land reform and nationalization. He repeated his declaration that he was not a communist and in January 1959 the US Secretary of State, John Foster Dulles, informed President Eisenhower that:

> *"the provisional government appears free from communist taint and there are indications that it intends to pursue friendly relations with the United States."*

Historians tend to agree that Castro was not a communist at this stage. Rather, he was a pragmatist whose policies were not so much governed by the doctrines of Marx or Lenin as by the needs of nationalism and Cuban independence, with a strong focus on political, social, and economic improvements designed to benefit the whole of society rather than just the wealthy elites. When he was introducing his agrarian reforms, for example, Castro even drew upon Catholic rhetoric by likening his policies to Christ's teachings, declaring that:

> *"They [Christ's teachings] did not prosper in high society, but germinated in the hearts of the humble people of Palestine."*

Despite the Catholic Church's history of support for the wealthy classes against the poor, Castro did not immediately move against organized religion as most communist rulers did. His economic reforms were, initially, seen as rather moderate, although this soon changed when he began nationalizing the large landholdings and other businesses of US corporations and wealthy Cuban planters. Nevertheless, even the US Vice-President Richard M Nixon stated, after meeting Castro in 1959, that Castro was not a communist and that he and the US could and should work together. The start of the US trade embargo in 1959–1960 pushed Castro into making a vital trade deal with the USSR, thus closer to the communists.

Events beyond Castro's control changed the situation further and, in May 1961 (immediately after the USA's failed **Bay of Pigs Invasion**), he publicly declared that the Cuban Revolution was a socialist one and that Cuba was a communist state. The move towards communism had, however, begun during the earliest days of the new government, when, recognizing the need for politically experienced officials, Castro gave members of the Popular Socialist Party (Partido Socialista Popular or PSP) positions of power. His brother Raúl was a communist and naturally had some influence over Fidel's decisions, but soon there was open resistance to him and to the other communists. Castro responded by removing these anti-communists from power and by November 1959 he had been mostly successful in this (a further four anti-communists were removed in 1960).

Bay of Pigs Invasion
On 17 April 1961 a group of anti-Castro Cubans who had fled to the USA launched an invasion of Cuba intended to overthrow Castro. Within three days they had been defeated and captured. Within a week, the world knew that the failed invasion attempt had been planned, funded and (at least in part) executed by the USA.

INRA
The National Institute of Agrarian Reform, established in 1959.

Directorio Revolucionario Estudantil (DRE)
The DRE had been an anti-Batista student movement. From c.1960–1965 they became an anti-Castro resistance group, joining the rebels in the Escambray Mountains. When those rebels were defeated, the DRE was also finished as a political threat. With dwindling numbers, and lack of success, the DRE eventually disbanded in December 1966.

While communist/Marxist influence is visible in some of his early policies (especially land reform and nationalization), Castro's social and economic policies were drawn from a more nationalist, pro-Cuban and anti-imperialist perspective. They needed to be radical in order to redress the inequities within Cuban society after centuries of domination by the Spanish and then six decades of corrupt governments working primarily in the service of the US corporations. As Antonio Núñez Jiménez, then head of the **INRA**, said to an American reporter in 1959, "We are only trying to move from feudalism to enlightened capitalism. Cuba is not ready for socialism."

In 1961 the 26 July Movement, the DR (the Directorio Revolucionario, the successor to the **Directorio Revolucionario Estudantil** or DRE) and the PSP were merged to form the Integrated Revolutionary Organizations (ORI), which became the Communist Party of Cuba (PCC) in 1965.

Castro's leadership of Cuba, 1959–1962

Becoming the leader of Cuba

A provisional government was appointed by Fidel Castro and the M-26-7 leadership, replacing the Batista regime in January 1959. The well-respected judge Manuel Urrutia Lleó became president and José Miró Cardona prime minister. They presided over a cabinet that included only three rebels (only one of whom came from M-26-7). Fidel Castro was appointed commander-in-chief of the armed forces.

At the same time, Castro also established an organization to oversee the rapid and efficient implementation of his proposed agrarian land reforms: the Office of the Revolutionary Plans and Coordination (ORPC). This body was made up of his closest confidants from the guerrilla war, including his brother Raúl and Che Guevara. Thus a dual-power governmental system was in place (something which both Lenin and Mao had put to good use in the past). By February 1959 Miró had resigned and Castro had been appointed prime minister in his place. It soon became apparent that true power lay with Castro and the ORPC.

In April 1959, while Castro was visiting other countries in Latin America and the USA, President Urrutia closed down the brothels and casinos in Cuba. Castro returned to Cuba to find protests and anger from these newly unemployed urban workers. Putting socio-economic considerations ahead of moral objections, Castro ordered the casinos and brothels to be reopened until alternative jobs could be found for these workers. This example highlights two of the major issues in Cuba in early 1959:

▲ Fidel Castro with Manuel Urrutia Lleó in 1959

1   the tension between the radical young revolutionary-turned-prime minister and the more conservative president

2   Fidel Castro's habitual method of leadership: once a decision was made in his head, he would simply act on it rather than debating and forming a political consensus.

This preference for action rather than words proved to be a constant feature of Castro's rule, supporting, to some degree, the accusation that he was a dictator. This accusation was further supported by his decision to suspend elections in order to allow time to consolidate the revolution and secure it against the ever-present threat of a US-funded counter-revolution or even an all-out invasion. Fair and free elections would, he promised, be held shortly. They weren't.

The following month, the National Institute for Agrarian Reform (INRA) was established, with former rebel troop leader and Marxist economist Antonio Núñez Jiménez at its head. The INRA was in charge of the agrarian reforms and answerable only to Castro. Within months, the INRA had absorbed the ORPC, thus becoming Cuba's real government and superseding Urrutia's provisional government.

This was just one of many examples of communists being given positions of power. Some M-26-7 members and other anti-Batista allies complained about the increasing influence of communism and in June a number of cabinet ministers resigned in protest. Pedro Díaz Lanz, the rebel pilot whom Castro had appointed as Chief of the Revolutionary Air Force in January, also resigned for this reason. While the staunchly anti-communist Urrutia condemned Lanz as a traitor, he took the opportunity to publicly warn against the slide towards communism. This provoked a power struggle between him and Castro. In an act of theatrical genius that revealed his understanding of his people, Castro resigned as prime minister and, in a televised broadcast, declared that this was in protest at President Urrutia's refusal to implement the social reforms that Cuba's poorest people needed. He went on to state that Urrutia was planning treason and that he would no doubt find "plenty of American agents to serve in his government". Castro achieved his anticipated result: an outpouring of spontaneous anger and demands for Urrutia's resignation.

Urrutia resigned in July and took sanctuary in the Venezuelan Embassy. His replacement, Osvaldo Dorticós, was more amenable to Castro's decisions and remained president until 1976. In December 1976 Castro replaced Dorticós and he remained President of Cuba until February 2008, when ill health prompted him to step down in favour of his brother Raúl.

Consolidating the revolution

As early as December 1960, Cuba was well on its way towards becoming a single-party state, with Fidel Castro as its unimpeachable "supreme leader" (*Máximo Líder*).

- Political parties were banned.
- Newspapers and radio stations were censored and forced to close if they angered the government.
- Communist-led trade unions were growing ever more powerful.
- All judicial appointees were made with Castro's approval.
- All legislative and executive power in Cuba was in the hands of the cabinet (appointed by Castro).

▲ Propaganda poster from 1976 showing Castro as a young man

Despite his promises to hold fair and free elections (unlike those held by Batista in 1954 and 1958), one of Castro's first acts (through Urrutia's provisional government) was to ban all political parties for at least four years. During his trip to the USA in April 1959, Castro announced that he would be suspending the elections. This was, like so many other laws of this time, intended to be a temporary measure to allow him to consolidate the gains of the revolution before the inevitable counter-revolutionary attempts by the USA and their allies.

Although this appears to be a dictatorial (and hypocritical) move by Castro, his reasoning was sound. Because of the traditionally chaotic, violent, corrupt nature of Cuban politics, he could not permit political parties and their armed gangs of supporters to wander freely around Cuba at a time when he was restructuring the weakened police and armed forces in order to maintain the security of the nation. Other political parties could also be easily bought by US corporate, criminal or government elements – after all, the Mafia had tried to buy the 1952 election for Batista. Furthermore, with CIA agents still active in the country, the threat of a US-sponsored coup was never far from his mind.

Castro explained his postponement of the elections by declaring: "real democracy is not possible for hungry people". Nevertheless, his enemies and former supporters alike have identified his failure to deliver the elections as one of the major failings of the years immediately after his victory.

Consolidating power

In 1963 the ORI became the United Party of the Socialist Revolution (PURS) and, by the time he was announcing the newly named Communist Party of Cuba (PCC) in 1965, Castro was its undisputed leader. Within a couple of years the Cuban government was stable and well established, able to deal with the various opposition elements through mostly democratic means. There were, however, some instances where Castro resorted to repressive measures. For example, in February 1968 his criticism of the USSR's policy of peaceful co-existence provoked opposition from hardline communists within the PCC. He dealt with this by arresting the leaders for sectarianism. The public example of their trial ensured that there was no more trouble from the PCC after that.

In 1972 Castro's unlimited power was reduced, with a number of his roles being shared among members of the newly enlarged executive committee of the Cuban cabinet. However, to all intents and purposes, he remained the spiritual figurehead of the nation. He was helped in this by the aggressive actions of the USA, which continued its embargo and terrorist attacks, all of which served to strengthen the public perception of Castro as Cuba's defender and the protector of their hard-won rights.

Research and thinking skills

Historians and other commentators from all sides of the political spectrum have argued fiercely about the rights and wrongs of Castro's actions during his rule over Cuba. One of the most important questions is whether Castro's decision to make Cuba a Marxist/communist state was deliberate or forced on him by the actions of the USA and, to a lesser degree, the USSR. Many sources, especially online historical summaries, portray their chosen side of the argument through:

- carefully selecting what information to include and what to omit
- deliberate blurring of the chronology to imply the "cause and consequence" chain that fits their agenda.

For greater understanding of the different viewpoints, read and compare the accounts of different historians. See the References and further reading section for the Castro section for some suggestions.

Castro's challenges, January 1959

Post-Batista Cuba faced a number of problems and challenges. Castro's solutions are listed below.

Problem	Solution
1 Inequities in land ownership	Radical land reform; nationalization of large landholdings
2 Inequities in society	Universal education and universal health care; improvement and enforcement of labour laws; removal of racist barriers to careers and promotion prospects; rent reductions of 30–50 per cent (March 1959)
3 The need for transparent social justice	Reform of judiciary and police; arrest, trial and punishment of members of the Batista regime (especially Batista's torturers and murderers); televising the trials and executions of the most notorious criminals from Batista's regime
4 Endemic corruption	Punishment of corrupt officials and policemen; increase in pay
5 Ownership or control of much of Cuba's economy by US corporations	Nationalization of industries
6 Economy in severe trouble (massive graduate unemployment; unfavourable trade conditions with USA; rural poverty; urban unemployment)	Creation of jobs in towns; temporary reopening of casinos and brothels; land reform/redistribution; economic ties with USSR after 1960
7 Lack of democracy	Reintroduction of parliamentary democracy; reinstatement of political parties; fair and free elections
8 Lack of a united vision for the "new Cuba" by anti-Batista forces	Banning of political parties; unification of the main groups (for example, M-26-7, PSP and DR to form ORI, eventually the PCC)
9 Potential counter-revolution from within Cuba	Banning of political parties; a people's militia (as a counterbalance to the army whose loyalty remained dubious); arrest of Batista loyalists; letting those who opposed the revolution to leave (at first)
10 Potential counter-revolution from outside Cuba	Strengthening of the armed forces; establishment of people's militia; cultivation of alliances/friendships with USSR; help for revolutionary groups inside those Latin American countries that had tried to destabilize Cuba
11 Potential invasion by foreign countries	As above; the Dominican coup attempt foiled (August 1959) through luck; defeat of the Bay of Pigs Invasion (April 1961)

Problem	Solution
12 Anxiety from domestic economic interests (Cuban planters, bankers and business elites) about what would happen	Reassuring them that he was not a communist (until May 1961); land reform aimed at weakening the biggest landowners in favour of the smaller ones; reiterating desire for continued trade with USA (until 1960–1961)
13 Anxiety from the middle classes (professionals such as doctors, lawyers, businessmen) about what would happen	Instructing victorious anti-Batista forces (in 1959) to respect private property and the rule of law; reiterating that he was not a communist (until May 1961); enforcing the law; nationalizing large landholdings (especially foreign-owned plantations); promoting Cuban-owned smaller plantations
14 Anxiety from foreign economic interests (most notably US corporations and the Mafia) about what would happen	Limited nationalization of industries/businesses (after 1960 this increased dramatically in reaction to US pressure); strengthened counter-inteligence services to catch CIA and Mafia agents
15 Economic destabilization attempts by the "Colossus to the North" (the USA) and its Latin American allies	Nationalization of industries; propaganda campaign to ensure loyalty to the revolution (short-term solution); education policies designed to ensure loyalty to the revolution (long-term solution)

Thinking skills

1 Create your own copy of the table on the previous page.

2 Cut out each problem and each solution to make a mix-and-match sorting activity to help you revise this topic.

3 Highlight the problems/solutions in a specific colour to indicate which factor they are most associated with (political, social, economic, military or other).

This will help you plan and construct an essay about how effectively Castro consolidated his control over Cuba after January 1959.

US actions in Guatemala

In the early 1950s, with the Cold War entering its early stages between the USA and the USSR, it was deemed imperative to American security that Latin American states remained firmly in the hands of pro-US leaders. Even if this meant that less-than-democratic methods were used to install and maintain these regimes.

There is increasing evidence about the role played by US corporations in directing US foreign policy at this time. For example, in 1954 the United Fruit Company's pressure upon the US government paid off and the CIA orchestrated a coup d'état against the democratically-elected (and highly popular) Guatemalan government of Colonel Jacobo Árbenz Guzmán. The main impetus for the United Fruit Company's efforts to remove the Guatemalan government were due to the labour laws brought in by Árbenz's government during the 1940s. These laws were intended to protect workers from the notoriously brutal conditions employed by the United Fruit Company (and other corporations). As a result of their loss in profits, these corporations pressured the American government into continuing their much-maligned involvement in Latin American affairs.

The CIA coup sparked a thirty-year civil war and brought untold misery to Guatemala and the region. Che Guevara witnessed firsthand the actions of the US-trained death squads and became convinced that the only way to combat American corporate imperialism in Latin America was through force.

Despite the best efforts of CIA investigators to prove the link between Arbenz and the USSR, the only evidence that could be found from all the Guatemalan documents seized after the coup was two unpaid bills (one for $12.35 and the other for $10.60) from a Moscow bookshop.

It has been suggested that the Director of the CIA (Alan Dulles) and the Secretary of State (his brother, John Foster Dulles) were the main driving forces behind encouraging US involvement in Guatemala. They both had significant business interests in the United Fruit Company. This is similar to the connection between Dick Cheney (US Vice-President 2001–2009) and the invasion and occupation of Iraq (2003–2011) which proved extremely profitable for Halliburton – a company which he had significant business interests in. The United Fruit Company is currently trading under the name Chiquita Brands International.

The US response to the Cuban Revolution, 1959–1962

The pervading fear among the revolutionaries was of a CIA-sponsored coup against them, exactly as had happened to President Arbenz in Guatemala in 1954. This, however, did not occur immediately. John Lewis Gaddis described the initial US response as "remarkably calm". For its role in the Guatemalan coup, the USA had been castigated in Latin America, where there was now a strong undercurrent of support for communist or communist-affiliated nationalist movements that promised to challenge the USA's influence. In 1958, for example, during a visit to Venezuela, Vice-President Nixon's motorcade was attacked by angry mobs. The US administration rightly surmised that to intervene in Cuba at this time would be potentially disastrous for relations with their Latin American neighbours, but that did not mean that the USA had written off the prospect of military intervention. According to the reporter Tad Szulc, President Eisenhower's National Security Council was discussing US military action as early as March 1959.

Dealing with opposition to the revolution

The early years of the Cuban Revolution saw Castro faced with opposition from a variety of groups:

- the Escambray rebels (War Against the Bandits, 1960–1965)

- members of the M-26-7 and other anti-Batista groups who opposed the move towards communism but did not take up arms

- the wealthy middle classes, who had hoped that their interests would be protected.

The growing influence of communists led to various forms of resistance to Castro from within Cuba. Some, like Huber Matos, were denounced as traitors and arrested. Others chose to take more direct action. This included some members of the DRE, the anti-communist and anti-Batista student group that had joined forces with Che Guevara's M-26-7 units in December 1958 during the fighting for the city of Santa Clara. During the revolution they had been active in the Escambray mountain region and, in 1960, they returned to their hideouts there, prepared to fight Castro's forces. Other disaffected rebels and Batista loyalists joined them, leading to a five-year guerrilla campaign (called the Escambray Rebellion or "War Against the Bandits") that ended in January 1965 with their utter destruction.

The Escambray Rebellion, 1960–1965

Following Castro's victory in January 1959, some soldiers still loyal to Batista decided to continue the fight from the Escambray Mountains. They were soon joined by others (including William Alexander Morgan) who disliked the pro-communist leanings of the new government and by peasant farmers disenchanted with the land reforms. The Escambray Rebellion (known in Cuba as *"Lucha contra Bandidos"*, the War Against The Bandits) was a guerrilla campaign similar in style to Castro's own Sierra Maestra campaign against Batista's forces. These rebels enjoyed far less popular support than the M-26-7 rebels had, but they were given the same US military aid, via CIA and Mafia agents, that the previous regime had enjoyed. However, after the debacle of the Bay of Pigs Invasion, the USA cut off funding and supplies to the rebels. Castro's counter-intelligence units were busily uncovering and arresting CIA agents and their networks, and so it was only a matter of time before Castro's numerically superior forces defeated the rebels (in January 1965).

Huber Matos (1918–2014)

Castro appointed Huber Matos, a former teacher and farmer who had been a brilliant rebel commander during the Sierra Campaign, as military governor of Camagüey province. In October 1959 he wrote a resignation letter, stating his concerns about the growing influence of the communists. His timing was unfortunate: his previous complaints to Castro about the communists had been ignored but this letter was sent two days after the appointment of Raúl Castro (the new government's most prominent communist) as Minister of the Armed Forces.

Matos (along with many of his officers) was immediately arrested for "rebellion", tried and sentenced to 20 years' imprisonment. As Balfour states: "The Revolution was beginning to devour its sons."

Castro also had to deal with external threats. For example, in August 1959 an anti-Castro coup organized by Dominican dictator Rafael Trujillo (probably acting on advice from the CIA) was foiled because William Alexander Morgan, one of the plot leaders, secretly informed Castro. All of this helped to convince Castro that the revolution was far from safe yet.

The saving grace for Castro came, ironically, from the USA. The constant threats and aggressive actions by the USA and Cuban exiles who had fled there meant that Castro was able to clearly identify himself as the bastion of Cuban defence against imperialist oppression. With the failure of the Bay of Pigs Invasion, his position was secure. The ensuing wave of nationalism and the incontrovertible evidence of the USA's intentions to undo the positive changes of the revolution led to anyone who criticized Castro being denounced as a traitor. The terrorist attacks by CIA agents and Cuban exiles just helped to confirm Castro's position as the saviour of Cuba.

William Alexander Morgan (1928–1961)

William Alexander Morgan was a US citizen who volunteered to fight against Batista and had been recruited to the M-26-7 when his rebel group joined forces with Che Guevara's during the Sierra Maestra campaign. The military training gained during his time in the US army (where he was possibly recruited by the CIA) served him well and he was soon promoted to the rank of *Comandante* – one of only three foreigners to hold that rank – the others being Eloy Gutiérrez Menoyo (Spanish) and Ernesto "Che" Guevara (Argentinian).

The US government has, unsurprisingly, denied claims that *El Yanqui Comandante* (as he was known) was an agent of the CIA. Morgan was one of the leaders of an anti-Castro coup organised by Dominican dictator Rafael Trujillo. However, Morgan had secretly informed Castro of the plot and it failed. Possibly due to the persistent belief of his involvement with the CIA, Morgan was implicated

in the March 1960 *La Coubre* explosion and, later, accused of gunrunning to aid the anti-Castro rebels in the Escambray Mountains. It was for the last of these that, in March 1961, he was executed by firing squad.

▲ William Alexander Morgan, US volunteer and suspected CIA agent, c. 1958

The USA's economic war on Cuba in the early 1960s

In response to the nationalization of plantations and foreign-owned businesses, in November 1959 the US government banned all exports to Cuba, in the hope that economic starvation would force Castro to adopt a more business-friendly stance. The USA was, by far, Cuba's biggest trading partner and the Cuban economy was almost entirely dependent on this link. However, the trade embargo had the effect of forcing Cuba into the eager arms of the USA's Cold War enemy, the USSR.

The Soviet premier, Nikita Khrushchev, had previously been uninterested in pursuing communist expansion in Latin America, preferring instead to consolidate the USSR's grip on Eastern Europe and paving the way towards better relations with the USA. When presented with an existing socialist state, however, it seemed too good an opportunity to pass up. With the US embargo threatening to cripple Cuba's economy, there was little alternative for Cuba but to turn to the USSR. Khrushchev agreed in 1960 to buy their sugar and provide weapons and oil in return. Soviet oil would now replace American oil in Cuba's refineries. The US corporations that owned the Cuban oil refineries refused to process Soviet oil and found themselves suddenly and unceremoniously taken over by Castro. This naturally shocked and angered the US government almost as much as the US corporations who had just lost their highly profitable multi-million dollar investments: its nearest overseas neighbour was becoming an ally of its greatest global enemy.

This deal with the USSR can be credited with saving the Cuban Revolution at a time when it was at its most vulnerable. The USA, now convinced that Castro was a communist, increased the intensity of the embargo against Cuba. Castro responded by accelerating the nationalization process. Land reform was underway and health care and education had both been made universally available. As far as Cuba's working class was concerned, Castro was their saviour and he had earned their loyalty by keeping his promises.

Military problems and solutions in the early 1960s

The ever-present threat of invasion by the USA, and the CIA campaign to destabilize the Cuban Revolution through terrorist attacks, meant that Castro had to ensure that Cuba was in a position to defend itself. The first step was to remove Batista loyalists from the army and other security services, through the Revolutionary Courts and public trials and executions of the worst of Batista's torturers and killers.

In October 1959 Castro used Huber Matos's so-called "rebellion" to consolidate his control over Cuba. He created armed militias to complement the existing state military and civil controls: the armed forces, the military counter-intelligence section, the police, and the secret police (which replaced the hated BRAC). It was these militias that helped to save Cuba in April 1961 when they delayed the Cuban exile landing forces at the Bay of Pigs long enough for the Cuban army to arrive and destroy them. Following this victory, Castro enjoyed the unquestioning loyalty of both the Cuban people and the military. He never lost the latter.

The Bay of Pigs invasion, April 1961

In April 1961, Kennedy sent 1400 Cuban exiles who were trained by the US military and the CIA to invade Cuba. These Cubans, known as Brigade 2506, were taken by civilian freighters and supported by US warships. About 200 paratroopers were also dropped by US planes painted in the Cuban air force colours.

The invasion was intended to spark a popular uprising amongst the Cuban people and to lead to the overthrowing of the Castro government. It failed dramatically when the Cuban militia discovered them and fought fiercely to prevent them establishing a beachhead. Although the militia were outgunned by the invaders, they bought valuable time for the Cuban army to launch a counter-attack. Castro took personal command of the fight, commandeering a tank and leading his forces in battle.

In an effort to maintain plausible deniability, the USA did not send any American troops to fight; they only provided intelligence and logistical support from their warships. The hoped-for uprising did not occur as Castro's police forces immediately arrested the most prominent anti-Castro activists in Cuba. Additionally, Cuban radio broadcast a warning to the people that invaders were attempting to undo the revolution, thus inspiring a massive surge of pro-Castro popularity.

After three days, the Cuban exiles were defeated. 118 were killed, 360 wounded and 1202 captured. On the Cuban side, casualties were far higher (mostly due to the indiscriminate bombing by the US warplanes) – over 4000 civilians, militiamen and police were killed or wounded with 176 soldiers killed and over 500 wounded. The captured invaders were paraded in front of the world's media and

▲ Fidel Castro personally leads the Cuban counterattack against the CIA-led Cuban Exiles during the Bay of Pigs Invasion (April 1961)

they publicly admitted that they had been trained, financed and equipped by the US. The US government were no longer able to claim the moral high ground in the Cold War.

The most significant effects of this failed invasion were the way it showed the world that Castro had been correct about US intentions. It led almost directly to the Cuban Missile Crisis of October 1962.

The threat posed by Castro's Cuba to the USA's allied dictatorships in Latin America did not go unnoticed. The Cuban Missile Crisis of October 1962 was a direct result of Castro's conviction that another US invasion attempt was inevitable. He was probably right in this view, as the US government was under intense pressure from Cuban exiles, US corporations and the Mafia to try again to depose Castro.

The Cuban Missile Crisis, 1962

Khrushchev placed Soviet nuclear missiles on Cuba as a bargaining chip to convince the USA, Britain, and France to withdraw from West Berlin – as well as to discourage another American invasion attempt against Cuba. The ensuing confrontation with the US escalated and brought both sides closer to a global nuclear war than ever before or since. The crisis was averted by the removal of the Soviet missiles from Cuba and American nuclear missiles from Italy and Turkey. West Berlin remained in US, British and French hands. Castro was furious when the Soviets reneged on their promise that their missiles would remain. President Kennedy's promise that the USA would not invade Cuba did little to reassure him – although, so far, successive US governments have honoured that promise (notwithstanding continuing attempts to kill Castro and to destabilize the Cuban economy through terrorist attacks).

▲ Map showing Soviet missile sites in Cuba at the time of the Cuban Missile Crisis, 1962

Throughout the 1960s, Castro embarked on a policy of assisting other anti-imperialist revolutionary groups, especially in Africa and Latin America. Che Guevara and Castro (and other veterans of the Sierra Maestra campaign) sent Cuban troops to assist rebel groups around the world, with varying degrees of success. Bored with his ministerial role, Guevara personally led some of these expeditions. In 1967, shortly after the failure of his 1963–1965 expedition to the Congo, Guevara led a mission to Bolivia where his group was ambushed and he was captured, tortured and executed by a CIA-led team of Bolivian rangers.

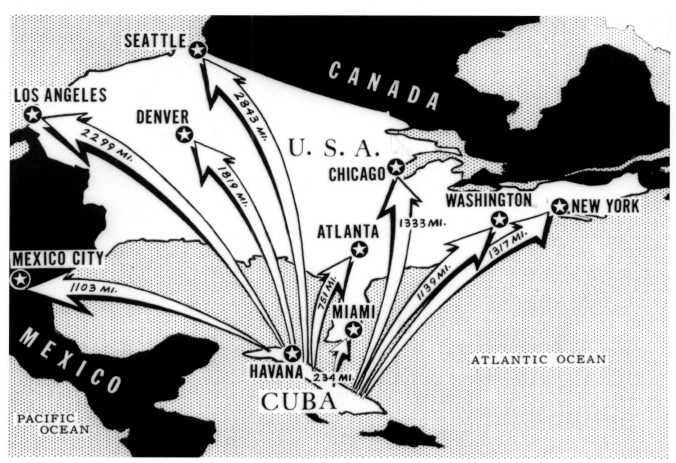

▲ An American cartoon from 1962 showing the potential danger of nuclear missiles on Cuba. Note how the image is angled to accentuate the size (and, therefore, perceived threat) of Cuba in relation to the USA.

In 1975, Cuban forces were deployed to Angola to help the left-wing Popular Movement for the Liberation of Angola (MPLA) against the US-backed South African and Zairean invasion forces. Such forces were supporting right-wing militants, the National Liberation Front of Angola (FNLA) and The National Union for the Total Independence of Angola (UNITA). After almost a decade of fighting, the two sides negotiated a ceasefire, but not before the war had earned itself the nickname of "Cuba's Vietnam" – a reference to the way that Cuban forces became mired in this war as Americans had been in Vietnam. One point of comparison, however, is that the Cuban government never had a shortage of volunteers for the Angolan expedition or the accompanying humanitarian mission.

2.3 Castro's domestic policies

Conceptual understanding

Key questions

→ In his economic and social policies, what was Castro trying to achieve for Cuba, and why?

→ What were the problems that Castro faced?

→ What were the results of his policies and how did he react?

→ To what extent did his policies change between 1959 and the early 21st century?

Key concepts

→ Significance

→ Consequences

Economic relations with the USSR

The shift from economic reliance on the USA to economic reliance on the USSR after 1960 brought with it a political shift, and Cuba drew ever closer to the communist ideology of the USSR. Although Cuba did not declare itself to be a communist state until after the April 1961 Bay of Pigs Invasion, in November 1960 raucous cheers from the Cuban delegation had punctuated Khrushchev's speech at the UN General Assembly in New York. At the same time, photographs of a grinning Castro embracing an equally cheerful Khrushchev outside the former's hotel in Harlem were seen all over the world.

The Cuban Missile Crisis of October 1962, however, soured this relationship. Castro felt that the USSR had used his country in a broader power play with the USA, disregarding the needs of the Cubans. With Khrushchev's withdrawal of Soviet nuclear missiles, Cuba was once again left vulnerable to the very real threat of a US invasion – its only protection being the US president's promise that this would not happen. However, by the end of 1968 the two nations were back on good terms (with Castro making the first move by publicly expressing support for the USSR's violent actions in Czechoslovakia in August 1968). Both Castro and Che Guevara had misgivings about the communist model espoused by Lenin, preferring instead to

▲ Fidel Castro embracing Soviet premier Nikita Khrushchev in 1960 when the two leaders met at the UN General Assembly in New York

create a system more suited to the Latin American environment in which they lived. However, by 1968, Guevara was dead and Castro was increasingly dependent on the USSR for Cuba's economic survival. The Cuban state therefore began to adopt many of the structures of the Soviet state.

Castro's communism

Historians (e.g., Ramonet, Balfour and Coltman) tend to agree that Castro was not a communist at this stage. Rather, he was a nationalist whose policies were less governed by the doctrines of Marx or Lenin and more so by the needs of nationalism and Cuban independence, with a strong focus upon political, social and economic improvements designed to benefit the whole of society rather than just the wealthy elites. When he was introducing his agrarian reforms, for example, Castro even drew upon Catholic rhetoric by likening his policies to Christ's teachings.

Despite the Catholic Church's history of support for the wealthy classes against the poor, Castro did not immediately move against organized religion as most communist rulers did. His economic reforms were,

initially, seen as rather moderate by most contemporaries, although this soon changed when he began nationalizing the large landholdings and other businesses of US corporations and wealthy Cuban planters. Nevertheless, even the US vice-president, Richard Nixon, stated after meeting Castro in 1959 that he was not a communist and that the US and Castro could and should work together.

Events beyond Castro's control changed this and, in May 1961 (immediately after the failed Bay of Pigs Invasion) he publicly declared that the Cuban Revolution was a socialist one and that Cuba was a communist state. However, even though the open declaration of Cuba as a communist state only took place in 1961, the move towards Communism had begun during the earliest days of the new government.

Economic problems and solutions

Prior to Castro's victory, the Cuban economy had suffered from unfavourable trade conditions with the USA, which had seen many Cuban planters and other businessmen shift their allegiance away from Batista. During his 1959 tour of the Americas, Castro promised to redress this situation. Coltman points out that wealthier Cubans had been hoping that "Castro would restore democracy without undermining the economic status quo". However, they were to be disappointed – though not to the degree that many Castro supporters had hoped for. Castro's promised agrarian reforms were more moderate than many had anticipated, possibly as a conscious decision to avoid antagonizing their belligerent neighbour to the north.

Unemployment in Cuba had been high before the revolution, especially in the impoverished rural areas. The work (only sporadically available) for many landless peasants had been back-breaking and poorly rewarded. Castro's policies changed this and peasants found themselves paid more fairly and given more rights and shorter working hours. By the mid-1960s there was even a labour shortage in Cuba. However, production fell in some areas because, according to some commentators, Castro's policies had removed the incentive for people to work hard – although this view does not take into account the effects of the US trade embargo against Cuba.

The 1970s saw Cuba following Soviet advice to allow greater liberalization in its economy, with decentralized planning and management as well as more material incentives in order to encourage greater productivity. With greater market freedom, however, came opportunities for corrupt officials to enrich themselves, leading to a growing sense of dissatisfaction, especially among the working classes. By 1985, however, Castro had decided that this liberalization had gone too far. He felt that the economic

plan proposed by the Central Planning Board in 1985 was ignoring the nation's economic needs. Humberto Pérez, the Moscow-trained economist whose department had pioneered this plan, was removed from office and a new committee established to create a new plan. The Rectification Campaign of 1986–1987 was launched with the intention of moving Cuba back towards a more centrally planned economy and was a determined effort to stamp out the corruption that had begun to set in.

The INRA, nationalization and land reform

As promised in his Moncada Programme of 1953, Castro was keen to implement reforms that would improve the lives of the peasants. His initial reforms adversely affected only the wealthiest landowners while providing short-term economic benefits for the vast majority of the Cuban population; the macro-economic impact would only be felt in subsequent years. The reforms involved nationalizing major industries (for example, public utilities, the power companies and the telephone company – all US-owned), drastically reducing rents, and breaking up large landholdings (with some exceptions such as sugar plantations) into smaller units and turning them into cooperatives similar to those in communist China in the 1950s.

Land was confiscated from large companies and then redistributed to the peasants. More than 200 000 peasants were given the title deeds to land on which they had previously worked for wealthy landlords. Compensation was paid to the former owners but, in a move that highlighted the corruption of the previous government, the value of the land (and, therefore, the level of compensation) was calculated by using tax office records. In order to dodge paying taxes, the US corporations had severely undervalued their land in their official tax returns. It was now this same value that was used by the Castro government in calculating the compensation that they would receive for the land that was nationalized. Incensed at having been caught in a financial trap of their own creation, many of these corporations exercised their influence over the US government and media to create a strongly anti-Castro message for US audiences.

Land reform was, in the eyes of the M-26-7 leaders, the path towards achieving the social justice that had inspired the revolution. They also had the example of the People's Republic of China to work from. With his victory in October 1949, Chairman Mao Zedong had introduced rapid agrarian (and, to a lesser extent, urban) reforms that had transformed the country and had led to the widely acclaimed successes of the First Five-Year Plan (1953–1957). The situation in Cuba was, of course, different but the same basic principle still applied:

- social and economic justice was long overdue

- the peasants were desperate for the promised improvements

- only rapid and radical action could achieve these aims before their patience wore out and turmoil ensued.

The nationalization of large plantations certainly irked the US corporations and the largest landowners as they lost their enormous profits. However, the majority of the Cuban business and banking sectors (as well as some of the middle classes and the more numerous smaller plantation owners) were supportive of Castro's agrarian reforms, which

---

The Rectification Campaign, 1986–1987

After following the advice from the USSR to liberalize the Cuban economy, Castro grew unhappy with the resulting return to corruption and inequality. The trade unions protested against being treated as a "production army" by the government. Their protest took the form of reduced productivity and worker absenteeism. Castro appeased them by publicly apologizing for his and his government's attitude, and launched the Rectification Campaign to undo these mistakes. This is indicative of the humility with which he conducted himself at times – a stark contrast to most leaders, authoritarian or otherwise.

The Agrarian Reform Laws

The Agrarian Reform Laws of 1959–1963 called for the nationalization of large landholdings (over 1000 acres for Cuban companies and over 3000 acres for foreign companies) and the most productive plantations. This allowed land to be redistributed among impoverished plantation workers and small plantation owners, or be taken by the government itself to be used as state farms or cooperatives.

promised a rejuvenation of their fortunes. By gaining their support, Castro succeeded in dividing his opposition and buying himself time to consolidate his position as ruler of Cuba.

Social problems and solutions

Castro was adamant that the Cuban Revolution was about improving life for all Cuban people. Although Batista had made inroads into addressing the racism that blighted Cuba, there were still marked differences between the opportunities for Cubans of African descent and those of European descent. Black Cubans were predominantly working class and had little to no hope of advancing, although Batista had (in the 1940s) begun the process that would allow the promotion of black soldiers. Castro extrapolated this into wider society, making it illegal to discriminate against people on the grounds of either gender or race. One area in which prejudice was still permitted, however, was sexuality. Castro has come under criticism for his intolerant attitude towards homosexuality.

Health care and education in Castro's Cuba

▲ Cuban schoolchildren with portrait of Che Guevara, 2004

Once in power, Castro quickly began implementing the promised social changes, including free universal health care and education. A massive vaccination programme began in 1962 and by 1971 polio, malaria and diphtheria had been eradicated. The centrally planned economy allowed investment in rural infrastructure (especially roads and electricity), which meant that the improvements to health care could reach even the most remote and needy areas. Castro also ensured that all Cuban citizens could access high-quality education up to and including university level. The literacy rate grew from 78 per cent in 1953 to 99.8 per cent in 2014.

Control of the media

After taking power in January 1959, Castro was quick to silence anti-revolutionary media. This was intended as a temporary measure and would, he promised, be revoked shortly. However, with the communists inciting outspoken criticism from his own supporters, Castro reneged on this promise, using the excuse given by dictatorial governments throughout history (and still used today): the interest of public security. In Cuba in 1959, the real threat of a US invasion or US-sponsored counter-revolution meant that the public security argument was probably valid, at least to some degree.

University professors and journalists who voiced their dissent at the increase in communist influence were threatened with dismissal and arrest. Newspapers, magazines and radio stations that spoke out against Castro or the communist influence were often threatened with closure unless they changed their political stance. Even former Castro allies (such as Carlos Franqui, who had run the invaluable *Radio Rebelde* during the Sierra Maestra campaign) disliked his leanings toward the communists. Castro's treatment of his critics, however, was not as brutal as that of Batista. For example, rather than being imprisoned or killed, Franqui was able to go into exile with his family. Nonetheless, Castro's methods still ran counter to his professed aims of establishing the long overdue fair and free Cuba of José Martí's dreams.

Cuban refugees

Since before independence, Cubans wishing to flee their homeland for whatever reason have travelled to Miami in Florida and the surrounding area, and a "Cuban exile" community has grown there. This community was already strong enough in the 19th century for José Martí to be able to go to them for help in financing his war of independence in 1895.

Since the revolution, there have been many flights to the USA from Cuba, especially by the educated and wealthy middle classes who feared that post-revolutionary Cuba would deny them their privileged positions. The largest emigrations have been:

— 1959–1960: Cubans worried about the change of regime and what it might bring.

— 1960–1962: Operation Peter Pan, in which the Catholic Church helped Cuban parents to send their children to be fostered in the USA.

— Oct–Nov 1965: the Camarioca Exodus. Castro announced that any Cubans wishing to leave for the USA could do so from Camarioca; 2979 Cubans left Cuba for Miami.

— 1965–1973: "Freedom Flights". Twice-daily flights from Cuba to Miami allowed Cubans with relatives in the USA to flee Cuba. According to the *Miami Herald*, 265 297 Cubans made this journey.

▲ The Cuban exodus from Camarioca, 1965

— Apr–Oct 1980: the Mariel Boatlift. Around 125 000 Cubans from across the social spectrum (but mostly young, male and working class) made it across to the USA, to flee the poor economic situation in Cuba.

— Jul–Aug 1994: the Malecón Exodus. Due to the economic and humanitarian crisis caused by the collapse of the Soviet Union, about 35 000 Cubans took up Castro's offer to emigrate to the USA after the Malecón protests showed the level of discontent.

Additionally, many Cubans who have tried to escape to the USA on homemade boats and rafts have drowned in the Straits of Florida and do not feature in the statistics.

Social control and repression

Many of the criticisms of Castro's rule in the early years centred on his dictatorial style, his harshness towards former members of the Batista regime, and, in particular, the banning of political parties and the promised elections that were never held. Both Castro and Guevara later admitted that mistakes had been in the immediate aftermath of the victory over Batista. However, Castro also responded to the international outcry over the trials and executions of Batista's henchmen by asking why they were complaining now when these same countries had been silent as these torturers had been committing their crimes. Castro justified the trials by declaring: "revolutionary justice is not based upon legal precepts, but moral conviction".

Castro's rapid, public punishment of criminals ensured that the Cuban Revolution did not descend into the chaos of violent reprisals and vigilantism. The televised trials and executions sent a clear message to the Cuban public: the new government would uphold the law and they would dispense justice. Thus, the Cuban Revolution did not suffer from the anarchy, public disorder and random violence of other sudden changes of government, such as after the Bolshevik Revolution in Russia, the liberation of France from the Nazis, or following Mao's victory in China.

These trials have been likened by some commentators to Stalin's show trials of the 1930s and criticized for the public way in which the most high-profile cases were conducted – in the national sports stadium in front of large audiences. The Castro government, however, has likened these trials and executions to the Tokyo and Nuremberg trials held to punish war criminals after the Second World War. Although Castro later admitted that the trials may have been conducted in the wrong way, he also pointed out that they had prevented the collapse of law and order.

Over the following years, Castro implemented the same sort of security apparatus that other dictatorships have used. It is unsurprising that the new Cuban government felt the need to establish a secret police and pursue a hardline approach to traitors and enemies, having incurred the implacable hatred of (to name a few):

- the US government, which saw it as a potential communist threat and a challenge to their hegemony in the region

- the US corporations that lost their Cuban investments

- the CIA, which saw it as a direct threat to their operations and influence in the region

- the Batista loyalists who had lost their power with the fall of the regime

- the Autenticos who wanted to return to power and hated the left-wing aspects of Castro's government

- the American Mafia, which had lost its lucrative drugs, gambling and prostitution trades

- the US-supported governments of other Latin American countries, which all feared the impact of Castro's example on their own repressed citizens.

From 1968, internal opposition also emerged within the PCC and from groups of intellectuals (such as the Varela Project): first it was against the growing ties with the Soviet Union; and, later, in the 1990s, it emerged during the Special Period.

The option of allowing malcontents to leave for the USA did reduce the need for repressive measures in Cuba. Although the free transfer of people between the two countries was impossible after the revolution, over the years many Cubans (of all social classes) made the decision to leave. On occasion, Castro even gave permission for Cubans to leave if they wished to. Referring to them as escoria (scum) and encouraging other Cubans to turn against them as traitors, Castro nevertheless managed to dilute the opposition to his regime by allowing these "exoduses".

One major criticism of Batista's regime had been its reliance on police brutality and intimidation to subjugate the populace. Castro had frequently spoken out against this and promised a far freer society in the "new Cuba". However, the threats to Cuba and to him personally meant that a degree of repression was needed in order to survive. For example, in August 1959, he had narrowly foiled a coup organized by the Dominican Republic and was sure that there would be many more US-sponsored attempted coups in the near future. He was, of course, correct: President Eisenhower had already (in 1959) authorized the CIA to plan and implement Operation Mongoose (also known as the Cuban Project) to remove Castro from power by any means necessary, short of a full-scale US military invasion.

Operation Mongoose (The Cuban Project)

In early 1960, President Eisenhower authorized a budget of US$1.3 million for the CIA to remove Castro from power. (Part of this campaign featured in the best-selling 2012 console game, *Call Of Duty: Black Ops*, earning strong condemnation from the Cuban government.) Some of the plots were very simple and relied upon Mafia or Cuban exile assassins infiltrating Cuba and murdering Castro with guns or bombs. However, his notoriously erratic movements made this very difficult. Some plots played on his love of scuba diving and involved giving him gifts of poisoned wetsuits or having an agent poison his breathing apparatus.

Other CIA plots involved targeting the Cuban economy itself, in the hope of provoking an uprising against Castro. These plans relied on terrorist tactics such as the indiscriminate bombing of targets (both civilian and military). From the 1960s until the 21st century, CIA agents or former agents (such as Luis Posada Carriles) conducted terrorist campaigns against Castro's government and people, including blowing up a civilian airliner (October 1976) and planting bombs in tourist hotels (September 1997).

According to the 1975 Church Committee (a US senate investigation into the activities of the CIA during this period), the CIA was involved in at least eight attempts to kill Fidel Castro between 1960 and 1965. According to Fabián Escalante Font, a retired Cuban senior counter-intelligence officer, there have been 638 attempts to kill Castro from 1960 to the present day.

The "Special Period in Time of Peace", 1989–c. 2000

The June 1989 Ochoa Affair created intense divisions within Cuban society, divisions that could have escalated Cuba's problems had it not been for the economic crisis that followed the collapse of the Soviet Union (1989–1991). This led to Cuba entering what Castro called the "Special Period in Time of Peace", thus once again using his charisma and popular appeal to call for Cuban unity in the face of adversity as an economic crisis hit Cuba.

The Council for Mutual Economic Assistance.

It was founded in 1949 as a direct response to the American Marshall Plan - what Soviet politicians referred to as "Dollar imperialism".

Dominated by the USSR, the main aim was to promote mutually-beneficial trade between communist and socialist countries.

The Ochoa Affair, 1989

The Ochoa Affair was possibly the most serious internal threat to the Cuban regime since 1959. A number of senior military leaders, including General Arnaldo Ochoa, were arrested for corruption and drug smuggling. Their trial saw several of them sentenced to long prison terms and Ochoa and three others sentenced to death. It has been speculated that General Ochoa had been planning a coup.

Class discussion

Why was Cuba so badly affected by the collapse of the Soviet Union in 1989–1991?

The USSR and, by extension, **Comecon**, had become the lynchpins of the Cuban economy; by 1989 approximately 80 per cent of both Cuban exports and imports came through the USSR. The collapse of the Soviet Union (1989–1991) therefore had an enormous impact on Cuba. The worst effects of this collapse were felt in 1990 and lasted until around 1996 but, despite the predictions of most non-Cuban commentators, Castro's Cuba survived. Balfour identifies a number of reasons for this:

- the absence of an organized and effective opposition
- general support for Castro and the leadership (even in the face of the socio-economic dissatisfaction of the early 1990s)
- the army's utter loyalty to Castro
- disloyalty to Castro and the regime being a punishable offence.

The government's control over the media and the persistent sense of gratitude for the positive effects of the revolution can also be added to this list (especially healthcare, social justice and education). The Cuban economy did not fully recover until around 2003. During this so-called "Special Period":

- Cuban GDP fell by 34 per cent
- oil imports dried up immediately, dropping to 10 per cent of pre-1990 levels
- loss of food imports led to famine (before 1990 approximately 63 per cent of Cuba's food imports came from the USSR)
- medical imports fell dramatically.

The government responded to the crisis, according to Balfour, in a piecemeal fashion. In October 1990 the "Food Programme" was launched with the intention of encouraging farmers to increase the food supply. There was mass mobilization of the unemployed, students and other volunteers to work on plantations. A recycling campaign and the reallocation of scarce funds into biodiversity research also began, combined with a nationwide austerity campaign designed to limit waste. With the sugar subsidies from the USSR gone, the economy also had to adjust, leading to a growth in tourism-related industries. State-owned farms (which had accounted for 75 per cent of Cuba's agricultural land) were downsized and agricultural cooperatives (*Unidades Básicas de Producción Cooperativa; UBPCs*) were created. By the mid-1990s Castro had agreed to allow US dollars to be used as currency – as they already were in the newly thriving black market economy.

Despite his protestations to the contrary, Castro was also forced to reintroduce capitalist elements to the Cuban economy. Farmers' markets (banned since 1986) were reintroduced and private ownership was allowed to a certain degree. (This is similar to the way that Deng Xiaoping and Liu Shaoqui allowed private food production to supplement state production on communal land as a means of rescuing China from the famine that followed the Great Leap Forward of 1958.)

The US reaction to the "Special Period"

Throughout this period, the possibility of a US invasion still loomed large in Castro's mind. In 1990 he said: "There may be other forms of aggression for which we must prepare. We have called the total blockade a 'Special Period in Time of War'. Yet, in the face of all these problems we must prepare and devise plans for a 'Special Period in Time of Peace'."

The US trade embargo already prevented US companies from dealing with Cuba, but the Helms-Burton Act of 1996 went further. It gave stiff penalties to foreign companies doing business in Cuba, which meant that they were dissuaded from investing in Cuba for fear of being sued, thus worsening the economic and humanitarian crisis.

The Helms–Burton Act, 1996

This act, officially called the Cuban Liberty and Democratic Solidarity (Libertad) Act, was brought into force at the height of Cuba's humanitarian and economic crisis. According to Balfour, it is "one of the most controversial bills in the history of the US". Its main stipulations were sanctions against:

- any US business that imported products originating from Cuba, even if sourced through a foreign intermediary
- any country, institution or business (including the World Bank) that traded with or extended loans to Cuba
- any foreign business that used resources previously owned by US corporations and individuals and that had been nationalized by Cuba.

Castro referred to this act as "that brutal and genocidal Helms Burton law", claiming that it was "harming the sovereignty of the rest of the world". However, he was also quick to point out that it was only serving to increase the growing global disgust at the USA and that it had not deterred foreign investment in Cuba.

The Act stipulated that the newly intensified embargo would not be lifted until:

- Castro's government was replaced by a transitional government (i.e. one friendlier to US business interests)
- all nationalized property was returned to its "original owners" (i.e. US corporations, individuals and the Mafia)
- compensation was paid to US corporations and individuals for their nationalized property.

This act was an example of the US government attempting to exploit its position as the world's only superpower after the collapse of the USSR in 1991. It naturally met with stiff resistance from other nations. The European Union instructed its member nations to ignore the Act (effectively declaring it illegal in international law) because it violated international free trade laws. The US government, realizing the limits of its power and the animosity the Act was generating, eventually agreed to ignore the clauses dealing with foreign companies or countries. It failed to prevent Cuba from gaining foreign investments and became a continuing source of resentment for both Cuba and the global community.

Many companies did invest in Cuba, primarily in the tourism industry, and this has helped to stabilize the Cuban economy since the 1990s. By the early 2000s around 160 000 American tourists each year were defying their country's ban on travel to Cuba to soak up the sun, history and "old-world charm". Tourists from other countries also flocked there, bringing in much-needed foreign currency and helping to achieve Castro's aim of reintegrating Cuba into the world community.

The Special Period and industrial production

The rapid modernization of Cuban agriculture, transport and industrial production since the 1960s had led to a reliance on Soviet oil imports. Cuba had sold its surplus oil to generate more income to spend elsewhere in the country. When oil was no longer forthcoming after the collapse of the USSR, transportation and industrial production ground to a halt practically overnight and many jobs dried up, creating unemployment across all social classes. The government distributed more than a million (Chinese supplied) bicycles in order to help people to move around, and ingenious alternatives sprang up such as *Camellos* ('camel buses'), which were 18-wheeler trucks specially adapted to act as buses.

▲ A *Camello* in Havana, Cuba

Castro changed the law to allow foreign companies to invest in Cuba through business partnerships. Hundreds of other businesses that were already starting to operate privately on the black market became legally sanctioned. State subsidies were removed in a number of areas and progressive taxation was introduced. The US dollar was permitted as currency, validating the fact that it was already being used throughout the black market that thrived after 1990.

The Special Period and agriculture

The loss of oil imports affected the agricultural sector in a number of ways. There was a massive decline in food production, leading to a famine that saw desperate people killing and eating almost all of Cuba's cattle as well as zoo animals. In 1992, state-owned plantations were reorganized and private ownership of plots was reintroduced. With the loss of the guaranteed Soviet market for Cuban sugar (at four times the market price), many plantations had to change their crops.

As well as a lack of petrol for farm machinery, stocks of pesticides and fertilizers – which had oil derivatives as an essential ingredient – declined. Australian permaculture experts came to Cuba to distribute aid and to teach techniques of sustainable agriculture. A number of urban rooftops were successfully turned into vegetable beds and the Cuban government made these compulsory. Students and unemployed Cubans whose jobs had depended on foreign trade were relocated to the countryside to help grow food.

The effects of these measures varied.

- The impending famine was alleviated to some extent.

- Due to shortages of animals, the Cuban diet shifted away from the traditional Latin American preference for high meat consumption to a more vegan diet.

- Farmers were once more allowed to sell surplus crops for private profit.

- The student volunteers, while generally eager to help, proved to be less than entirely useful when they abandoned entire harvests to rot as they returned to sit their exams.

Cuba's traditional exports of tobacco, citrus fruits, nickel and sugar were now having to compete on a global market without the price protection that the USSR had supplied. As the Cubans sought out new markets, they also found a high demand for their biotechnology – a direct long-term result of the educational improvements introduced after the revolution.

The Special Period and society

According to a 2013 study published in the well-respected *British Medical Journal*, the effects of the Special Period on the Cuban population were not entirely negative. While for the first time since the revolution of 1959 Cubans were facing malnutrition and other poverty-related illnesses, the move from meat consumption to eating vegetables (coupled with reduced access to processed foods) led to a significant decrease in cardiovascular diseases and diabetes. In conjunction with the increased use of bicycles as a result of the fuel shortage, there was a noticeable improvement in general health and a population-wide average weight reduction of 5.5 kilograms per person.

In August 1994, there was a public demonstration against the poverty gripping Cuba at the time. It is unclear whether it was a genuinely spontaneous demonstration or whether there had been some involvement of anti-Castro agents from the USA. Either way, the demonstration in the Malecón district of Havana was the first protest of its kind since the end of Batista's regime in 1959. It led to the third major exodus since 1965, with an estimated 35 000 people boarding rafts and ramshackle boats to undertake the perilous journey across the Straits of Florida to start a new life in the USA.

Balfour points out that, despite the cutbacks to food subsidies and public spending, the poor in Cuba enjoyed a far greater level of protection than the poor in almost any other country at this time – both in the developing world and the developed world. Universal health care and universal education remained as constants and Castro was determined to protect the integrity of the post-revolution society that he had helped to construct. By the mid-1990s, the economic chaos and misery for the poor in other former eastern bloc countries was being used as a warning against demands to shift the Cuban economy closer to an unrestricted capitalist model. Faced with the global collapse of Soviet-style socialist economies, Castro instituted economic reforms while being careful not to fully liberalize the economy.

Nevertheless, the egalitarian nature of Cuban society was still eroded. Those who had access to US dollars (for example, from generous relatives in the USA) enjoyed a distinct advantage over those who did not. For many Cubans, the continued achievements of Cuba (for example, the highest ratio of doctors per capita and one of the lowest rates of infant mortality in the world) were small comfort compared to the food shortages and the lack of consumer goods.

The Special Period and politics

Despite their situation, the Cuban population remained behind Castro and still saw him as a bastion of strength against their aggressive neighbour to the north. The consistency of his position also helped to ensure the popular support of the people of Cuba's Latin American neighbours (if not the US-supported regimes of these countries).

The continued use of US economic muscle to bully Cuba and the threat of a return to the "bad old days" of Batista served to entrench support for Castro's regime among those Cubans who could remember a time before 1959. However, for the younger generation, the economic crisis of the Special Period was a sign that things needed to change. Demands for political and economic reform were growing and Castro began to accede to some of these wishes. This met opposition from conservative elements within the party and the military.

To appease these elements of the leadership, party members who pushed too loudly for reform were removed, suggesting that (despite his position and charisma) Castro was not able to claim full dictatorial control over Cuba. This period also saw a change in the rhetoric about the Cuban Revolution, moving away from comparisons with the Bolshevik Revolution of October 1917 and highlighting Latin American nationalism instead. There was also a resurgence of public support for the ideologies of Che Guevara, calling upon justice and egalitarianism as the cornerstones of the Cuban Revolution.

There were, of course, limits to the freedoms that the Cuban leadership would tolerate. With the example of the effects of perestroika on the Soviet Union and the eastern bloc, Castro was unwilling to allow too much political reform in Cuba. The Centre for the Study of America, an internationally respected research centre that examined Cuban relations with Latin American countries, had suggested reforms of the Cuban economic and political systems. In March 1996 it was investigated for being in the service of the USA and its leading members were moved from their positions to other centres. Although this punishment was less harsh than those used by other dictators or regimes against their opponents, the message was still clear: Cuba would not be abandoning its political and ideological orthodoxy.

> ### Luis Posada Carriles (aka Bambi)
>
> Cuban-born Posada (b. 1928) knew Castro while they were both university students. Following the revolution, Posada was involved with anti-Castro groups before being arrested. On his release from prison, he fled to the USA from where he helped the CIA to plan the ill-fated Bay of Pigs Invasion in April 1961. Determined to overthrow Castro, he was trained in terrorism methods by the CIA and, since 1964, he has been involved in many terrorist attacks against Cuba or Cuban interests in Latin America (including the 1976 bombing of Cubana Flight 455, which killed 73 civilians). Throughout his career, Posada has been supported by the CIA and the US-based right-wing Cuban exile group, the Cuban American National Foundation (which itself has close links to the CIA). Posada currently lives in Miami and is treated as a hero by many members of the hardline Cuban exile community there.

The end of the Special Period

By mid-1996 the changes of the Special Period were coming under attack by Raúl Castro (no doubt with the full support of his brother) and some of the reforms were being reversed. Taxes on some private enterprises (for example, the *paladares*, the family-run restaurants) were increased and the cost of self-employment licences also went up. After 1996 there was a concerted effort to reverse some of the economic changes and return Cuba to a more centralized economy.

Castro's Cuba, 1996 to 2008

Around this time, the economic cooperation with Spain came to an end as the new neoliberal government of José María Aznar sought to align itself more closely with the USA. The European Union tied its economic assistance to Cuba to increased liberalization measures within politics and the economy. The Cuban tourism industry also suffered at this time, as a series of terrorist bombings against tourist hotels killed an Italian-Canadian tourist and wounded 11 others. The bombings were the work of a Cuban-born former-CIA agent, Luis Posada Carriles.

In January 1998 Castro achieved a major public relations coup by arranging for Pope John Paul II to visit Cuba. This signified not only the tacit support of the Catholic Church for Cuba but also a recognition that the Cuban brand of socialism did not hold the same anti-religiousness of the Russian form on which it was claimed to have been modelled. It was not an entirely pro-Castro visit, however, and the Pope did not refrain from criticizing the regime during one of his four public masses. As a result of the Pope's visit, the release of 300 prisoners was negotiated and there was greater tolerance of Church activity.

With the December 1998 Venezuelan election victory of Lieutenant Colonel Hugo Chávez, Castro gained another ally in the region. Chávez referred to Castro as his mentor and claimed:

> *"Venezuela is travelling towards the same sea as the Cuban people, a sea of happiness and of real social justice and peace."*

Venezuelan oil was soon being sold to Cuba at preferential prices and, by 2004, the two nations had signed a mutually beneficial trade agreement.

After George W Bush became US president in 2000, US–Cuban relations took a turn for the worse. Bush declared in 2002 that Cuba was part of the "Axis of Evil" (namely, countries that the USA accused of sponsoring terrorism – somewhat ironic considering the prolonged CIA terrorist campaign against Cuba – and, by implication, intended to fight against). Cuba began to brace itself for another invasion attempt or some other attempt to destabilize the country. Suspicion fell on a pro-democracy movement, the Varela Project, that had collected 11 000 signatures on a petition for political reform and increased free-market economics. The Cuban government responded with a counter-petition calling for the socialist nature of the Cuban constitution to be made a permanent feature. This petition gathered over 8 million votes (about 99 per cent of the Cuban voting public). In March 2003, around 75 members of the Varela Project were arrested for taking money from foreign agencies for political purposes, many of them being given long sentences.

Additionally, as Castro declared, the world was growing tired of the US's bullying. This led to increased support for Cuba from other Latin American countries and the establishment of trade links with other nations (for example, Iran and post-apartheid South Africa). From 1998 a wave of left-wing electoral victories swept Latin America – the so-called "Pink Tide". The term "pink" refers to economic and social policies that were seen as more moderate than the dreaded communist policies that the USA had been so desperately and brutally trying to prevent from emerging. Within six years of Chávez's electoral victory (according to the BBC in 2005), more than three quarters of the Latin American population were living under democratically elected left-wing governments. Many of their leaders had expressly cited Fidel Castro and Cuba as their examples. Ironically, in their fear that Castro's 1959 victory would precipitate a domino effect in Latin America, the USA had enacted policies that had pushed Castro into adopting communism and helped to spread these views to the continent.

Castro's legacy

In February 2008, after a long illness, Fidel Castro eventually stepped down as leader of Cuba, handing power to his brother Raúl. During his long period in power, Castro had succeeded in changing Cuba and, as a result, the world itself. His impact on the Cold War was entirely disproportionate to the size of his nation. The fact that he outlasted the Soviet Union is testament to both his personal qualities and to the resilience of his nation.

Class discussion

Think back to the beginning of the Castro section. How accurate was Castro when he claimed that they had made mistakes in the early days of the Cuban Revolution?

Justify you answers with reference to specific examples.

ATL Research and communication skills

1 Construct a detailed essay plan for one of the exam-style questions listed at the end of this chapter.

2 Swap essay plans with your partner.

3 Verbally explain how you intend to construct your essay, explaining which points of information belong in each paragraph and why.

4 Your partner should ask questions and state where they struggle to follow your ideas.

5 Make notes on how to improve your essay plan.

6 Spend five to ten minutes perfecting your essay plan.

7 Write the essay within 45 minutes.

Exam-style questions

Answer the following essay questions with reference to Cuba and, where applicable, another authoritarian state of your choice.

1   "Successful economic policies were essential for the maintenance of power by authoritarian leaders." With reference to one authoritarian leader, to what extent do you agree with this statement?

2   Compare and contrast the impact on religious groups of the policies of two authoritarian states, each chosen from a different region.

3   To what extent was the success of an authoritarian leader due to their control of the media?

4   Compare and contrast the use of propaganda and the media in the rise to power of two authoritarian leaders, each chosen from a different region.

5   Discuss the importance of the use of force in consolidating an authoritarian leader's maintenance of power.

Constructing the essay

Question

With reference to two or more authoritarian rulers, each chosen from a different region, discuss their role in helping their party to gain power.

Analysis

Focus on answering the question: in a Paper 2 exam you have 45 minutes per essay, so it is a good idea to address the most significant aspects of your answer earlier in the essay, and then other aspects in descending order of significance.

Understand the language you use: do not use "long words" and convoluted phrases to try to sound clever. This is simply showing off and examiners usually see through this ploy. You will struggle to convey your message if you use phrases or language you have not fully understood.

To become familiar with more complex vocabulary, it is best to prepare by:

- reading history books and journal articles (e.g., *History Today*) to increase your exposure to academic styles of writing (this is also useful for the extended essay)

- practising using complex terms and phrases in your essays and acting on your teacher's feedback.

Structure paragraphs carefully: to write well-structured paragraphs, a good mnemonic to follow is **PEEL**:

- **P** = Point – your topic sentence where you briefly state the point you are making

- **E** = Evidence – develop the point, providing evidence to support your argument

- **E** = Explanation – evaluate the importance of this point in terms of what the question is asking

- **L** = Linkage – a concluding line relating your argument back to the question

Sample answer

Adolf Hitler's 1924 speech at his trial for the Munich Putsch (November 1923) was similar to Fidel Castro's October 1953 speech during his trial for the Moncada and Bayamo attacks (July 1953). Both leaders were on trial for attempting treason yet both delivered speeches that had no hint of an apology. Instead, they both challenged the legitimacy of the regime they had tried to lead a coup against.

There are clear echoes of Hitler's speech in the content and tone of Castro's. For example, Hitler concluded his 1924 speech with a reference to the "Goddess of History" who would find him and his co-defendants not guilty. Castro's speech of October 1953 echoed this sentiment in its eponymous concluding line "History will absolve us." Both speeches reveal the belief that the judges are not worthy to pass judgment on the person delivering the speech. Both Hitler and Castro subscribe to the belief that their actions will be judged by a higher power (akin, on some level, to a divine power) than the judges appointed by the regime they have tried to overthrow.

More significantly in terms of the question, the results of both speeches were similar. The 1924 trial catapulted the leader of the relatively obscure National Socialist German Worker's Party in Munich to prominence with the German people and even brought him to the attention of an international audience. Similarly, with his articulate speech in October 1953, Castro went from being one of many outspoken critics of Batista's 1952 coup to the face of the new breed of politically energized Cuban youth who were pressing for change through any means, rather than simply contenting themselves with verbal condemnation of Batista.

However, neither Hitler nor Castro rose to power immediately after their trials and these speeches. In both cases the trials helped bring them to public prominence, which helped them gain popularity and spread their message in the following years. Arguably, their later successes were, therefore, built on the recognition they gained as a result of the speeches they gave at their trials. In this way, both Hitler and Castro were helped in their rise to power by their trial speeches but it would be inaccurate to claim that these speeches were the main reasons for their later success.

Examiner comments

Although the information provided here is accurate and interesting, the student has begun to deviate from the question being asked. This in itself is not a problem so long as you make it directly relevant to the question by the end of the paragraph or section of the essay.

The third sentence of the third paragraph ("Similarly, with his… of Batista") is too long and includes too much information, which can confuse the reader. It is best to use short, simple sentences. To make the information easier to understand, a better way of writing this might have been:

Castro's speech at his trial had a similar effect. Previously, he had been just one among many outspoken critics of Batista's coup. Their verbal condemnation of Batista's coup was not enough. Castro's speech and his actions put him at the forefront of the politically energized Cuban youth who wanted deeds, not words.

The final paragraph concludes with an effort to link the point to the question and to evaluate its importance in light of the question. Although this is good, it could have been done more concisely. Do not waste precious exam time in unnecessary repetition.

3 CHINA — MAO

The global context

For more than two thousand years, until the 19th century, China avoided contact with other nations and was largely isolated from the outside world. By tradition, the Chinese believed that China was the Middle Kingdom at the centre of the earth. This instilled in them a sense of confidence in their independence and culture, but by the 1840s this was beginning to change with the encroachment of foreign nations. These external powers had a thirst for resources and influence in China and their successful incursions would expose weaknesses in China's traditional political system.

Starting with the Opium Wars (1839–1842), in which the British defeated Chinese forces, China was forced to open up to the West. Great Britain, France, Germany, and Russia were militarily and industrially advanced powers and they wanted to set up commercial bases for trade and for their Christian missionaries to have the right to operate in China. In addition, Japan was

emerging as the dominant power in Asia, as a result of the Meiji restoration of 1868. Japan had defeated China in the Sino-Japanese War of 1894–1895, seizing Taiwan and Korea from China. Japan would play a considerable role in the struggles for power in China during the 1930s and 1940s.

These incursions culminated in a series of "unequal treaties", which allowed foreign merchants control of China's import and export trade. Shanghai had large foreign-controlled districts. Russia claimed Manchuria in 1900; France had seized Indo-China by the 1890s. In 1898, the USA announced its "open door policy" with regard to foreign spheres of influence in China. This would mean that the USA could trade freely within China's borders. The German acquisition of railroad building and mining rights in Shandong soon followed. By 1900 more than 50 Chinese "treaty ports" were in foreign possession.

Timeline

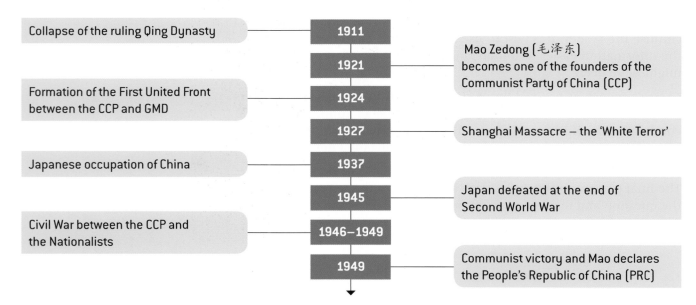

Year	Event (left)	Event (right)
1911	Collapse of the ruling Qing Dynasty	
1921		Mao Zedong (毛泽东) becomes one of the founders of the Communist Party of China (CCP)
1924	Formation of the First United Front between the CCP and GMD	
1927		Shanghai Massacre – the 'White Terror'
1937	Japanese occupation of China	
1945		Japan defeated at the end of Second World War
1946–1949	Civil War between the CCP and the Nationalists	
1949		Communist victory and Mao declares the People's Republic of China (PRC)

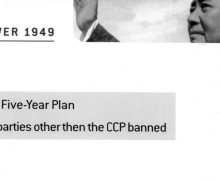

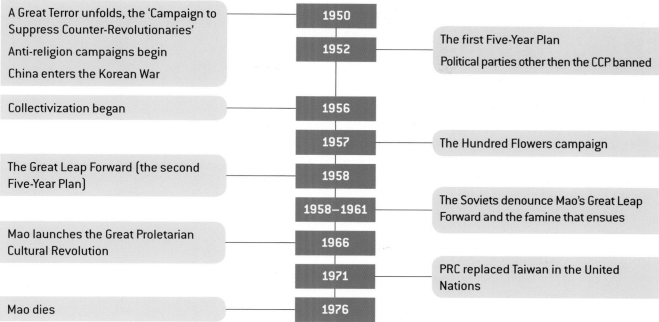

A Great Terror unfolds, the 'Campaign to Suppress Counter-Revolutionaries'

Anti-religion campaigns begin

China enters the Korean War

1950

1952

The first Five-Year Plan

Political parties other then the CCP banned

Collectivization began

1956

1957

The Hundred Flowers campaign

The Great Leap Forward (the second Five-Year Plan)

1958

1958–1961

The Soviets denounce Mao's Great Leap Forward and the famine that ensues

Mao launches the Great Proletarian Cultural Revolution

1966

1971

PRC replaced Taiwan in the United Nations

Mao dies

1976

▲ Henri Meyer for Le Petit Journal, 16 January, 1898

Conceptual understanding

Key questions

→ What were the political, military, economic and social conditions that helped Mao come to power?

→ How important was Mao's leadership in the victory of the Chinese Communist Party in 1949?

Key concepts

→ Causes

→ Perspectives

The establishment of the People's Republic, 1949

On 1 October 1949 Mao Zedong, Chairman of the Chinese Communist Party (CCP), stood on a balcony of the old imperial palace in Beijing (formerly known as Peking) to proclaim the formal establishment of the People's Republic of China (PRC). This moment marked the victory of the Chinese communists over their enemies after two decades of civil war. China was braced for a dramatic break with the past.

Mao was leader of the People's Republic of China until his death in 1976. During that time, he established a single-party state by authoritarian means. His policies transformed the political, economic, and social structure of China. Millions of lives were lost a result of this upheaval, as well as those who were victims of his purges during the climax of the Cultural Revolution of 1966–1976.

Few major figures of the 20th century have been as controversial as Mao. In the early decades of his rule, he was known in China and neighbouring countries as a talented guerrilla leader and visionary. Many people in China today still display a portrait of Mao in pride of place in their home. They view Mao as the liberator of China who restored national pride. By contrast, in the West, Mao is often regarded as a despot who used his own brand of communism (Maoism) to establish totalitarian rule. The extent to which you consider Mao a liberator or oppressor of China is worthy of debate once you have investigated his story.

▲ Mao Zedong, founder of the People's Republic of China

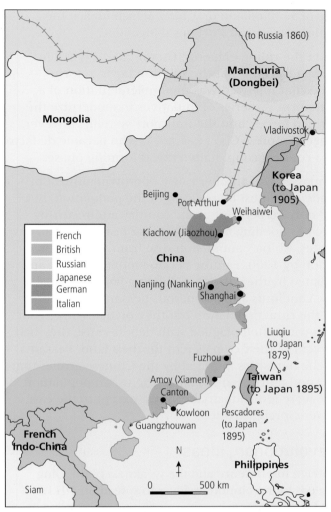

▲ The areas of China controlled by foreign powers during the 19th century

Conditions in China before 1911

Until the 19th century, China was a very conservative nation. The emperor was the supreme ruler at the top of a strict hierarchy in which everyone knew their place. His right to rule derived from the "mandate of heaven", which permitted him to put down any opposition or threats to his power. For more than two millennia, Confucian values were at the heart of Chinese society. Based on the philosophy of the "great sage" Confucius, these values were a way of building harmony and making people accept the social order without complaint. China was a feudal country, with the majority of the population, the peasant class, at the bottom, and power and wealth in the hands of the landlords, the ruling clans, and the aristocracy.

The increasing presence of foreign imperialists in China during the 19th century provoked the people's resentment against the ruling Qing (Manchu) dynasty. A series of large-scale rebellions erupted and the imperial rulers, based in Beijing, struggled to keep control of the country. The most serious rebellions were the Taiping Rebellion (1850–1864) and the Boxer Rebellion (1898–1900). During the latter, the Boxers murdered missionaries and Christian converts. The foreign powers eventually crushed the Boxers by sending a 50 000-strong international relief force.

The Chinese language

There are two commonly used systems for transcribing Mandarin into Western text: the older Wade-Giles system and the more recent Pinyin. Pinyin provides a more simplified version of how words should be pronounced and is used throughout this chapter. Thus it will be Mao Zedong not Mao Tse-tung, and Guomindang, not Kuomintang. However, Chiang Kai-shek is the exception and is most commonly known by the Wade-Giles term, and not by Jiang Jieshi as it appears in Pinyin.

Meiji Restoration

In Japan the Meiji Restoration of 1868 marked the accession of a new emperor, Meiji, and the beginning of Japanese modernization. Enormous changes were made to Japan's system of government and armed forces and the country embarked on a programme of industrialization. Many educated Chinese saw Japan as a model that China should emulate.

Class discussion

A key aim of the rebellions of the late 19th century was to achieve "a revolution against the world to join the world". What do you think this meant? Does this phrase have any resonance today?

The Dowager Empress Cixi (慈禧太后) 1835–1908

Cixi, who effectively controlled the Chinese government for 47 years, from 1861 until her death, was a conservative, resistant to reform and western ideas. Although Cixi did eventually follow the blueprint of the "Hundred Days of Reform", many historians suggest that she did too little too late to save the empire from collapse. Before her death she named the infant Puyi – who would become the last emperor of China – as her successor.

TOK discussion

Orthodox biographers blame Empress Cixi for weakening the empire. They focus on her role in encouraging the failed Boxer Rebellion, her role in halting reform and her anti-western ideas. However, Jung Chang, in her book *Empress Dowager Cixi: The Concubine Who Launched Modern China* (2013), claims that Cixi was in fact a modernizer who did eventually implement reforms and loved learning about foreign ways. Had she lived a little longer, Chang argues, China might have become a stable constitutional monarchy.

Why do you think historians have such different perspectives of Cixi?

Sun Yatsen (孙逸仙 or 孙中山) 1866–1925

Sun Yatsen came from a peasant background but he was educated in the West and was a Christian. In 1894 he founded the first anti-imperial organization and campaigned for a republic. He became the first leader of the republic after the revolution of 1911, but resigned in March 1912 to avoid civil war. In August 1912, the nationalist Guomindang (GMD) Party was formed, with Sun as its leader.

They imposed a fine of $330 million on China, which fuelled the national sense of bitterness against foreign subjugation.

Pressure mounted on the ruling emperor, Guang Xu (光绪帝), to act. His advisers persuaded him that the solution lay in reform and modernization. What followed was the implementation of a "Hundred Days of Reform", a series of initiatives to modernize the bureaucracy, the armed forces, and the transport system. However, the powerful Dowager Empress Cixi (慈禧太后), who became de facto ruler in 1861 after a ruthless coup, halted this reforming phase.

The poverty of the masses was another cause of growing unrest in China. Peasants made up almost 80 per cent of the population, but arable land covered only 10 per cent of the country and recurring natural disasters such as flooding made it hard for peasants to survive. According to estimates, China's population rose from 120 million in 1712 to 440 million by 1900. Famine became more frequent and hunger was exacerbated by the custom of dividing land among all the sons of a family. Landlords and prosperous peasants constituted only 10 per cent of the rural population but they owned 70 per cent of the land. Peasants were often plagued with debt because they had to pay 50 to 80 per cent of their crop as rent for their land. Peasants also had to endure the hardships imposed by the Chinese armies that periodically ravaged and plundered the land. The urban population was small and there were few industrial centres, except to the east, and most of them were foreign-owned.

The spread of revolutionary ideas

Bitterness against foreign interference and the weakness of the Qing dynasty sowed the seeds for revolutionary ideas to spread. In 1911, peasants, townspeople and students began a revolutionary uprising in central China. Sun Yatsen (孙逸仙, later 孙中山) was the leader of the young revolutionaries. His revolutionary league, founded in 1905, was built on three principles: nationalism, democracy, and improving the people's livelihoods through socialism.

The 1911 Revolution and the creation of the republic

In the army units of the south, revolutionary conspiracy spread, which culminated in the toppling of the Qing rulers, China's last imperial dynasty, in October 1911. Sun Yatsen was abroad at the time, but returned to China in December. The Revolutionary Alliance in Nanjing appointed him president, but the revolutionaries were not strong enough to wrest full control away from the imperial government without military support. What sealed the fate of the Qing dynasty was the decision of the most powerful imperial general, Yuan Shikai (袁世凯), to broker a deal with the rebels. Yuan promised to support the revolution on condition that he, rather than Sun Yatsen, took over as president. Sun Yatsen had little choice but to agree. On February 1912, following the abdication of the infant emperor, Puyi (溥仪), the Republic of China formally came into being.

President Yuan Shikai

Yuan Shikai's commitment to the revolutionary cause was soon to be tested. In 1913 he called parliamentary elections. When the Revolutionary Alliance, now called the Guomindang (National People's Party, GMD or 国民党), won the elections, Yuan Shikai exposed his reactionary credentials by banning the GMD. In 1914, he shut down parliament and proceeded to rule China as if he were emperor. To make matters worse, he proved no more able than the Qing to stand up to foreign aggression. In 1915, he submitted to most of the "Twenty-one Demands" imposed on China by Japan. These demands included the transfer of some German privileges in Shandong to Japan and the granting of rights to Japan to exploit mineral resources in southern Manchuria.

Yuan Shikai died in 1916, leaving China weak and divided.

The warlord period, 1916–1927

After the death of Yuan Shikai, there was no effective central government in China until 1927. There was a government in Beijing, which foreign powers recognized, but its authority did not extend over much of China. Power was in the hands of powerful regional generals, or warlords. War between rival warlords made conditions very tough for the peasants. They had to pay high taxes and their land was looted and pillaged by invading armies. Anarchy and division within China made it easier for outsiders to interfere. The Chinese empire was weakened by the loss of Tibet, Xinjiang, and Outer Mongolia.

Later, Mao wrote:

During my student days in Hunan, the city was overrun by the forces of rival warlords – not once but half a dozen times. Twice the school was occupied by troops and all the funds confiscated. The brutal punishments inflicted on the peasants included such things as gouging out eyes, ripping out tongues, disembowelling and decapitation, slashing with knives and grinding with sand, burning with kerosene and branding with red-hot irons.

Sun Yatsen and the GMD remained in a shaky position, having attempted to set up a government in Guangzhou in southern China. Sun planned to launch a northern military expedition to reunify China but he depended on the support of local warlords. In 1922, Sun fled to Shanghai.

The May Fourth Movement, 1919

The end of the First World War increased Chinese humiliation. China had provided the Allies with 95 000 labourers to help with the war effort against Germany in 1916. Most of them were peasants from remote villages and it is estimated that as many as 20 000 may have died on European soil. This support was given with the expectation that Shandong would be returned to China after the defeat of Germany.

ATL Communication skills

Discuss why you think Sun Yatsen's Three Principles – nationalism, democracy and the people's livelihood – were popular. Which groups of people would find these ideas appealing?

ATL Communication skills

Mao grew up with four main influences on his thinking: Japan, the ruling elites, the western powers and the warlords. Reflecting on the story so far, discuss the part played by each of them in shaping his ideas.

Comintern

Communist International, the body set up in 1919 in Moscow to spread communism worldwide.

Marxist

A believer in the theories of Karl Marx (1818–1883). Marx explained history as the continuous conflict between the exploiters and the exploited; the elites in power could only be removed through working class revolution, of which the final stage would result in an equal society or communist utopia.

However, the Treaty of Versailles, signed in 1919, gave Japan the German concessions in China. This prompted student protests in Beijing on 4 May 1919, followed by nationwide demonstrations. Thousands of students denounced the Twenty-one Demands. The protesters felt that China had been betrayed by the western powers and were furious at Japanese expansionism.

The emergence of Mao and the CCP

The May Fourth Movement paved the way for the emergence of the Chinese Community Party (CCP, also known as the CPC) in 1921. Formed in Shanghai, the party was led by Chen Duxiu (陈独秀) and Li Dazhao (李大钊). It originally numbered 12 delegates, representing 57 members. The Russian **Comintern** had encouraged the formation of the CCP and had sent agents to China. One of the founding delegates was Mao Zedong, an assistant librarian at Beijing University. He had been involved in the 4 May demonstrations and was a **Marxist** convert, having read a Chinese translation of Karl Marx's *Communist Manifesto*.

Neither the GMD nor the CCP was in a strong enough position to achieve power in China in the early to mid 1920s. Large areas of China were still under warlord control, but Sun Yatsen was determined and he returned from exile to Guangzhou with two alliances in mind that would strengthen the Nationalist cause. Firstly, the Christian warlord Feng Yuxiang (冯玉祥) now had control of Beijing. He was broadly supportive of GMD policies and had the military strength to reinvigorate the fortunes of the GMD. In addition, the CCP was a disciplined political party, and those on the left of the GMD were sympathetic to some of the CCP's ideas. A merger of the parties had the potential to broaden the national appeal of the GMD.

The First United Front

With Russian Comintern support, the CCP was encouraged to form an alliance with the GMD. Although there were ideological differences between the two parties, they were united in their determination to defeat the warlords; it was evident that a communist revolution could not be achieved unless the warlords were defeated and foreign interference was crushed. In 1924 the GMD and the CCP formed the First United Front. The CCP formed a bloc within the GMD and was very much the inferior partner, accepting GMD control and discipline.

The formation of the United Front had a remarkable effect on CCP membership: its numbers rose from 57 members in 1921 to 58 000 by 1927. The GMD also saw increased support and was further strengthened by the establishment of the Whampoa military academy in 1924. Under the command of Chiang Kai-shek (蒋介石), the academy provided a military force to support the political aims of the GMD. After the death of Sun Yatsen in 1925, and after a brief power

struggle, Chiang Kaishek became leader of the United Front. This was a significant step. Chiang Kaishek was on the right of the GMD and suspicious of the CCP. His rival Wang Jingwei (汪精卫) leaned much more to the left and, had he become leader, may have been more intent on preserving the United Front.

The decision was made to put into place Sun Yatsen's plans to unite China in a military campaign against the warlords. The Northern Expedition, numbering approximately 100 000 men, left Guangzhou in May 1926 with three targets in mind: Fujian, Jiangxi, and Nanjing.

Meanwhile, Mao was becoming more active within the GMD and CCP in Shanghai. He returned to Hunan in 1926 to organize peasant associations to support the United Front campaigns against the warlords. Mao was less concerned about national CCP issues and among the peasants of Hunan was seen as their leader against the warlords and the landlords. This would play a significant part in Mao's rise to the leadership of the CCP.

Chiang Kaishek (蒋介石) 1887–1975

Chiang Kaishek trained in the military and was an early nationalist supporter. He joined the uprising to overthrow the imperial government in 1911. After the death of Sun Yatsen, Chiang became leader of the GMD. The First United Front was formed with the CCP in 1924, but Chiang turned on the communists in 1927 and went on to establish a government in Nanjing. Chiang reluctantly joined the Second United Front in 1937 to resist the Japanese invasions. After the defeat of Japan, civil war between the GMD and CCP resumed. The GMD were defeated in 1949 and Chiang was forced to retreat to Taiwan.

▲ Chiang Kaishek, nationalist leader

The Northern Expedition, 1926–1928

The Northern Expedition, led by Chiang Kaishek, made rapid advances against the warlords and within months GMD/CCP forces were poised to take Nanjing and Shanghai. Chiang could hardly claim full military success against the warlords, since he had brokered deals with several of them on condition that they support the GMD. Yet, with this success, tensions within the alliance began to emerge. Communist activism in the countryside and the cities had played a significant part in the success of the Northern Expedition, but Chiang increasingly saw this as a threat. He was concerned that the fomenting of strikes could undermine his middle-class support. He also had to contend with a renewed power struggle within the GMD as Wang Jingwei launched a bid for leadership.

The White Terror, 1927

Chiang Kaishek wanted to reassert his authority and the supremacy of the GMD by turning on the communist bloc of the United Front. In the spring of 1927, with the support of landlords, warlords, secret societies, criminal organizations, and Western groups still in China, he used military force to "purge" communist organizations in Shanghai. This was followed by violent confrontations in Wuhan and Hunan, where union members, communists and peasant associations came under attack and thousands were killed. These events became known as the "White Terror". As the United Front collapsed, Wang Jingwei renounced his claim to GMD leadership and gave his support to Chiang. The Manchurian warlord Zhang Zoulin (张作霖) seized control of Beijing and joined forces with the GMD.

Chiang then established a nationalist government in Nanjing, marking the beginning of the Nanjing decade (1928–1937) in which China was torn apart by civil war. The survival of the CCP hung in the balance, and its fate would partly be decided by the decisions and actions of Mao Zedong.

▲ The provinces of China, and the route of the Long March of the Red Army to Yanan, 1934–1935

The Jiangxi Soviet, 1927–1934

Mao survived the White Terror and retreated with CCP forces to the mountains of Jiangxi province in the southeast of the country. Here he established his base as the Jiangxi Soviet territory, which had a population of a million, and this was where the **Red Army** developed a strong guerrilla force to resist the extermination campaigns of the GMD. Mao was dedicated to achieving a peasant revolution, an aim that

Red Army
This was the original name of Mao's communist troops, later to be known as the People's Liberation Army (PLA).

contradicted the position of the Comintern and the pro-Moscow factions in the CCP, which believed that the urban workforce should lead the revolution. Mao frequently defied orders from Moscow that instructed the CCP to base its activities in the towns rather than the rural areas.

Mao's position on the direction a future communist revolution should take became clearer with his 1928 "Land Law": land was taken from the landlords and distributed among the peasants. Mao advocated moderate land reform, although a more extreme policy was implemented after 1931, when land was confiscated from richer peasants.

The Futian Incident, 1930

It was also during the Jiangxi period that Mao applied a calculated brutality against his rivals. In the "Futian Incident" of 1930, some 4000 Red Army troops were tortured and executed on Mao's orders. Mao regarded them as rebels who were plotting against him, and it is likely that he suspected they supported other potential leaders in the party. Mao's authoritarian methods against opposition would be a key trait in his rise to the forefront of the party and would also be very evident in the way he would rule China.

Source skills

The Futian Incident

It was the first large-scale purge in the Party, and took place well before Stalin's Great Purge. This critical episode – in many ways the formative moment of Maoism – is still covered up to this day. Mao's personal responsibility and motives, and his extreme brutality, remain a taboo.

Jung Chang and Jon Halliday. 2005. *Mao, The Unknown Story*. Jonathan Cape. p. 100.

Do not kill the important leaders too quickly, but squeeze out of them the maximum information; then from the clues they give you can go on to unearth others.

Mao Zedong, quoted from a secret document found in the party archives.

Question

With reference to their nature, origin and purpose, assess the value and limitations of the following extracts in explaining Mao's rise to the leadership of the CCP.

The Long March, 1934–1935

The GMD was the official government of China but it was weakened by the Japanese invasion of Manchuria in 1931. Chiang Kaishek was determined to crush the communists and he persisted in his extermination campaigns rather than resisting the Japanese.

In 1934, GMD forces encircled the Jiangxi Soviet. Chiang hoped to starve the CCP into defeat and capitalize on his change in military tactics. The "blockhouse" strategy meant building defensive fortifications to consolidate the position of his armies as they hunted down the CCP. This resulted in heavy defeats for the communists and led to Comintern adviser Li De (李德) who was, in fact, German – real name Otto Braun, persuading the Revolutionary Military Council to abandon guerrilla methods. Mao was relegated from the leadership but the GMD encroached even further.

ATL Self-management skills

Construct a visual summary or spider diagram to show the importance of Mao's leadership in the CCP victory of 1949. Consider ideology, persuasion, coercion, violence and propaganda.

The CCP faced annihilation and was forced to retreat. About 100 000 CCP troops fled from the besieged Jiangxi Soviet and headed for Yanan, Shaanxi, in the northwest of the country. This was the Long March: an epic journey of nearly 11 000 kilometres (7000 miles). The March took more than a year, and would provide the CCP with an inspiring legend to draw on and use for propaganda purposes. One famous episode was the crossing of the threadbare Luding Bridge, when 22 soldiers swung across the Dadu River gorge while under fire. In reality the Long March and its results were much bleaker than the legend: only 20 000 of the troops survived. However, the March would play an essential part in communist folklore and there is little doubt that once again, the CCP had shown resilience against the odds.

There is evidence that Mao was not the initial leader of the Long March, or even selected to take part in it. It has been suggested that at the Zunyi Conference held in January 1935, Mao Zedong made a crucial comeback to the party leadership by arguing that the CCP should return to guerrilla methods. Supported by Zhou Enlai (周恩来), Mao outmanoeuvered his opponents, such as Otto Braun and the Comintern members, and took military control of the First Front Army. This change in leadership and strategy was a disappointment to the Soviets, who argued that there was not a fair vote. Although this change was significant, Mao's rise to the leadership of the CCP was by no means a foregone conclusion.

TOK discussion

Chinese, Western and Soviet historiography have conflicting narratives of the events at the Zunyi Conference, so it is difficult to get an accurate record of what happened. Archives detailing the events were not opened until 1985 and the details of who attended and how the new leadership was elected are still in dispute.

Discuss how the events and outcomes of the Zunyi Conference are likely to have been portrayed in China, the USSR, and also in the West. How can we decide which version of events is most valid?

ATL Thinking and communication skills

Examine the propaganda poster below, which shows the Red Army crossing the Dadu River during the Long March.

Discuss how this event has been depicted and the ways in which this may contrast to the realities of the Long March. (Alternatively, you could search online for an alternative Long March propaganda poster, download it and annotate the key elements of the image.)

▲ A propaganda poster showing the Red Army crossing the Luding Bridge over the Dadu River in 1935

TOK discussion

Discuss how propaganda influences the way we perceive historical knowledge.

Yanan, 1935–1945

After the surviving marchers settled in Yanan, Mao began to impose his personal authority on the CCP. With a combination of political and military skill – as well as violent repression – Mao would overcome three challenges:

- potential leadership bids from his opponents and attempts by the Comintern to dominate the party

- the need to rebuild the CCP support base, win popular support and increase military recruits

- the ideological struggle within the party.

The methods that Mao used to overcome these challenges would be a template for CCP success against the Japanese (1937–1945) and against the GMD in the Civil War of 1946–1949. These methods allowed Mao to consolidate his position within the party and emerge as the undisputed leader of China.

Mao won over the peasants with land redistribution and rent controls, as well as campaigns to wipe out corruption and improve literacy. His appeal went beyond the peasant class, however: he also reached out to the "national bourgeoisie", the "petite bourgeoisie", and industrial workers. Peasants participated in "revolutionary committees", and by the 1940s Mao had advocated the tactics of the **mass line**, whereby the CCP developed a close relationship with the people. CCP cadres were to live among the peasants and learn from them and help them. This converted many to the cause of Mao.

> **mass line**
> CCP policy aimed at increasing and cultivating contacts with the broad mass of the people and showing the leadership role of the party.

The "Six Principles of the Red Army" were:

1 Put back all doors when leaving a house.

2 Rice-stalk mattresses must all be bundled up and returned.

3 Be polite. Help people when you can.

4 Give back everything you borrow, even if it is only a needle.

5 Pay for all things broken, even if only a chopstick.

6 Don't help yourself or search for things when people are not in their house.

As Japanese incursions into China increased, Mao's nationalist stance against the oppression of the invaders also won popular support. CCP membership rose from 40 000 in 1937 to 1.2 million by 1945.

Mao wrote a number of political and philosophical works in Yanan, which put his own stamp of authority on the party. A series of "rectification campaigns" in 1942 led to the removal of potential opposition. Anyone suspected of being disloyal to the ideas and beliefs of Mao was forced to confess their "crimes" and was publicly stripped of their possessions or posts. Strict censorship rules cut Yanan off from outside contact, while enemies of Mao were denounced. "Self-criticism" sessions were held, at which everyone was encouraged to air their doubts and secrets. Not to speak invited suspicion, but to self-criticize for too long could result in demotion and punishment. A leadership cult began to emerge in 1943, and Mao adopted the titles Chairman of the Communist Central Committee and Chairman of the Politburo. CCP ideology was officially referred to as "Mao Zedong thought".

Mao's ideology

Mao Zedong thought was based on a "sinified" version of Marxism. In the first half of the 20th century China had undergone very limited industrialization compared with Russia. While Karl Marx had written off the peasantry as incapable of revolutionary consciousness and the Russian Communist Party affirmed Marx's emphasis on the industrial proletariat as the principal revolutionary class, Mao argued that the peasant masses in China *were* capable of overthrowing feudalism and going on to create a socialist society. From the 1920s, Mao's belief in this two-stage revolution also went against Marxism, which advocated a one-stage revolution of the proletariat class.

During the 1930s, the "28 Bolsheviks" and the Comintern met Mao's ideas with scorn, but Mao won the argument by interpreting Marxism and applying it to China's situation. In 1940, Mao published *On New Democracy,* in which he defined the Chinese communist revolution not as a class movement but as a national one. This united the urban and rural masses against Japanese incursions. The brutality of the rectification campaigns, in which more than a thousand party members were imprisoned and tortured to extract confessions, became broadly acceptable, partly through fear and also through Mao's potent ideological arguments. In 1942 he wrote, "Some comrades see only the interests of the part and not the whole. They do not understand the Party's system of democratic centralism; they do not understand that the Party's interests are above personal and sectional interests."

The Japanese occupation, 1931–1945

"The Japanese are a disease of the skin, but the communists are a disease of the heart", said Chiang Kaishek in 1941. After invading Manchuria in 1931, the Japanese consolidated their control of the province by installing as puppet ruler China's last emperor, Puyi, who had appealed to Japan to help him get his throne back. Chiang Kaishek was slow to respond to further Japanese incursions, seemingly too distracted by his extermination campaigns against the communists. Therefore the CCP were credited with forging the Second United Front in 1937 to fight Japan, the common enemy. This followed the Xian Incident in 1936, in which Chiang Kaishek's second in command, Zhang Xueliang (张学良), refused orders to attack the communists and placed Chiang Kaishek under house arrest. Zhang had received a letter from Mao, Zhou Enlai and Zhu De (朱德), urging him to bring an end to the civil war and unite with the communists to defeat Japan. Chiang reluctantly agreed, but it would be the CCP that had established stronger nationalist credentials than the GMD.

Thinking and communication skills

Draw a visual summary or spider diagram to show how Mao Zedong became leader of the CCP. Explore the themes of propaganda, violence, and Mao's military abilities, ideology, popular appeal, and policies. Then consider the significance of each factor.

Class discussion

How similar and how different is the story of Mao's rise to the leadership of the CCP compared to that of Stalin in the USSR?

Source skills

▲ Cartoon of Japan invading China

Question

What can you learn from this source about Japan's actions in the 1930s?

In 1937, Japan launched a full-scale invasion of China and set up a government in Nanjing. The entire eastern seaboard of China fell under Japanese control and this had a devastating impact on the Chinese. Although the nation was more united than ever, the Sino-Japanese war would play a crucial part in weakening the GMD and strengthening the position of Mao and the CCP.

In 1941, the GMD army turned on the communist armies in the south, which lost Chiang Kaishek vital support at home and abroad. Initially, the Soviet Union was the only country to give assistance to China but after 1941 the USA sent approximately $500 million of military aid to China. A number of missions were sent to try and reinvigorate the Second United Front but Chiang was stubborn, and this widened the gulf between the GMD and the CCP.

Chiang Kaishek's GMD was weakened by corruption, but Chiang appeared to ignore the reports that GMD troops were selling food on the black market; often the rice sacks would be half full of sand. Conditions for the GMD soldiers were terrible. The peasants were particularly hit by conscription, and faced sickness and starvation. Many of the soldiers tried to flee to the CCP so some were tied up at night to prevent them deserting.

Chiang's leadership became increasingly dictatorial. He was titled Generalissimo and used his secret police to arrest, torture, and execute civilians. Expressions of discontent were repressed and many intellectuals turned to the communists. The economy was in decline,

The Rape of Nanjing, 1937–1938

The Rape of Nanjing, also known as the Nanjing Massacre, describes the mass murder and mass rape committed by Japanese troops during the Japanese occupation of Nanjing. Hundreds of thousands of people were killed and figures suggest that 30 000 to 80 000 rapes took place. The event is still a raw memory for many Chinese and it affects Sino-Japanese relations even today.

which damaged the main base of GMD support, the middle class in the cities. Inflation spiralled out of control, but Chiang's answer was simply to print more money, which led to hyperinflation. Some cities had different exchange rates. The government increased taxes, which were mostly levied on the peasants. All this gave Mao and his ideas, which he was promoting in Yanan, moral credibility over Chiang Kaishek.

Mao and the CCP could exploit the Japanese advance because the GMD was forced southwards and was spread too thinly to prevent the CCP from controlling much of the countryside and northern China. By the end of the Japanese war, the CCP controlled an area populated by 90 million Chinese. Mao later admitted that the Japanese occupation had saved the Chinese communists.

In 1945, after the dropping of two atomic bombs on Hiroshima and Nagasaki, the Sino-Japanese war came to an abrupt end. China rejoiced in victory but any hopes that a GMD–CCP coalition would usher in an era of peace soon faded, as a new world emerged with the Cold War in Europe, which defined the increasingly hostile relationship between the USA and the USSR. These superpowers had conflicting aims in China. With the retreat of Japan, the USSR wanted to strip Manchuria of its industrial resources. The USA was concerned that Soviet influence in China would lead to China's dominance in Asia.

In 1946, President Truman sent Secretary of State George Marshall to China to try and broker a deal between the GMD and CCP. It was Truman's hope that political stability would ensure a non-communist-controlled China. A truce was agreed but by July, both sides had reverted to civil war.

The Chinese Civil War, 1945–1949

The odds of a CCP victory were initially very slim. The GMD armies outnumbered the CCP by four to one; it also had an air force and was better equipped for conventional battle. The GMD was recognized by other powers (including the Soviet Union) as the legitimate government. The USSR provided aid and military assistance and tried to curb Mao. The GMD controlled most of the larger cities and the railway network at the outset of the war, and by 1947 had taken Yanan from the communists.

By 1948 the direction of the war began to change as CCP troops used their guerrilla training to capitalize on their hold of northern China and the rural areas. The CCP had also received weapons from the former Russian occupation forces, taken from the Japanese armies. By June 1948 CCP troops were almost equal in number to the GMD. The CCP secured control of northern China and made incursions into the cities, despite Stalin's orders that the cities should be given to the GMD. The USA provided limited aid to the GMD, but had withdrawn support by 1948 when it became clear that the GMD cause was lost.

The CCP won popular support while the reputation of the GMD was in disrepute for corruption, inflation and repression. CCP troops were disciplined and Mao had used party propaganda to good effect. Mao and the CCP had a broad appeal among the peasants but atrocities were committed against those who did not conform. Anying (毛岸英), Mao's oldest son, was sent to the countryside to take part in the suppression of the peasantry and force them to fight for the CCP against the GMD. He described the CCP atrocities as worse than anything he had seen while studying in the Soviet Union. He wrote that the party cadres were "thugs" and "the dregs of society".

Chiang Kaishek made some strategic mistakes that cost him the war. He sent his best troops to Manchuria before establishing control of northern and central China. Communication between his generals was not fluid and supply lines were poor. By 1948 the GMD had lost Manchuria. By then, Mao's cult of leadership had reached epic proportions and inspired confidence in the CCP. GMD defectors providing them with weapons further bolstered them; and Lin Biao's (林彪) military expertise was crucial in making the Red Army into a strong fighting force.

By January 1949, the CCP controlled Beijing, followed by the south and west. Realizing that defeat was imminent, Chiang Kaishek resigned the presidency and began to move his government base to **Taiwan**. Mao and the Communists proclaimed victory and focused on the next steps of their consolidation of power.

Taiwan
From 1945 until his death in 1975, Chiang ruled Taiwan, a group of islands to the east of China, as the Republic of China (ROC). Until 1971, many western nations and the UN recognized Taiwan as the only legitimate government of China with a seat on the Security Council.

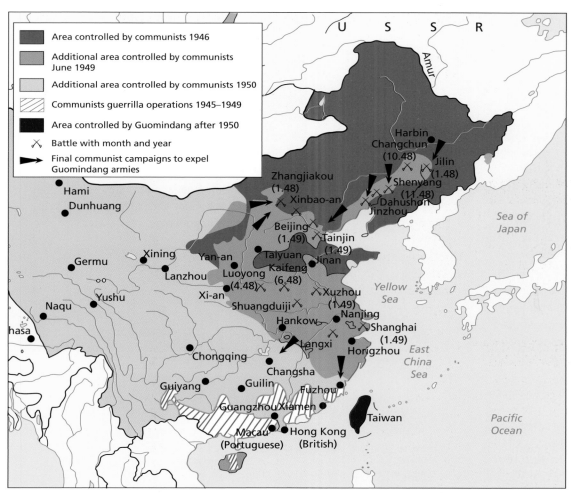

▲ The stages of the Chinese Civil War, 1945–1949

ATL Self-management skills

Construct a case to explain Mao's rise to power, from different historical perspectives. You could copy and fill in a version of the following table. Some boxes have been started for you.

Historical perspectives on Mao's rise to power		
Perspectives of the historians	**Likely ideas**	**Facts and ideas to support this perspective**
Intentionalists explain events by focusing on the decisive impact of particular individuals or events.	Mao shaped the course of China's history. Mao's actions and ideas explain his rise.	Mao was a founding member of the CCP in 1921. Mao's ideology and strategy were crucial to the survival of the CCP in 1934 because of the Long March. Mao was also crucial to CCP success because...
Structuralists (or Functionalists, as they are sometimes known) react against the intentionalist approach and build up a picture of what happened through meticulous research, often at the grassroots level.	China had a long history of political upheaval and this affected many different groups of people in China. The Revolution of 1911 did not achieve the desired effect. Peasant associations were crucial to CCP success.	
Marxists work from the standpoint that economic forces are the main causal factor in historical change and development.		
Revisionist approaches are relatively recent and challenge what had been up to then accepted as **orthodox** or even definitive interpretations. In China, the orthodox view of Mao's rise to power as a liberation from imperial aggression and civil conflict still prevails. In the West, orthodox views during the Cold War centered on Mao's rise being controlled by Moscow.	Historians can challenge orthodox views of Mao, which were developed during the Cold War. The end of the Cold War allowed archives (many held in the USSR) on Mao to be opened and viewed by scholars. Historians, especially those outside China, can look beyond propaganda and the official CCP party view.	Mao's rise was not orchestrated by Moscow... Mao's guerilla tactics and military leadership were crucial... Secret documents and accounts have revealed the importance of Mao's brutality against his opponents...

1 October 1949: Mao Zedong proclaims the People's Republic of China

Conceptual understanding

Key questions

→ What methods did Mao use to consolidate his power?

→ How did Mao establish and maintain an authoritarian state?

→ Why did the Sino–Soviet rift happen?

→ How successful was Mao's foreign policy?

Key concepts

→ Change   → Causes

→ Perspectives   → Significance

→ Continuity

Chairman Mao and the People's Republic

After declaring the formation of the People's Republic of China (PRC) in October 1949, Mao Zedong and the CCP took hasty measures to secure full political control of the country. Although a sense of victory and relief electrified the nation, the communists also faced stiff opposition, both from within the country and on the international stage. Mao Zedong and the communists had promised to free the country from imperialism, smash class divisions and further the revolution. Expectations across the country were high, so the CCP was under pressure to quell opposition and satisfy national hopes.

Although many were jubilant, the country was still politically and economically unstable after decades of war and division. The CCP faced a number of urgent challenges:

- Chiang Kaishek and the nationalists continued fighting before fleeing to Taiwan in December. From here they posed an invasion threat.

- The United Nations accepted the nationalists in Taiwan, not the CCP, as the legitimate government of China.

- Opposition parties within China still existed and posed a threat to CCP control.

- Many party **cadres** were trained as a guerrilla force, and had not acquired the skills to govern.

- The communists feared that separatist elements on China's remote borders would undermine unity.

- Expectations were high in a war-weary nation used to inflation, unemployment, and corruption.

- There were serious rebellions, especially in the south, by villagers who wanted to resist grain requisitioning and imminent land reform.

cadres
Devoted Communist Party workers who spied and reported on fellow CCP members and the public.

The declaration of the People's Republic of China

I was so full of joy that my heart nearly burst out of my throat, and tears welled up in my eyes. I was so proud of China, so full of hope, so happy that the exploitation and suffering, the aggression from foreigners, would be gone for ever. I had no doubt that Mao was the great leader of the revolution, the maker of a new Chinese history – an onlooker in the crowds when Mao declared the PRC.

Source: F. Dikotter in *The Tragedy of Liberation*.

Question

What is the message conveyed by this source?

reunification campaigns
A means for the CCP to secure full control of China and its borders; claims that these areas were historically part of China are contested to this day.

Research and discuss the claim that Tibet is historically part of China. Why do historians disagree? Is there such a thing as historical fact?

Moderate beginnings

The communists aimed to bring stability after decades of turmoil and had little choice but to ask the former government servants and police to stay on initially. The Chinese middle classes provided the civil servants and the industrial managers and, on condition of their loyalty to the PRC, were convinced to stay. Under the slogan "New Democracy", a new era of cooperation began and only the most hardened enemies of the regime were stamped out.

The structure of the PRC

In order to administer the country, China was divided into six regions, each governed by a bureau of four major officials:

- Chairman
- Party secretary
- Military commander
- Political commissar.

Officers of the People's Liberation Army (PLA) filled the last two posts, which put China effectively under military control. Central authority rested with the Central People's Government Council. This comprised 56 leading party members, mostly veterans of the Yanan years. Six of them served as vice-chairman under the Chairman of the Council, Mao Zedong. Mao was the undisputed leader in government.

The reunification campaigns

The CCP feared that nationalist elements could weaken a united China. Religion posed a particular threat to communist control because it fuelled resistance to a centralized communist authority. In order to secure China's borders, PLA units were sent to annex the outlying parts of China in a series of **reunification campaigns**. They invaded regions to the west and south of China. In October 1950, PLA forces entered Tibet. The Tibetans had a significantly different racial, cultural and religious identity from the Chinese. Tibetan Buddhists identified with the authority of their spiritual leader, the Dalai Lama. Around 60 000 Tibetans fought to defend their autonomy but they did not have the weapons or the training to match the PLA, who took full control of Tibet within six months. This marked the beginning of a regime of terror and suppression in Tibet. (See the Tibetan Uprising of 1959 on page 139.)

The PLA invasion forces acted with similar brutality in Xinjiang, a distant western province with a large Muslim population bordering Soviet-controlled Outer Mongolia. The CCP feared Xinjiang falling into Soviet hands or even becoming part of a separatist movement, supported by neighbouring Muslim states. By 1951 the PLA had secured full control of the province, while at the same time securing CCP authority in Guangdong in southern China, the traditional base of the GMD.

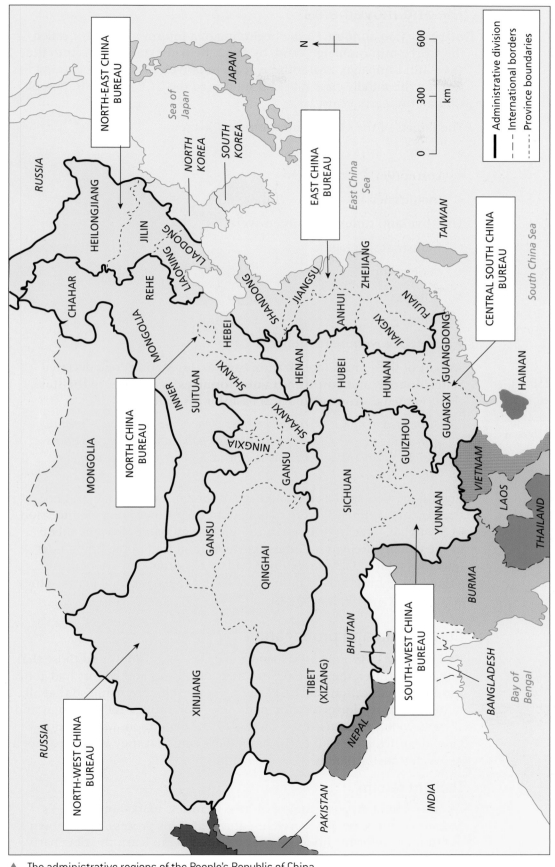

▲ The administrative regions of the People's Republic of China

The anti-movements

In 1951, Mao announced the beginning of a reform movement called the "three-anti campaign" and, by 1952, he had extended this into the "five-anti campaign". After three years in power, Mao was beginning to turn on the middle class that had supported the CCP administration of China in its early years.

The targets of the "three-anti campaign" were:

* waste

* corruption

* inefficiency.

The "five-anti campaign" targets were:

* industrial sabotage

* tax evasion

* bribery

* fraud

* theft of government property.

As part of these mass mobilization campaigns, Mao Zedong declared **reactionaries** and **counter-revolutionaries** as enemies of the state. Mao claimed a strong ideological basis for his actions:

> *"Our present task is to strengthen the people's state apparatus – meaning principally the people's army, the people's police and the people's courts – thereby safeguarding the national defence and protecting the people's interest."*

English became seen as the language of foreign exploitation and no transactions in English were tolerated. In the former French concession of Shanghai, streets were renamed and foreign names became taboo in the cinema. Religion, Chinese customs, and traditions came under ferocious attack. Jazz was banned and, as the attack on intellectuals gained pace, hundreds of thousands of books were burned because they were vestiges of the feudal past.

Censorship and propaganda

By February 1949 most newspapers were out of business and those that remained printed the same news. Once journalists and editors had gone through re-education, the CCP could rely on self-censorship so that all news reports conformed to the party line. Communist rallies, songs, and slogans widely advertised the success of the revolution. Many Chinese people participated with enthusiasm, believing that they were a part of a national transformation.

Thought reform

All over China, in government offices, factories, workshops, schools, and universities, people were "re-educated". This process, also known as "thought reform", involved everyone having to learn the new party

reactionaries and **counter-revolutionaries**
Those deemed to be the remnants of the "bureaucratic capitalist class". Essentially, the middle classes (bourgeoisie) posed a "counter-revolutionary" threat to the communist revolution. Mao regarded the destruction of the bourgeoisie as essential for the revolution, in which only one class, the proletariat, or revolutionary workers, would exist.

doctrine and transform themselves into "new people". Many were forced to write confessions and admit past mistakes, often in public. As Frank Dikotter wrote, "By the end of 1952 virtually every student or teacher was a loyal servant of the state".

The Great Terror

In the early years of communist rule, the CCP could easily identify the "enemy" because of the household registration system, which was started by the nationalists in areas they wanted to secure control of during the civil war. A household could be a family or any collective unit such as a factory dormitory or hospital department. Under the CCP, in addition to household registration, every individual was given a class label and ranked as "good", "middle", or "bad" on the basis of their loyalty to the party. These labels would determine a person's fate for decades to come because children would inherit the same status as the head of their household. This labelling became a key method of ensuring conformity.

Local party officials turned China into a nation of informers. People turned in their neighbours, hopeful of reward. Friends **denounced** one another to show their allegiance to the regime. Children reported on their parents. Every street had officially appointed "watchers" who kept the CCP informed of anything or anyone suspicious. Those belonging to "bad classes" were interrogated by the police.

Vulnerable classes of people were deemed to be threats to the revolution and a drain on resources. These included paupers, beggars, pickpockets and prostitutes, millions of refugees, and the unemployed, who sought refuge in the cities. According to recent archive evidence that has come to light in China, by the end of 1949 some 4600 vagrants in Beijing had been sent to re-education centres and government reformatories.

Labour camps

There were many prison camps scattered across the remotest parts of the country. This network is sometimes called the *laogai*, an abbreviation of *laodong gaizao*, or "reform through labour". These forced labour camps – modelled on the Soviet gulag – dated back to the early days of the CCP and at the height of the Great Terror the number of prisoners swelled when many "counter-revolutionaries" were sentenced to hard labour. By 1955, the number of people sent to the camps hovered at 2 million; nine out of ten were political prisoners. Judicial procedures were dispensed with altogether, so that people could be arrested and disappear into the camps without trial. Conditions in the camps were very harsh and torture and hunger were common. The average number of prisoners held in the camps each year during Mao's time was 10 million; during Mao's rule some 25 million people died in these camps.

ATL Communication skills

There were three main class labels: good classes, the middle classes, and bad classes. Discuss which of the following groups would have fallen under each class label:

revolutionary cadres, the petty bourgeoisie, landlords, revolutionary soldiers, middle peasants, intellectuals and professionals, revolutionary martyrs, industrial workers, capitalists, rich peasants, poor and lower-middle peasants.

Write down your conclusions under each class label.

denunciation

This was a key method of turning on the "enemies" of the revolution. Many denunciations were very high profile. In 1955, Hu Feng, an intellectual critical of the communist attack on writers, was denounced in the *People's Daily*. Mao personally wrote commentaries against him. Hu Feng was tried in secret and imprisoned for being a counter-revolutionary until 1979.

Mass killings

The new regime's most dangerous enemies were imprisoned or quietly executed. Others were interrogated or kept under surveillance. In the early 1950s, thousands of "counter-revolutionaries" – spies, underground agents, and criminal bosses – were interrogated. In Shanghai and Guangzhou (Canton), the CCP turned on gangs and **triads** in a violent killing campaign and about 90 000 were executed. Mao issued quotas for how many per thousand should be killed and many cadres were eager to reach or even surpass them. Official figures have recently come to light, but many killings were not recorded. The lowest estimates suggest a national killing rate of 1.2 per thousand.

triads
Chinese secret societies, usually criminal, involved in drugs, gambling and prostitution.

TOK discussion

Look at the figures in the table to the left. How should a historian assess the reliability of statistics?

Class discussion

Compare Mao's use of terror to that of other dictators.

Total executions reported in six provinces, October 1950–November 1951		
Province	**Total killed**	**Death rate (per 1,000)**
Henan	56 700	1.67
Hubei	45 500	1.75
Hunan	61 400	1.92
Jiangxi	24 500	1.35
Guangxi	46 200	2.56
Guangdong	39 900	1.24
Total	301 800	1.69

Source: Report by Luo Ruiqing, Shaanxi, 23 August 1952

Land reform

Many peasants rejoiced in the arrival of land reform, which had already happened in many parts of China before 1949. Land was confiscated from landlords and redistributed among their former tenants. "Speak bitterness" campaigns and violence were used to humiliate, punish, and wipe out the landlords as a class.

Between 2 million and 3 million landlords were killed as feudal China came under attack. In 1953 peasants were organized into mutual-aid teams, encouraged to share their tools and livestock. No sooner had peasants gained a plot of land than it was pooled into a cooperative; they had only nominal ownership of their land. Those that resisted were labelled class enemies. Villagers were locked into cooperatives at a rapid pace. This made it easier for the party to requisition grain and develop a state monopoly over supplies. There was hunger and famine because state levies were high. By 1954 party cadres and militias succeeded in taking more grain than ever before. Such sweeping reforms across the countryside were heralded as a remarkable achievement for the communists.

▲ An alleged "landlord" facing a People's Tribunal minutes before being executed by a shot in the back in a village in Guangdong, July 1952

The one-party state

In 1949 there had been over ten separate political parties in China. These included the Left GMD, the Democratic League and splinter parties that had broken away from Chiang Kaishek's nationalists. In a number of political purges, combined with the mass campaigns against "imperialists" and "counter-revolutionaries", these parties were removed. By 1952, only the CCP was authorized to exist.

The Communist Party claimed that power rested with the people and that party officials and the government were servants of the nation. They made much of the claim that elections for party officials were held at a local level, and that the Chinese people elected the members of the National People's Congress (NPC), which was responsible for deciding national policy. In reality, party officials oversaw the election process so that anybody critical of Mao would have little chance of making a stand.

Real authority rested with the **Politburo** and the National People's Congress simply rubber-stamped its decisions. Mao Zedong was Chairman of the Party and would also hold the office of President of the PRC until 1959, which confirmed his supremacy in the party and country at large. This was justified on the basis of **Democratic centralism.**

The Constitution of 1954 put in place a framework for the development of a legal system in China. A committee of the NPC controlled the appointment of judges and each citizen was granted the right to a public trial. Equality was guaranteed before the law. In reality, none of this was practised until after Mao's death.

Politburo
This was an inner group of 20 or so leading members of the CCP.

Democratic centralism
A concept developed by Lenin and which Mao adapted to China, which maintained that although all communists were revolutionaries, only the leaders were educated in the science of revolution. In China's case, this meant accepting the ultimate authority of Mao Zedong.

Power struggles

Despite the growth of his authority, Mao Zedong grew increasingly paranoid and feared that his position was under threat. This was because of a number of challenges, including:

- the impact of the Korean War (1950–1953)
- the hardships caused by the First Five-Year Plan to boost the economy through rapid industrialization (1952–1956).

The Korean War, 1950–1953

At the end of the Second World War, the Korean Peninsula was occupied by US forces in the south and Soviet Union forces in the north, effectively dividing the nation into two at the 38th parallel. In 1948, two nations formed — the communist Democratic People's Republic of Korea (North Korea) and the Republic of Korea (South Korea).

In June 1950, North Korea invaded South Korea in an attempt to seize its territory. The United Nations, led by the United States, intervened on the side of the South Koreans, but the South Korean capital, Seoul, quickly fell. By mid-September, North Korea occupied all but a small corner of South Korea surrounding Pusan.

1 **Maximum North Korean advance:** 15 September 1950

UN counterattacks

2 UN forces led by US General Douglas MacArthur invade at Inchon on 15 September 1950. By November, US forces occupy most of North Korea, including its capital.

3 **Maximum United Nations advance:** 24 November 1950

China enters war

4 **China enters the war:** 24 November 1950, UN forces withdraw into the south.

5 **Maximum Chinese/ North Korean advance:** 21 January 1951

Stalemate

6 The war continues for two more years until a truce is announced with a no man's land along the 38th parallel: 27 July 1953

▲ A timeline of the Korean War, 1950–1953

From 1910 until 1945, Korea was under Japanese occupation. After the defeat of Japan at the end of the Second World War, the north was "liberated" by Soviet troops and the south by American troops. The 38th parallel divided the peninsula. Because of the Cold War rivalry that emerged at the end of the war, the USA and the USSR could not reach agreement over reunification and they established opposing systems of government. Stalin wanted to support the communist regime of Kim Il-Sung in the north and President Truman ensured that the south was non-communist under the leadership of Syngman Rhee.

In 1950 the North Koreans attempted to bring about reunification under the communist banner with an invasion of the South. President Truman was committed to the policy of containing the spread of communism and he convinced the **United Nations (UN)** Security Council to allow a UN mission to take action and drive back the communists from the South. Zhou Enlai condemned it as an "imperialist invasion".

The US State Department believed that Stalin and Mao orchestrated the communist invasion of South Korea. After the "loss" of China in 1949, the idea that communism was a **monolithic** force was very powerful. We now know that although Mao did support the invasion, he did not initiate it. In fact, Mao's priority at this time was to pull in the People's Liberation Army (PLA) units for the reunification campaigns in Tibet and beyond. He may have had an invasion of Taiwan in mind and wanted to test Stalin's resolve as an ally.

Mao was kept in the dark about Stalin's motives. It is likely that Stalin wanted to provoke the USA. He was boycotting the UN Security Council over their refusal to recognize the PRC as the legitimate government of China. He had backed the invasion of the South, but had indicated to Kim Il-Sung that he would not "lift a finger". It seems that Stalin was playing Cold War politics.

Once the UN forces had pushed the North Koreans back towards the 38th parallel, Mao realized that the Americans were unlikely to stop pushing north. The prospect of a Western victory over the North stirred Mao into action and he worked hard to persuade his military commanders to send in Chinese troops. Lin Biao wanted to concentrate PLA efforts on crushing China's internal enemies, but Mao won the day by arguing that by taking North Korea, the USA could have ambitions to invade China. Mao was determined that the boundaries of the **Bamboo Curtain** should not be crossed.

Some historians have suggested that by sending Chinese troops to fight the Americans, Mao was hoping to gain Soviet technology and equipment. He was certainly taking a risk. There was the possibility of a nuclear stand-off with the USA, but Mao called the threat of nuclear weapons a mere "paper tiger". By the end of 1950, a quarter of a million PLA troops under the command of Deng Dehuai had crossed into Korea. During the course of the war, the number of Chinese troops would rise to 3 million.

In China, efforts to mobilize the masses began with a campaign called "Resist America, aid Korea, preserve our homes, defend the Nation". Zhou Enlai became an eloquent spokesman for the "Hate America" campaign, supported by relentless propaganda. In 1952, China accused the United States of waging germ warfare in Korea. These claims grabbed world headlines. Once an international commission had confirmed

United Nations (UN)
An international organization formed in 1945 with the aim of preventing conflict between nations.

monolithic
The idea that the spread of global communism was controlled by Moscow.

Bamboo Curtain
The border between communist China and its non-communist neighbours – similar to the notion of the Iron Curtain.

CCP leaders

Zhou Enlai (周恩来**) 1898–1976** became Premier and Foreign Minister in 1949. He was an able diplomat and was seen as a moderating influence during the Cultural Revolution.

Lin Biao (林彪**) 1907–1971** was a communist military leader who played a key role in the CCP victory in the civil war. He was instrumental in creating the cult of Mao and directing the PLA during the Cultural Revolution. Lin died in a plane crash, following what may have been an attempt to oust Mao.

that one diseased vole had been found in Manchuria, the Chinese propaganda machine went into overdrive. Since General MacArthur had openly considered the use of the atomic bomb, the use of biological weapons seemed plausible. Panic swept the nation and, from north to south, people were urged to kill the "five pests" considered as possible sources of disease, namely flies, mosquitoes, fleas, bedbugs and rats.

In May 1953, a resolution in Moscow concluded that the PRC allegations about the American use of germ warfare were false.

The impact of the Korean War on China

When a truce was called in 1953, Mao Zedong could claim a huge propaganda victory and this bolstered his prestige at home and abroad. Not only could Mao be credited with the Chinese troops' success in pushing UN troops back to the 38th parallel, but it was also he who had persuaded the communist leadership to take action in the first place.

Official figures calculated by UN and Soviet experts put the number of Chinese deaths at nearly a million, although these figures were not issued in China. The casualties included Mao Zedong's oldest son, Anying. The USA announced that it would defend Taiwan and its seat on the UN as the official representative of the Chinese people, ruing out any attack on Taiwan by the PRC.

China's economy had been severely hit as a result of the war. In 1951, military expenses amounted to 55 per cent of government spending. Party cadres requisitioned grain from the peasants and many peasants hid their supplies through fear of starvation. The urban economy also suffered; it would take a decade to make up for losses in production. The pressure to repay Stalin for Soviet supplies provided for the war effort only worsened the pressure on the budget.

Mao and Stalin

Tensions had always existed between Mao and Stalin: Stalin failed to provide support to the CCP during the civil war; there were also ideological disagreements between Stalin and Mao. Stalin believed that the industrial workers, not the peasants, should pioneer a Marxist revolution. Despite this, in 1949 Mao announced that China should "lean to one side" and emulate what Stalin had achieved in the Soviet Union.

Stalin and Mao signed the Sino-Soviet Treaty of Alliance in 1950. The USSR supported China with a $300 million loan, which allowed China to begin economic reform. This came at a high price because of the strict terms of interest levied by Stalin on China. Mao later stated that getting financial aid from Stalin was like "getting meat from the mouth of a tiger". Mao did not want to rely on any foreign power, and eventually repaid this debt entirely.

The flow of Chinese party members to the Soviet Union and of Soviet experts to China was considerable. Soviet technicians helped build roads, bridges, and industry across the country, while the CCP cadres learned about political organization in the Soviet Union. The Sino-Soviet Friendship Association spread the message throughout China: "The Soviet Union's Today is our Tomorrow." Stalin's death in 1953 prompted a power struggle within the USSR, after which Khrushchev emerged as leader. Relations with China would significantly alter after this.

Party purges

By 1954, plans to industrialize China were well under way. At the same time, Chairman Mao grew concerned about potential rivals within the party. In an act reminiscent of the Futian Incident of 1930, Mao turned on two provincial CCP leaders, Gao Gang (高岗) 1902–1954 in Manchuria, and Rao Shushi (饶漱石) 1900–1975 in Shandong. He claimed that these

party officials had abused their positions and established "independent kingdoms". The Central Council dismissed both from their positions. Gao Gang eventually committed suicide and Rao Shushi languished in prison. A witch-hunt followed as other leaders were denounced and sent to prison camps for "treachery" and "splitting the party". Mao's motives were complex but they served as a reminder to all party members to tow the line.

> **Class discussion**
>
> How similar or different was Mao's reaction to threats to his authority within the party compared to that of another dictator?

> **Source skills**
>
> *Historians (too) have sometimes confused the abstract world presented by propaganda with the complicated individual tragedies of revolution, buying all too readily into the gleaming image that the regime so carefully projected to the rest of the world. Some have called the years of liberation a "Golden Age" or a "Honeymoon Period" … But … the first decade of Maoism was one of the worst tyrannies in the history of the twentieth century, sending to an early grave at least 5 million civilians and bringing misery to countless more.*
>
> Frank Dikotter, Chair Professor of Humanities at the University of Hong Kong, in *The Tragedy of Liberation* (2013).
>
> **Questions**
>
> 1 In what ways might this source represent a revisionist view?
>
> 2 In the light of this source, discuss the challenges facing historians investigating the early years of the PRC.

Mao's grip on power, 1955–1976

By 1955, Mao appeared to be at the peak of his power, having put his own stamp on the country and asserted his authority in the party. As industrial and agricultural reform gained pace, the New China appeared to glow on the international stage. Yet China was also on the cusp of enormous political upheaval. Mao wanted to fulfill the ideals of the revolution, but he grew increasingly paranoid about losing his grip on China. In the decades ahead, Mao would take his power to new heights.

The registration system

Throughout 1955 the power of the CCP over the population increased. The state took more control of the countryside to requisition more grain. More peasants were placed into cooperatives. Although peasants nominally owned their plots of land, land usage was pooled with other villagers. Where there was resistance, the militias responded with violence. Many peasants left the countryside for urban areas to supplement their income and escape famine; in all, about 20 million people became rural migrants. Attempts by the State Council to stem the flow failed, so in June 1955 Zhou Enlai extended the household-registration system to the countryside. This was like the internal passport system introduced in the USSR decades before. It essentially tied millions of rural residents to the countryside, while urban residents held on to certain rights and entitlements. Anyone wanting to change residence needed a migration certificate. Ration cards had to be presented at local grain stores where peasants were registered. Local officials kept dossiers on every individual and used them to maintain political and social control over the Chinese people.

> **Types of registration system documents**
>
> Danwei: a permit to work
>
> Hukou: a certificate entitling a family to obtain accommodation
>
> Dangan: a dossier held by local party officials containing personal details and records of every individual

> **Class discussion**
>
> Discuss how the registration system was able to strengthen CCP control of China. How was this method used in any other authoritarian state?

The impact of de-Stalinization

In 1956, the new Soviet leader Nikita Khrushchev launched a bold attack on Stalin, who had died three years earlier. He denounced Stalin's "cult of personality" and held him responsible for his brutal purges, mass deportations, and the torture of loyal party members. He also criticized Stalin for his agricultural reforms and the reckless pace of collectivization. His speech sent ripples across the Soviet satellite states in central and eastern Europe. In Poland and Hungary, people took to the streets demanding political and economic reform. In China, there were strikes and protests in urban and rural areas.

Khrushchev's speech denouncing Stalin had a considerable impact on Mao, who saw that it could easily be interpreted as an attack on his "cult of personality" and his agricultural reforms. In September 1956, references to Mao Zedong thought were removed from the CCP charter. The cult of personality was denounced and the shift to collective leadership encouraged. Mao needed to divert criticism away from his style of leadership and his perceived failures if he was going to maintain control.

The "Hundred Flowers" campaign

In early 1957, with the slogan, "Let a hundred flowers bloom, let a hundred schools of thought contend", Mao encouraged open criticism in the party and the country. At first, criticism was mild but then leading party figures, and even Mao Zedong, came under attack. Critics accused the party of corruption and lacking realism. Fearing it had gone too far, Mao called a halt to the campaign and turned on his critics. He then launched the **anti-rightist movement** to force his biggest critics, both intellectuals and party members, to redact their criticisms. Deng Xiaoping (邓小平) led the campaign. More than half a million people were labelled "rightists". Many committed suicide, were executed or sent to the countryside for re-education. Even high-ranking members were targeted as "poisonous weeds". Zhou Enlai, one of Mao's most loyal supporters, was forced to confess his responsibility for slowing reform to the party. The only way to escape denunciation was to conform to Mao's wishes.

> **anti-rightist movement**
> A series of campaigns from 1957 to 1959, in which critics of Mao were labelled "rightists" and endured public denunciation and humiliation.

> ### Deng Xiaoping (邓小平) 1904–1997
> A revolutionary of the Long March who became Secretary General between 1954 and 1966, Deng was purged in the Cultural Revolution of 1966 and again in 1976 after the Tiananmen Incident, but he rose to power in 1978 and remained leader of China until his retirement in 1992.

Historians debate the reasons why Mao launched the Hundred Flowers campaign:

- Jung Chang, in her 2005 biography of Mao, argues that it was a deliberate trick by Mao. By allowing open criticism, Mao's critics were easily exposed so that he could then root them out. This was part of a wider ploy to control the party and wider society.

- Lei Feignon, a US scholar, has revised this view, by arguing that Mao's motives were more pragmatic. He argues that the Hundred Flowers campaign was Mao's attempt to encourage criticism against the bureaucracy. He was against its growing influence and wanted its inefficiencies to be publicly identified.

- Jonathan Spence, a widely respected authority on China, argues that the Hundred Flowers campaign was the result of confusion within the party over the pace of industrial and agricultural reform.

> **Class discussion**
> Discuss whether Mao was driven by ideology, pragmatism, or a thirst for power by launching the Hundred Flowers campaign.

Whatever his motives, by rooting out opposition, Mao had strengthened his position in the party and the wider country. His leadership was further bolstered by Khrushchev's military clampdown on dissent in Hungary in 1956. This served to justify his decision to suppress the opposition.

The Purge of Peng Dehuai

In 1959, Mao's position came under threat. At a party gathering in Lushan, Peng Dehuai (彭德怀), the PRC's Minister of Defence, spoke openly about the famine in the countryside caused by agricultural reform (see the Great Leap Forward on page 150). The famine would eventually claim the lives of 40 million people. This was an opportune time for other party members to speak out against Mao's reforms. None did. In fact, the opposite happened when delegates praised Mao's leadership and denounced Peng as a troublemaker. Mao equated Peng's criticism with treason and purged him from the party.

The Tibetan Uprising of 1959

In 1959, Tibet rose up against the Chinese occupation. Ever since the PLA invasion of 1950, the Tibetan resistance had been forced underground. The famine caused by Mao's agricultural reforms had reached Tibet and millions faced starvation. The Chinese authorities met the national uprising of the Tibetan people with suppression and mass arrests. The Tibetan religion came under attack and the state intensified its control of the Tibetan way of life. The Dalai Lama fled to northern India, and it was from here that he would campaign on the international stage for Tibetan independence. Tibetans were banned from mentioning the Dalai Lama in public. The CCP encouraged Chinese settlement in Tibet and many Tibetan religious practices were banned. In 1962 the **Panchen Lama** issued a report claiming that 20 per cent of the Tibetan population had been imprisoned and that half of them had died in prison. Mao denied the claims and had the Panchen Lama arrested. Zhou Enlai later admitted that the report was a fair and accurate portrayal of Chinese policy in Tibet.

> **Panchen Lama**
> Highest ranking Lama after the Dalai Lama.

The Cultural Revolution, 1966–1976

In 1962, Mao Zedong slipped into the background of the party, in the knowledge that his reputation had been damaged as a result of the Great Famine. President Liu Shaoqi (刘少奇) and CCP General Secretary Deng Xiaoping were instructed to save the countryside and stop the famine; their supporters reversed collectivization in Gansu and Qinghai. The growing popularity of Liu and Deng within the party became a threat and Mao began to regret retreating into the political background.

In 1966, in order to reassert his authority over the Chinese government and the country, Mao launched what became known as the Great Proletarian Cultural Revolution. This mass political upheaval, orchestrated by Mao, would result in genocide, class war, cultural destruction and economic chaos. It led to further purges of those considered disloyal to the principles of the revolution and enabled Mao to return to the forefront of the CCP as the undisputed leader of China.

> **Liu Shaoqi** (刘少奇)
> **1898–1969**
>
> Liu was a revolutionary who succeeded Mao as President in 1959. He was purged as Mao's successor during the Cultural Revolution in 1968 and died in harsh conditions in 1969.
>
> **Chen Boda** (陈伯达)
> **1904–1989**
>
> A leading communist intellectual, Chen helped Mao carve out the Maoist ideology.

The Little Red Book

In the early 1960s, Lin Biao, one of Mao's most loyal supporters, compiled the "Little Red Book" in collaboration with Chen Boda (陈伯达). The original title was *Quotations from Chairman Mao Zedong* and it was a compilation of the thoughts and sayings of Mao since the 1920s. The

Research and communication skills

Find a translated version of *The Little Red Book* on the Internet. It is available on the Marxists.org website.

1 Select a chapter from *The Little Red Book* and pick out two memorable or significant quotes. Put together a presentation so that you can share your quotes with the rest of your group. Annotate and discuss your ideas about the meaning behind each quote.

2 Why do you think Mao's ideas in *The Little Red Book* were so appealing to its readers?

3 Should *The Little Red Book* be described as faith? How valid is secular faith as a way of knowing?

Gang of Four

This powerful faction of the CCP was responsible for implementing the harshest and most radical policies of the Cultural Revolution. The Gang was made up of Jiang Qing and her three staunchest allies: Zhang Chunquiao (张春桥), Yao Wenyyuan (姚文元), and Wang Honwen (王洪文).

Central Cultural Revolution Group (CCRG)

This 17-member body included the Gang of Four and would play a key role in directing the Cultural Revolution.

preface read: "Study Chairman Mao's writings, follow his teachings, and act according to his instructions." Lin Biao made *The Little Red Book* central to the training of PLA soldiers and it also became a secular bible, selling over 750 million copies throughout China. It enshrined Mao Zedong as cult leader, was a social necessity in schools and at home, and became a vital point of reference in resolving disputes.

The Purge of Wu Han

In 1965 Lin Biao launched a series of attacks to blacken the name of Wu Han (吴晗), a playwright who was critical of Mao. The attacks were triggered by Wu Han's play, *The Dismissal of Hai Rui from Office*. The play was set during the era of the Song dynasty (960–1279) and told the story of a court official who defied the orders of a cruel emperor. Maoists interpreted the play as a criticism of Mao's dismissal of Peng Dehuai for opposing Mao's reforms and revealing the truth about the Great Famine. Distraught at the attacks, Wu Han committed suicide in 1969.

Power struggles in the CCP

The Wu Han affair highlighted the divisions emerging within the CCP. Maoists on the left of the party were growing in prominence. Jiang Qing (江青), a former actress in Shanghai and also Mao's wife, was a fervent hardliner. She was a dominant figure in the Shanghai Forum, a group of uncompromising radicals who advocated the toughest measures against Mao's opponents. Jiang Qing was one of the **Gang of Four,** the most extreme members of the Shanghai Forum. Jiang launched an attack on the moderates Liu Shaoqi and Deng Xiaoping, demanding that they, along with key artists and writers, should be removed from their positions for their disloyalty to Mao's revolution. The targeting of "counter-revolutionaries" had begun.

The Shanghai Forum argued that the PLA should root out all those who were "taking the capitalist road". In 1966 this began with the purge of the Group of Five, a set of moderate officials led by Peng Zhen (彭真), the mayor of Beijing. The **Central Cultural Revolution Group (CCRG)**, a subcommittee of the Politburo that had been set up in May 1966, would play a key part in these purges. Mao soon defined the enemy within as "counter-revolutionary revisionists" and notified the CCP that, unless steps were taken, they threatened to "turn the dictatorship of the proletariat into the dictatorship of the bourgeoisie". The Cultural Revolution had begun.

The events of the Cultural Revolution

The purges within the party became part of a national movement when Lin Biao, acting on Mao's instructions, used poster campaigns in universities to ignite students and radical teachers. Students and teachers abandoned their classes and attacked those who had strayed from the revolutionary path.

In July 1966 Mao made a timely and extraordinary comeback to the forefront of Chinese politics. In a carefully staged event, the 73-year-old chairman was photographed swimming across the Yangzi River. This was a symbolic choice because, in Chinese tradition, the nation's greatest river was regarded as a life force. This powerful image filled newspapers and newsreels across the country and inspired national adulation.

In August 1966, Mao called on members of the CCP to renew the class struggle and remove revisionists from the party. He relegated Liu Shaoqi in the party ranking and promoted Lin Biao to second in command. Effectively, he had nominated Lin Biao as his successor.

ATL Thinking skills

A number of factors help to explain why Mao launched the Great Proletarian Cultural Revolution. Some of these factors relate to Mao's ideology and others to his thirst for power.

Discuss each of the statements below and decide whether they link to Mao's ideology, his thirst for power, or even both.

1 Mao believed in permanent revolution. He feared that the CCP had been infected by "neo-capitalism" and would cease to serve a genuine purpose unless the party and country were cleansed of the enemy.

2 The downfall of Nikita Khrushchev in the USSR in 1964 – partly for economic failures – concerned Mao, who feared that the same could happen to him.

3 Mao thought that Khrushchev and his successors had betrayed the revolution by encouraging warmer relations (detente) with the West.

4 Mao wanted to eliminate all forms of opposition and preserve his own position.

5 Mao wanted to toughen up younger party members and make them hardened revolutionaries.

6 Mao built the revolution with the support of the peasants. He despised intellectuals and bureaucrats and saw them as a threat.

Jiang Qing (江青) 1914–1991

Both Mao Zedong and Jiang Qing left their spouses to marry each other in 1938. Mao allowed Jiang to enter the political fray in 1959 because she was a potent advocate of Maoist ideas. Jiang would become a brutal enforcer of cultural reform and she led ferocious attacks against "counter-revolutionaries". After Mao's death in 1976, Jiang and her associates were blamed for the worst excesses of the Cultural Revolution and put on trial. Jiang was sentenced to death, after claiming that, "I was Mao Zedong's dog. I bit whomever he told me to bite." The death sentence was commuted to life imprisonment in 1983. Jiang committed suicide in 1991.

Class discussion

Discuss why you think the youth of China held Mao in such high regard.

Rallies

On 18 August 1966, a mass demonstration organized by Lin Biao and Chen Boda took place in Tiananmen Square. Over a million people, mostly in their teens and twenties, waved their copies of *The Little Red Book* and chanted slogans in worship of Mao, such as, "Mao Zedong is the red sun rising in the east" and "Chairman Mao, may you live for a thousand years!" A further seven rallies took place over the following months. Mao did not need to be present for all of them because by then the cult of Mao had been cultivated so effectively. Lin Biao claimed that Mao was "remoulding the souls of the people".

The Red Guards and the destruction of the "Four Olds"

On 1 August 1966, Mao Zedong had urged the students at Qinghua University to "bombard the headquarters". By doing this, Mao was galvanizing the young to target the "enemies" of the revolution. At the August rally, Lin Biao identified "four olds" for the young to attack:

- old ideas
- old culture
- old customs
- old habits.

▲ The Tiananmen Square demonstration, August 1966

The youth were enthused by the call and would fanatically follow these orders. Many felt that they were defending the revolution and its leader who had liberated China from foreign humiliation and oppression. The cult of Mao was rising to new heights.

Source skills

Read the following extract from an author writing from self-imposed exile:

When Chairman Mao waved his hand at Tiananmen, a million Red Guards wept their hearts out as if by some hormonal reaction. Later on we were conditioned to burst into tears the moment he appeared on the screen. He was divine, and the revolutionary tides of the world rose and fell at his command.

Source: Suola Liu, *Chaos and All That*, p15. 1994. University of Hawaii Press.

Question

With reference to the Cultural Revolution and the cult of Mao, how far can it be argued that emotions distort reality?

Research and communication skills

Research the propaganda posters of the Cultural Revolution. You could use the following website:

http://chineseposters.net/themes/cultural-revolution-campaigns.php.

Design a presentation to show how propaganda was used to direct the Cultural Revolution. Make sure that you include the following:

1 Annotate a copy of your chosen poster. Look at its use of colour and other symbolism to reveal its meaning.

2 Identify the slogans in the poster.

3 Consider why posters like this wielded so much power.

Devout young people, mobilized by Mao, formed themselves into a paramilitary social movement they called the Red Guards. The Red Guards denounced their parents, and smashed and tore up any remnants of the Confucian past by destroying thousands of historic and cultural sites. They took control of public transport and the media, condemning any sign of bourgeois thinking. Schoolteachers, university staff, and intellectuals were denounced as rightists and forced publicly to confess their class crimes.

The Ministry of Public Security officially sanctioned the actions of the Red Guards and also provided them with information on the five categories of targets:

- landlords
- rich peasants
- reactionaries
- bad elements
- rightists.

The Cultural Revolution touched the remotest parts of China. Millions would be tortured or beaten to death and many more would have their lives irreparably damaged.

▲ The caption on this poster from around 1966 reads: "Hold high the great red banner of Mao Zedong Thought to wage the Great Proletarian Cultural Revolution to the end — Revolution is no crime, to rebel is justified"

Class discussion

Discuss why you think Mao enlisted the young to carry out the Cultural Revolution.

ATL Research skills

A student who had attended the rally at Tiananmen on 18 August 1966 became disenchanted with the movement and horrified by its excesses. She later wrote a letter to Mao, in which she said:

The Cultural Revolution is not a mass movement. It is one man with the gun manipulating the masses.

Source: Jung Chang and Jon Halliday, *Mao, The Unknown Story*, p547. 2005. Jonathan Cape.

Why is it difficult for historians to find out about opposition to the Cultural Revolution?

The attacks on Deng Xiaoping, Liu Shaoqi and other moderates

Even those who had devoted their lives to the CCP became targets of the Red Guards. In October 1966, following another Red Guard demonstration in Beijing, Mao let it be known that Deng Xiaoping and Liu Shaoqi were not following the party line. Wall posters denounced them as revisionists.

Liu and his wife were dragged from their government residence and publicly beaten. Liu was then forced to confess his crimes in a series of "struggle sessions". He was imprisoned and, denied medical treatment for his diabetes, eventually died in solitary confinement. Deng was denounced in public by jeering Red Guards and then put into solitary confinement. He was eventually sent to perform "corrective labour" in Jiangxi Province in 1969. The Red Guards threw Deng Xiaoping's son from an upstairs window, leaving him permanently paralyzed.

As the moderates within the CCP were removed, the influence of Lin Biao and Jiang Qing increased. They were bolstered by the appointment of Kang Sheng (康生) as head of the PRC's secret police. He was chosen, at Mao's bidding, for his ruthlessness and was the key instigator of the purges against the upper echelons of the CCP. Mao retreated from the city as Lin Biao, Jiang Qing, and Kang Sheng informed the Red Guards of the ministers and officials marked out for intimidation and attack. At the trial of the Gang of Four in 1980, it was stated that the Red Guards murdered more than half a million CCP officials.

The Cultural Revolution abroad

In 1967, Chinese militants were behind violent attacks in over 30 countries outside China. Mao wanted to provoke anti-imperialist unrest in the British colony of Hong Kong. He urged Zhao Enlai to send in Chinese terrorists to destabilize the region to force the British to retaliate. Despite the death of five policemen and the explosion of 160 bombs, the British authorities did not react with hostility, so there was no mass demonstration against British rule.

The PLA and the Red Guards' move to the countryside

By 1968, it appeared that the Red Guards were getting out of hand. Civil strife in China increased as the Red Guards turned on one another, competing over their level of devotion to Mao. Industrial production had been gravely affected; schools and universities had been closed since 1966 so that students could join the Red Guards and attack "counter-revolutionaries". Orders were given for the People's Liberation Army (PLA) to take over this hunt for "counter-revolutionaries" from the Red Guards who then became part of a great campaign "to go up to the mountains and down to the villages". The ease with which they followed this order reveals how China's rebellious youth were still under the control of the government. The campaign urged the Red Guards to go and live among the peasants and learn about the hardships of life endured by 80 per cent of the population. Although Mao did believe that those of privilege should learn "the dignity of labour", it is likely that the campaign was also necessary to save the urban areas from anarchy and chaos and restore order.

Between 1967 and 1972, over 12 million young people – students and secondary school graduates –moved from the towns into the countryside. Many were unprepared for the hardships they faced and they began to question their idealism and even the goodwill of Mao Zedong. (Their resentment of their situation was to contribute to an eventual decline in support for the Party.)

The "Cleansing the class ranks" campaign, 1968–1971

The PLA carried out its responsibilities for rooting out "counter-revolutionaries" with violent zeal. The CCRG, with Jiang Qing's Gang of Four, played a key role in their campaign to "cleanse the class ranks". Committees were established across China to remove any forms of capitalism. Hundreds of thousands of people were tortured and killed. Mao left Jiang and the extremists in control, even though he still had the authority to rein in the violence.

The Fall of Lin Biao, 1971–1972

By the early 1970s, disillusionment with the Cultural Revolution began to set in. It was still too dangerous openly to oppose Mao but as his health was increasingly in question, a power struggle for the succession began. Mao became paranoid about Lin Biao's influence within the party. Lin, Mao's nominated successor, was ordered to submit to self-criticism. Although it is difficult to find information on the circumstances

Class discussion

How responsible was Mao for the Cultural Revolution? Are some dictators more responsible for causing violent upheaval than others?

Why did Mao leave the direction of the Cultural Revolution in the hands of other party members?

of his downfall, it appears that Lin feared that his life was under threat and reluctantly plotted to remove Mao from power. Once the plot was leaked to Zhou Enlai, Lin Biao made a desperate bid to escape to the USSR by plane. His plane crashed in Mongolia, killing all on board. It is not known whether this was an accident or sabotage.

The decline of the Cultural Revolution

The story of Lin Biao's fall was not reported until 1972. The news reports claimed that the former PLA helmsman was a traitor and a spy who had conspired against the country. The impact was widely felt in China and people began to question such a dramatic shift in the reputation of a man who had been so loyal to Mao and the revolution.

As the minister who had foiled Lin's plot to remove Mao, Zhou Enlai's prestige increased. He enlisted his ally Deng Xioaping to return from exile and resume his position as Party Secretary. It was now in Deng's favour that he had been a victim of the Cultural Revolution. The rise of the moderates was met with fury by the Gang of Four, who denounced Deng and Zhou as a "the pragmatist clique".

The Tiananmen Incident

In 1976 Zhou Enlai died of lung cancer. At his memorial in Tiananmen Square, a large-scale demonstration in support of Zhao's moderating policies took place. The crowd was dispersed after bloody confrontations with the police. The Politburo blamed the Tiananmen Incident on "rightist agitators" and dismissed Deng Xiaoping. Deng retreated to Guangdong province in southern China to wait on events.

In 1976, after years of failing health, Mao Zedong died. In the power struggle that ensued, the Gang of Four was removed and the Cultural Revolution came to an end. By 1978, Deng Xiaoping would emerge as paramount leader of China.

> **ATL Thinking skills**
>
> Did Mao's style of leadership mark a change with China's past rulers or did Mao provide a sense of continuity with China's past?

> **ATL Self-management skills**
>
> 1 Create a diagram to summarize the Cultural Revolution. Include the following headings: Aims; Methods; Targets; Victims; Instigators; and Results.
>
> 2 Make a list of the different opponents to Mao's policies and rule. How did Mao silence and eliminate his opposition?
>
> 3 Produce a visual summary or spider diagram to show the methods that Mao used to consolidate his dictatorship. Consider legal methods, force, leadership, censorship and propaganda, reform, treatment of opposition and foreign policy.

Mao's foreign policy

Mao wanted China to gain recognition as a powerful independent state on the world stage. He wanted to show the Chinese people that the communist revolution would restore national pride and prevent any repeat of the imperialist aggression of the past. Although his policies were far from consistent, China did retain its independence as a nation. This section explores how far Mao's approach to relations with other countries strengthened or weakened his position.

战无不胜的马克思列宁主义、毛泽东思想万岁!

▲ The caption of this Chinese poster from 1967 reads: "Long live the Invincible Marxism, Leninism and Mao Zedong Thought!"

The Bandung Conference, 1955

In April 1955, representatives from 29 governments of Asian and African nations, including China, gathered in Bandung, Indonesia, to discuss peace and the role of their countries in the Cold War, economic development, and decolonization. China played an important role in the conference: by 1955, in the aftermath of Stalin's death, Mao appeared to be the leader of the communist world and countries that were non-aligned in the Cold War recognized him as their leader on the world stage.

By the 1970s Mao was less concerned with matters in the developing world because China's status on the world stage had dramatically improved, but it would take years for China to get to this point.

The Sino–Soviet rift, 1958–1976

Mao's alliance with Stalin in the Korean War played a part in strengthening Mao's consolidation of power. By 1956, Nikita Khrushchev had emerged as Stalin's successor and his denunciations of Stalin weakened Mao's position and contributed to the turmoil of the Hundred Flowers Campaign. Mao was fearful of the Soviet Union's improved relations with the West and China's subsequent isolation. He accused Khrushchev of revisionism and betraying the revolution, a point that was brilliantly argued by Deng Xiaoping at the Conference of Communist Parties in 1957. Tensions increased when both sides failed to find agreement, even when Khrushchev visited Beijing in 1958. In that year, Mao was braced for war with Taiwan. In response, the USA prepared to retaliate, so Mao backed down, blaming the Soviets for not offering their support. Khrushchev denounced the CCP as reckless.

The PRC deliberately pursued policies against the USSR in Albania and Yugoslavia. Diplomatic relations were severed at the Moscow Conference of 1961, when Zhou Enlai and the Chinese delegation walked out. Fierce Sino–Soviet propaganda played on the bitter recriminations between

ATL **Thinking skills**

Consider the message of the poster above. Why do you think foreign policy was essential to Mao's leadership of China?

both countries, as each side jockeyed to humiliate the other on the world stage. What was really at stake was which of the two powers would be the leader of worldwide revolution.

By the mid-1960s, all Soviet experts and advisers were withdrawn from the PRC. Despite this, China produced its first hydrogen bomb in 1964 and, to the alarm of the Soviets, Mao announced his willingness to use it. Relations continued to deteriorate under Khrushchev's successor, Leonid Brezhnev. The lowest point in relations was in 1969, when a relatively minor incident sparked a war on the Sino–Russian border. Only the threat of nuclear war ended the conflict.

The Sino–Soviet rift lasted until Mao's death in 1976. His eventual successor, Deng Xiaoping, adopted a more tolerant approach to the USSR and the West.

Relations with the US

The CCP victory of 1949 ushered in decades of tension with its traditional western imperialist enemy, America. Anti-American campaigns intensified during the Korean War and the Cultural Revolution. Tensions were heightened by China's moral and diplomatic support of the USA's enemies during the Vietnam War. Like Stalin, Mao always feared that the western powers would launch an attack on China. He devised a defensive strategy for China, known as the "Third Line". This was a plan for a vast network of fortifications across China, both above and below ground, to withstand heavy bombardment.

Mao steered China on a new course in 1971, when he invited the US table tennis team to play in China. Zhou Enlai and Henry Kissinger steered negotiations, which became known as "ping-pong diplomacy". By warming to the USA, Mao aimed to undermine the position of the USSR as a world power. He was also prompted to begin a Sino–American detente because the United Nations had accepted China's seat on the Security Council. China now had the power of veto to block Soviet-initiated resolutions.

Mao invited President Nixon to China and greeted him in 1972. This parting of the Bamboo Curtain was a major diplomatic success for both former rival nations. Although much still divided the two countries, the PRC crept out of isolation. By 1979 both countries had established full diplomatic relations.

Relations with other nations

China's relationship with India was initially based on mutual border agreements, but tensions concerning borders took them to war in 1962. Relations were strained when China supported Pakistan in the 1965 war with India. Relations between India and China were not stabilized until after Mao's death in 1976.

Relations with the West showed little mutual respect. The UN heavily criticized Mao for his hardline policies in Tibet. Relations with Taiwan were always hostile and, despite Mao's attempts to regain Taiwan for the Chinese mainland, Taiwan has remained independent to this day.

> **ATL Thinking and communication skills**
>
> 1 Construct a timeline of Mao's foreign policy and explain how each event strengthened or weakened Mao's position.
>
> 2 Debate whether Mao's foreign policy was a success or a failure.

When he took power in 1949, Mao seems to have had a genuine aspiration to improve the conditions of the people. Significant challenges faced the PRC in the transformation of the economy and society of China. Perhaps the greatest of these challenges was the pressure to reach Mao's revolutionary goals and targets when those who spoke the truth about any problems were labelled "defeatists" or "rightists", and then purged, punished, or wiped out. Mao's reforms undoubtedly made gains but, with the human tragedy of the Great Leap Forward and the disruption of the Cultural Revolution, it is clear that politics often got in the way of progress. This chapter explores the extent to which Mao's reforms were creative or destructive.

The Chinese Communist Party's economic policies

When the Chinese Communist Party (CCP) came to power in 1949, the inflation rate was out of control, at 1000 per cent. By 1951, the inflation rate had been reduced to a more tolerable 15 per cent. This was achieved by cuts in public spending, increased taxation on urban residents and replacing the old Chinese dollar with a new currency, the renminbi or yuan.

The first Five-Year Plan, 1952–1957

Mao was determined that China would industrialize on a similar scale to the Soviet Union. For the revolution to succeed, China needed to become a **command economy** and, to that end, in 1952 China's first Five-Year Plan was introduced. The country now had a potentially huge industrial workforce because of mass migration from the countryside into the towns: between 1949 and 1957, China's urban population doubled from 57 million to 100 million.

command economy
An economic system in which the means of production are publicly owned and economic activity is controlled by a central authority. Central planners decide on the goods to be produced, allocate raw materials, fix quotas for each enterprise, and set prices.

In the Sino-Soviet agreement of 1950, the USSR agreed to provide China with economic assistance. This assistance included the provision of resources and advisers for the transformation of the economy. China had to pay for this with high-interest loans, which soured relations between Mao and Stalin. Only 5 per cent of the capital sent to China was genuine industrial investment.

Under the first Five-Year Plan, coal, steel, and petrochemicals were targeted for industrial production. The development of the transport industry was a key priority and a number of ambitious civil-engineering projects were undertaken. One impressive example was the construction of a vast road and rail bridge across the Yangtze River at Nanking. At all levels of command, from party officials to industrial managers and workers, the pressure to reach industrial targets was immense. The figures were most likely to have been exaggerated, but even when western analysts have filtered them, the results of the first Five-Year Plan are notable.

Source skills

The first Five-Year Plan, 1953–1957

Indicator (unit)	1952 Data	1957 Plan	1957 Actual	1957 Actual as percentage of plan
Gross output value (in million 1952 yuan)				
Industry (excluding handicrafts)	27 010	53 560	65 020	121.4
Producer sector	10 730	24 303	34 330	141.0
Machinery	1404	3470	6177	178.0
Chemicals	864	2271	4291	188.9
Producer sector less machinery and chemicals	8462	18 562	23 862	128.5
Physical output				
Coal (mmt)	68.50	113.00	130.00	115.0
Crude oil (tmt)	436	2012	1458	72.5
Steel ingot (mmt)	1.35	4.12	5.35	129.8
Cement (mmt)	2.86	6.00	6.86	114.3
Electric power (billion kwh)	7.26	15.90	19.34	121.6
Internal combustion engines (thousand hp)	27.6	260.2	609.0	234.2
Hydroelectric turbines (kw)	6664	79 500	74 900	94.2
Generators (thousand kw)	29.7	227.0	312.2	137.5
Electric motors (thousand kw)	639	1,048	1,455	138.8
Transformers (thousand kva)	1167	2610	3500	134.1
Machine tools (units)	13 734	12 720	28 000	220.1
Locomotives (units)	20	200	167	83.5
Railway freights cars (units)	5792	8500	7300	85.9
Merchant ships (thousand dwt tons)	21.5	179.1	54.0	30.2
Trucks (units)	0	4000	7500	187.5
Bicycles (thousand units)	80	555	1,174	211.5
Caustic soda (tmt)	79	154	198	128.6
Soda ash (tmt)	192	476	506	106.3
Ammonium sulphate (tmt)	181	504	631	125.2
Ammonium nitrate (tmt)	7	44	120	272.7
Automobile tyres (thousand sets)	417	760	873	114.9
Sulphuric acid (tmt)	149	402	632	157.2
"666" insecticide (tons)	600	70 000	61 000	87.1

▲ Source A: Statistics for the first Five-Year Plan

Note: mmt = million metric tons; tmt = thousand metric tons.

From Jonathan Spence, *The Search for Modern China*.

Questions

1 What does this table of statistics suggest about the success of the first Five-Year Plan?

2 With reference to its origin and purpose, assess the value and limitations of the statistics for historians examining Mao's economic policies.

▲ Constructing a rudimentary smelting steel furnace, 1958

backyard furnaces
Every family was urged to make a smelting device by hand. Small blast furnaces were built in backyards to make steel, but lack of knowledge of the steelmaking process meant that the results were usually unsatisfactory.

The Great Leap Forward, 1958–1962

The Great Leap Forward was the term Mao used to describe the second Five-Year Plan of 1958–1962. His aim was to turn China into a modern industrial power in the shortest amount of time. Although Mao had seen the peasants as the vanguard of the revolution in 1949, he rested the future of China on the industrial workers. China was then largely an agricultural nation, lagging behind the West, but Mao had ambitions to overtake the industrial output of the capitalist world at rapid speed.

By 1958, Mao was resenting China's reliance on the USSR and tensions in the alliance had begun to emerge. The transformation of the economy was essential if China was going to become more independent. Targets were set for agriculture and industry, but it would take the efforts of the people to succeed. Two great soldiers would lead the nation to economic triumph: "General Grain" and "General Steel". The former would wage the battle to increase China's food supplies while the latter would turn China into a successful industrial economy.

The plan was that the collectivized peasants would produce a surplus of food, to be exported abroad. The profits would then be injected into China's industry. In this way the workers would create a modern industrial economy capable of surpassing the industrial powers.

Enormous construction projects were undertaken to show what the human hand could achieve. The propaganda machine went into overdrive, with news of singing workers dressed in identical blue uniforms as they achieved the remarkable with only basic tools and little machinery. The expansion of Tiananmen Square in Beijing began in 1957 and was completed within two years. Mao was determined for it to be larger than Moscow's Red Square and, at 44 hectares in area, it is still the fourth-largest city square in the world.

Projected figures for the Five-Year Plan changed frequently and there was considerable reliance on the idea that faith in human will would meet or even surpass targets. One example of where such lofty thoughts met with failure was the **backyard furnaces** campaign. Mao believed that producing massive amounts of steel would transform the economy. Iron and steel would not only be made in China's foundries and mills, but also in small family kilns. The Chinese nation was galvanized for the backyard steel campaign, building and smelting in a frenzy of national ambition. Jubilant officials reported back to Mao on how the Chinese people had answered his bidding. Mao became known as the "emperor of the blue ants". The reality was that little quality steel was being produced by all this goodwill: homemade steel, smelted from pots and pans, was useless. The authorities kept this quiet.

State-owned enterprises

For ideological and pragmatic reasons, industry was brought under government control. Private firms and companies could no longer exist to make their own profits and instead worked for the state as state-owned enterprises (SOEs). Wages, prices, and production targets were to be fixed by the state.

The SOEs were given state subsidies and the workers received a guaranteed wage. The problem was that there was little incentive for the SOEs to become efficient and highly productive. Any surplus was given to the state. The advantage for workers was that the system provided them with an "**iron rice bowl**". This included the provision of accommodation and medical and health benefits.

Class discussion

What were the ideological and pragmatic reasons for introducing SOEs?

iron rice bowl
The system for guaranteeing jobs and protecting wages.

Source skills

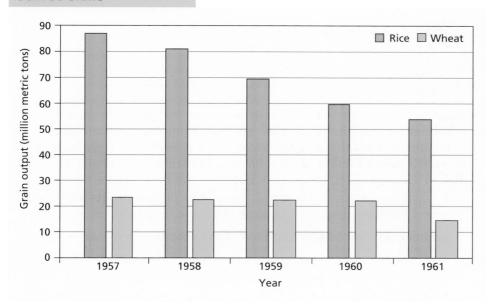

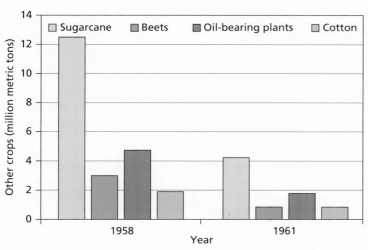

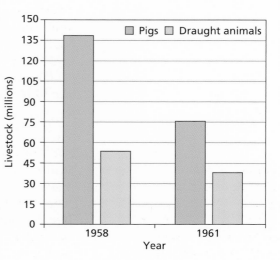

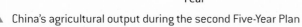

▲ China's agricultural output during the second Five-Year Plan

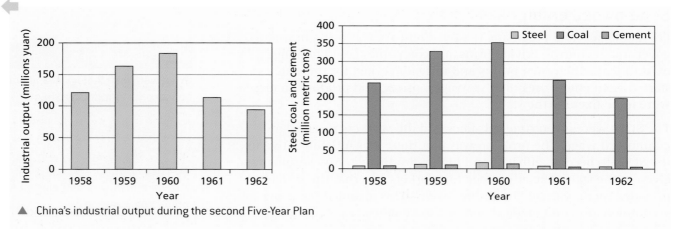

▲ China's industrial output during the second Five-Year Plan

From Jonathan Fenby, *The Penguin History of Modern China*

Questions

1   What does this source suggest about the success of the second Five-Year plan?

2   Use the sources here and on page 149 to compare and contrast the success of the first and second Five-Year Plans.

---

quality control
The system for monitoring production to ensure that products are of a consistent standard.

applied communism
Planning according to Marxist principles, which includes the ending of private ownership and state control of the economy.

Although some of the production figures look impressive, there were fundamental weaknesses in the second Five-Year Plan. The production of materials was not reflected in an increase of manufactured goods. China lacked the managerial know-how and technical skills required to fully transform the economy. The two guiding principles of **quality control** and **applied communism** were hindered by these underlying weaknesses.

A number of other factors hindered Mao's economic reforms:

- In 1960, the USSR stopped providing technical assistance. This resulted in the closure of half of China's 300 industrial plants.

- The reforms were ideologically driven, so political slogans got in the way of common sense.

- Mao's leadership played a part in limiting progress because he would not accept responsibility for failure. Mao blamed bourgeois elements for sabotage and poor administration but he refused to accept that his policies were at fault.

- Mao did not have the scientific expertise required to make his policies work and he believed that the effort of China's vast population would accelerate change, rather than sound economic planning.

Mao's intuition and blind faith was often a rallying call for action, but this would soon end in catastrophe.

The Great Famine, 1958–1962

"When there is not enough to eat, people starve to death. It is better to let half the people die so that the other half can eat their fill."

Mao Zedong, March 1959, at a meeting with other Party leaders in the Jinjiang Hotel, Shanghai

As you have read in the previous chapter, Mao's land reforms were key to his consolidation and control of China. The reforms also tied in with Mao's industrial plans: Mao wanted to revolutionize food production so that he could increase China's industrial workforce.

The state ownership of the land, known as **collectivization**, was achieved in five steps:

1   The landlords were wiped out and land was redistributed among the peasants.

2   Peasants were encouraged to work as "mutual aid" teams

3   Peasants were organized into cooperatives.

4   The household registration system limited peasant movement.

5   The peasants were forcibly arranged into communes and the private ownership of land ended.

By the mid-1950s, steps 1 to 4 had been achieved but there were reports that the increased production of grain was not reaching the urban workforce. State planners were also acutely aware that China had a severe labour shortage, despite migration to the cities. Between 1956 and 1958, China's collectives were amalgamated into a number of large **communes.** This was an integral part of the Great Leap forward:

●   Throughout China, 70 000 communes were established.

●   Each commune had 750 000 brigades and each brigade included some 200 households.

●   The PRC central government controlled farming methods, the sale and distribution of produce and the setting of prices.

●   Private farming was brought to an end.

Mao claimed that his land reforms were in tune with the wishes of the peasants. Any resistance was crushed and Mao put the blame for any failure on the peasants. Although the peasants had been the vanguard of the revolution in 1949, Mao's doubts about the peasant class would result in their ultimate betrayal: the agricultural expertise of the peasants was replaced by **Lysenkoism**, which became official policy in 1958.

Attempts to eradicate pests according to the ideas of Lysenkoism produced absurd results. The whole population was called on to end the menace of sparrows and other birds that ate crop seeds. Birds were driven off the land when households came out of their home, making as much noise as possible by clanging plates, pots, and pans. Thousands of birds were destroyed, with tragic results: there was an explosion of the crop-eating insect and vermin population, which ate the grain stocks. State officials also continued to requisition grain. Opposition was futile, even when hunger ensued. The peasants who resisted or tried to return to their old farming ways were labelled as "rightists" and ended up in the prison camps.

Most provinces of China were affected by the famine that followed, when as many as 45 million people died of starvation. In the famine provinces of central China there was an arc of misery, from Shandong in

collectivization
Originally adopted by the Soviet government in the 1920s and 1930s, this policy forced the peasantry to give up their individual farms to join large, state-owned collective farms.

TOK discussion

Investigate the importance of interpretation in history by exploring an alternative view of these words expressed by Mao (www.maoists.org/dikottermisinterpretation.htm).

commune
An organized region where the collectives were grouped together.

Lysenkoism
Trofim Lysenko was a Soviet researcher who claimed to have developed techniques to grow enormous yields of "super-crops" like rice, barley, and wheat. It was later realized that his ideas were fraudulent, but because Stalin accepted Lysenko's ideas as scientific truth, Mao did the same. Farmers were forced to follow Lysenko's flawed ideas.

the east to Tibet in the west. Parents sold their children and cannibalism was rife, but China's leadership did not act. Part of the problem was that officials continued to claim that production targets were being met. Speaking the truth was far too dangerous, as you have already seen with the purge of Peng Dehuai.

Mao eventually came to accept what was happening but he still did not take responsibility. Instead, he blamed:

- the peasants for hoarding food
- local officials for being incompetent
- bad weather, which had affected harvests.

Mao's reputation was tarnished and, confronted by Liu Shaoqi and Deng Xiaoping, he withdrew from the political frontline. Liu and Deng revoked Mao's reforms to allow private farming to operate again. Eventually food supplies improved and the famine came to an end, but Mao would punish both Shaoqi and Deng later on, for going against what he saw as Marxist ideals.

ATL Communication and research skills

Research the causes and impact of the Great Famine and produce a presentation of your conclusions. Find out about the following:

1 The human impact and how the peasants tried to survive

2 What the Chinese leadership claimed were the causes of the famine

3 Examples of propaganda produced during the Great Leap Forward

4 What historians say about the causes of the famine

This website is a good starting point: http://factsanddetails.com/china/cat2/sub6/item2854.html

---

Religious policies

Communism's official view of religion is that it is a capitalist invention, deliberately cultivated by the classes in power to suppress the exploited masses. In Mao's China, religion was to be replaced by loyalty to the party. Mao saw religion as a poison and this anti-religious zeal was evident as soon as the CCP won power in 1949.

Christian churches were forced to close and their property was confiscated. Ministers were physically attacked and foreign priests and nuns were expelled from China. Religion was condemned in propaganda posters and through loudspeakers. Slogans against **Buddhism** and Christianity became commonplace. China's traditional faiths, Buddhism and Confucianism, were banned from being practised openly and nobody was allowed to wear religious clothes. **Ancestor worship** was also ruled out. Songs and dances and traditional festivals were replaced with political meetings and **agitprop** performances organized by the party, to preach the message against landlords, Confucians, and priests. Maoism was encouraged as the new faith.

Buddhism
An ancient religion that emphasizes the individual's journey to enlightenment.

ancestor worship
The practice of honouring dead ancestors.

agitprop
An abbreviation for "agitation propaganda" used to impose political ideas through entertainment.

To give an appearance of tolerance, some churches were allowed to remain open as long as they "did not endanger the security of the state". These establishments were known as the "patriotic churches". The clergy had to profess open support for the communist regime and accept the government's right to appoint clergy and dictate doctrine. China's religious policy led to a permanent rift between the Vatican and the PRC. The Pope rejected the patriotic churches and refused to accept clergy appointed by the Chinese state.

During the Cultural Revolution of 1966–1976, religion was attacked as one of the "four olds" and further clergy were persecuted. Confucianism was denounced and the name of Confucius was linked to anyone targeted by the authorities. The CCP attack on religion was also motivated by a fear of religious separatism in Xinjiang and Tibet. The CCP used invasion and repression to control these provinces. They also tried to dilute the ethnic and religious populations in these areas by settling large numbers of Han Chinese there. By 1976, this migration policy had met with only partial success.

Policies affecting women and the family

Historically, Chinese women had been among the most repressed in the world. Imperial China had been a **patriarchal** society; Confucian ideals held that a woman must obey her husband. It was very rare for women, like the Dowager Empress Cixi, to hold positions of power. The medieval practice of **footbinding** was still practised in some parts of China and in rural China it was commonplace for women to be forced into arranged marriages. Many women were sold into marriage, at a price based on how many children she was likely to have. Before the establishment of the PRC it was legal and not unusual for a husband to have **concubines,** which meant that even a married woman was subordinate.

In 1919 Mao wrote a series of articles condemning arranged marriage as "indirect rape" and, during the 1930s and 1940s, Mao continued to give the impression that he was a firm believer in women's rights. The party under him outlawed footbinding in parts of China where it still survived. In the 1950s Mao claimed "Women hold up half the sky" but the PRC was very much a male-dominated system. Few important Party posts went to women and female comrades were still expected to do domestic chores.

In 1950, the PRC introduced the Marriage Reform Law. It included the following changes:

1 Concubinage was abolished.

2 Arranged marriages came to an end.

3 The paying of dowries was forbidden.

4 Women (and men) who had been previously forced to marry were permitted to divorce.

5 All marriages had to be registered with the state.

Class discussion

Why was Buddhism in particular targeted by the Chinese state?

Class discussion

Compare the aims and methods of Mao's anti-religious policies to those of another dictator.

patriarchal
Dominated by men.

footbinding
Men regarded small feet as erotic, so it was customary for girls, even peasant girls, to have their feet broken and tightly bound at a very young age, so that their feet resembled a "lotus flower". This agonizing practice was prevalent until the 1930s as a means to make girls attractive for marriage.

concubinage
The practice of men keeping women as mistresses (concubines).

Source skills

Propaganda poster

Look at the poster below.

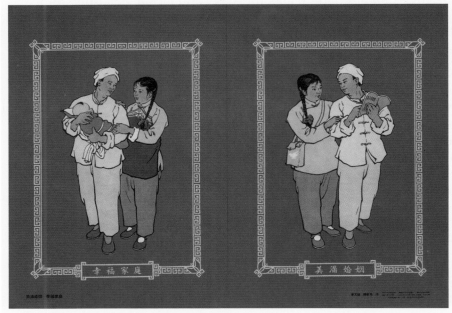

▲ A happy marriage, a happy family, 1955

Question

What does this poster suggest about the impact of the Marriage Reform Law?

The new marriage reforms were jubilantly received and many women divorced and remarried a number of times. Social disruption followed, as some women took as many as four husbands in as many years. The government added a special clause to People's Liberation Army (PLA) regulations so that soldiers had the legal right to override their wives' request for a divorce.

At first, many women benefited from Mao's land reforms. During the land redistribution campaigns of the 1950s, women were granted land in their own name. This was a significant break with tradition whereby only men controlled property. However, the gains were short-lived because of the collectivization of agriculture, which took away the rights of both men and women to own land.

Because women were officially regarded as equals to men, the number of working women quadrupled between 1949 to 1976, from 8 to 32 per cent. There were gains for many women where the work was fitting, but others were unsuited to the demands of heavy physical labour and felt no better off than before.

It was difficult to challenge ingrained ideas about women and their role. The historic practice of **female infanticide** continued because most Chinese couples believed that boys brought honour and economic benefits and that girls were a drain on resources. The notion of female equality was not well received in Xinjiang province, where Muslim culture dictated that women must be obedient to male family members and restricted to the domestic sphere.

female infanticide
The killing of newborn girls.

During Mao's dictatorship, women made up only 13 per cent of the membership of the CCP. The percentage of women deputies in the National People's Congress did rise from 14 to 23 per cent but there is little to suggest that the CCP was making the required efforts to make politics a realm that women were encouraged to enter.

Collectivization involved a deliberate attack on the traditional Chinese family. Mao said that it was necessary to destroy the family for the good of the state. Children were told to refer to Chairman Mao as their father and to relegate personal love below their loyalty to the Party. In many communes married couples were segregated and only allowed to see each other for conjugal visits. Many women who were wives and mothers saw their role become redundant.

Women suffered most during the famine years as they scrambled to provide for their children. Many had to decide which child would have to starve so that the rest could survive. It was often better for a woman to divorce her husband and look for a husband elsewhere to increase the odds of survival. For this reason the divorce rate soared in the famine-struck provinces of China. Many children were left motherless and ended up abandoned. This affected girls and, as the famine worsened, boys also. These children were vulnerable to exploitation by CCP officials. Prostitution thrived as women offered themselves in return for food and, in some parts of China, officials set up brothels for special use by Party members.

During the Cultural Revolution, the traditional nuclear family was attacked as one of the "four olds". Under the banner of the Red Guards, normal everyday family life was denounced and destroyed.

Although the population of China almost doubled during Mao's time, later leaders introduced measures to restrict the number of births.

Mao's cultural policies

"The Cultural Revolution was not just a disaster for the Party, for the country, but for the whole people. We were all victims, people of several generations. One hundred million people were its victims."

Pufang, Deng Xiaoping's son, 1996

From the 1930s, Mao had made it very clear that China's culture needed to reflect the values of a proletarian society. When the PRC was established, censorship and propaganda became a crucial means of achieving this. The duty of creative artists was to serve the people. Thousands of books were burned because they were deemed to be politically incorrect and the war on foreign cinema and western music was relentless.

It is a good idea to review the aims and impact of the Cultural Revolution of 1966–1976 (see page 155) before you consider how it affected the lives of creative artists: writers, painters, musicians, and filmmakers.

During the years of the Cultural Revolution, Jiang Qing, Mao's wife, became, in Mao's words, the "cultural purifier of the nation". Only literature, art, and media that promoted Chinese themes were allowed. This included opera–ballets that told the story of the triumph

ATL Communication and research skills

Foreign films were ousted and replaced by Russian ones such as *Lenin in October* (1937), *The Great Citizen* (1938), and *The Virgin Lands* (1958). Research these films and prepare a brief presentation to explain why they were thought acceptable.

of the proletariat over its class enemies. Jiang's war against genuine artistic expression became fanatical. Children were urged to knock the heads off flowers to show their contempt for bourgeois concepts of beauty.

Any creative artists who resisted were sent to labour camps for "re-education". Only Deng Xiaoping dared to suggest that the purpose of creative artists was to entertain, but his words were lost as intellectuals and creative artists were unwilling or too afraid to resist the destruction of China's traditional culture.

Literacy, language and education

In 1949, the majority of the peasants were illiterate or barely literate. Mao made the education of the masses a priority soon after achieving power and by the mid-1950s a national system of primary education had been established. By 1976, the levels of literacy had risen from 20 per cent in 1949 to 70 per cent.

The success of Mao's educational reforms can be partly attributed to the reform of the Mandarin language in 1955. Historically, the pronunciation of Mandarin had varied in different parts of China, and communication was also hindered because the language was so difficult to write. This is because it did not have an alphabet and instead consisted of **ideograms**, not letters. To write the language, you needed to learn words separately.

To improve this, the PRC introduced a written form of Mandarin that all speakers and writers of it could recognize and use. The result was **Pinyin,** a system that characterized Mandarin sounds into symbols. For the first time, spoken Mandarin could be written in a standardized form.

Mao's literacy and language reforms were largely successful in their time, but the system of education as a whole made little advance. During the Cultural Revolution, about 130 million young people stopped attending school or university and about 12 million of them were sent into the countryside to work. Even when educational establishments re-opened, creativity and critical thinking were greatly undermined because the priority was to produce students who conformed to Party ideals. Mao's eventual successor, Deng Xiaoping, later questioned whether students in China were capable of reading a book.

Class discussion

What do you think were the values of a proletarian society?

ideogram
A picture or character symbolizing the idea of a thing without indicating the sounds used to say it.

Pinyin
A standard phonetic system for transcribing Mandarin.

Class discussion

Compare the aims and policies of Mao's educational reforms to those of another dictator.

ATL Research and communication skills

Go to the Chineseposters.net website. Select a number of themes related to Mao's economic and social polices (1949–1976). There are many collections related to propaganda campaigns and reforms affecting health, women, education and the economy. Research a campaign and present your findings.

a   Describe and explain the message of a propaganda campaign poster.

b   Explain any additional information you have learned about the aims and impact of Mao's social and economic reforms.

Health reforms

One of the biggest challenges facing the PRC in 1949 was the lack of universal access to healthcare. The new government aimed to direct medical care to the remotest areas of China.

From 1949 onwards, based on their experiences in Jiangxi and Yan'an, Mao and the communists introduced a number of campaigns, called "patriotic health movements". These involved government-funded schemes to provide people with basic advice on health and hygiene. Local populations launched huge communal efforts to eradicate insects and drain swamps to prevent the spread of diseases like dysentery and malaria. Many more doctors and nurses were trained throughout the 1950s so that large numbers of people could receive professional medical care for the first time.

The Cultural Revolution damaged health reform because doctors were targeted for their bourgeois lifestyles. Politics increasingly came before good medical practice as doctors, fearful of being attacked, were swept along by the fanatical zeal of the Red Guards. Showing pain was condemned as a bourgeois reaction and in some cases doctors no longer used anesthetics and analgesics. Many women were denied painkillers during childbirth.

By the late 1960s, a crash programme for training doctors was introduced. Trainee doctors would engage in months of intensive practical study and would then go to live with the peasants. By 1973 over a million new doctors had been trained. Known as **barefoot doctors,** these young idealists greatly improved the lives of peasants by providing medical treatment, often free of charge. In the long term, however, a full national health service was not established during the era of CCP rule.

> **Class discussion**
>
> Should Mao be remembered as a liberator or an oppressor of China?

> **barefoot doctor**
> Health worker who provided medical care in rural areas.

ATL Communication skills

Discuss how each of the following factors create problems for students studying Mao Zedong's dictatorship:

- By tradition, China's ruling authorities view the purpose of history as justifying the present.

- Before 1976, everything published in China praised Mao Zedong without reservation.

- Mao has not been entirely criticized and rejected by his successors.

- In China, the Cultural Revolution is viewed as a closed topic.

- Chinese textbooks are not allowed to dwell on the negative aspects of China's history.

- Since the 1950s, western sinologists have sought to convey the truth about China.

- Since the 1990s, many Party archives have been opened in Russia and, most recently, in China.

- Authors like Jung Chang have been criticized for being too critical of Mao because of their own experiences.

Exam-style questions

Answer the following questions with reference to China and, where applicable, another authoritarian state of your choice.

1 Examine the methods used by one authoritarian leader in his bid for power.

2 Analyse the methods used by an authoritarian leader to consolidate his dictatorship.

3 Assess the role of terror and force in maintaining power in two authoritarian states.

4 Account for the effectiveness of internal opposition to two leaders of authoritarian states.

5 Evaluate the role of ideology in the policies of two authoritarian leaders.

6 Examine the status of women in two authoritarian states.

7 Examine the role of the arts in two authoritarian states.

8 Examine the role of education in two authoritarian states.

9 Analyse the global impact of one ruler of an authoritarian state.

Evaluation

Question

Evaluate the domestic social and cultural policies of Mao.

Analysis

An evaluation question requires you to make a full appraisal of the theme or argument under discussion. The term "evaluate" is similar to words like "criticize" and "analyse". The examiner is looking for answers that weigh up the strengths and limitations of the issue under discussion. You could look at evaluation as a detailed process of debate and exploration, in order to reach an informed judgment.

It is essential to "unpack" an evaluation essay question carefully, for two reasons. Firstly, a question about Mao's domestic social and cultural policies incorporates a number of social themes including education, health and policies affecting women. The cultural themes include religion, minority groups and the arts. All of these themes link to Mao's political reforms. For example, the Cultural Revolution was about purging opposition to Mao, but it also included cultural policies affecting media and the arts. Under time pressure in the exam, you need to avoid writing in too much breadth by carefully selecting detailed knowledge from each theme.

It is a good idea to organize your essay into themes related to Mao's social and cultural policies. The essay requires you to showcase your descriptive knowledge and also balance that with an assessment of their strengths and limitations. You must demonstrate a factual grasp of the dates, changes, and effects of Mao's policies while tailoring your essay to explore the debates about their degree of success.

The second reason why you must unpack the question carefully concerns how you should evaluate Mao's domestic policies. Evaluation requires an awareness of the aims and motives behind the policies and a view on how or if the goals/objectives were reached. This opens the opportunity for debate using the evidence and indicating different perspectives. A good starting point is to measure the impact of Mao's policies against his aims. It could be argued that Mao's policies were ideologically successful and fulfilled his aims, but that their practical impact was often catastrophic or extremely limited.

Sample answer

When Mao seized power in China in 1949, his overriding aim was to establish a communist revolution that would dramatically transform all levels of Chinese society. His social policies related to education and health were implemented for pragmatic reasons. They met with some success in addressing basic human needs that had been historically neglected. Other social policies, especially those relating to women, in theory could be viewed as liberation from patriarchy, but the family came under vicious attack, and against the backdrop of commune life and famine, many women faced new struggles. Mao's cultural policies aimed to wipe out religion, assert control over minority groups and eliminate freedom of artistic expression. These changes were driven by a devout sense of ideology and desire for control and the results were immensely destructive. The Cultural Revolution for example, had a disastrous impact on China's political, economic and cultural development. Although Mao's aims were arguably achieved, they resulted in great human suffering and loss of life, which is emphasized in the work of Mao's critics and Western historians. The grave limitations of his domestic social and cultural policies continue to be underplayed in China where debate on most of these issues is closed or where other personalities are blamed for any failings.

Examiner comments

This is a strong introductory paragraph. The student's opening sentences address the scope of the question directly. It is clear which examples of domestic social and cultural policies/themes will be explored. The student has indicated a general line of argument to show that some domestic reforms met with relative success, whereas others were extremely limited. The candidate has commented on the motives for Mao's domestic reforms and, importantly, will be explaining why some policies succeeded where others did not.

The student could have indicated factors such as China's history of violence or the fanaticism of others and their impact on Mao's policies, although these are likely to be explored in the body of the essay. The mention of "great human suffering" could have included an example, such as "loss of religious freedom" or "oppression in Tibet". The mention of "loss of human life" might have been elaborated with "an estimated 1.5 million lives lost as a result of the Cultural Revolution" – it is always useful to have a compelling statistic to make a point more resounding.

The candidate has avoided the common mistake of saying that some historians think one way while others think another. Instead, the candidate has indicated which schools of thought exist on the subject and why their perspectives on Mao's domestic social and cultural policies are different. It would be as well to mention that some of Mao's domestic reforms were well received by many sectors of the population, but it is still a challenge to quantify this, given the censorship and propaganda that propped up his reforms.

4 GERMANY – HITLER

The global context

Authoritarian states – states in which the ruling regime is not accountable to the people and in which political pluralism and civil rights are restricted or simply abolished – take a variety of forms. In the case of Germany this was a totalitarian state, in which one party, driven by ideology, sought to exert control over every aspect of the life of its citizens and exercised a monopoly of power.

The emergence of an authoritarian state in the form of an ideologically driven totalitarian movement was not unique to Germany. The First World War acted as a catalyst for change in every nation that participated, whether on the side of the victors or the vanquished. The new authoritarian regimes of the first half of the 20th century (in Russia, Italy, and Germany) were given their

opportunity because of the massive economic, social, and political disruption caused by the conflict and disillusionment produced by the terms of peace. The destruction of older state systems led to the emergence of regimes that, through repressive measures, attempted to wield complete control over every aspect of the life of a nation.

Italian fascism served as a model for Hitler in the early years of his movement. The factors explaining the rise of fascism in Italy (1919–1925) show similarities with those that helped promote the growth of National Socialism in Germany. Germany's case (1919–1934) illustrates how a totalitarian regime emerged after a brief period of democratic government following the First World War.

Timeline

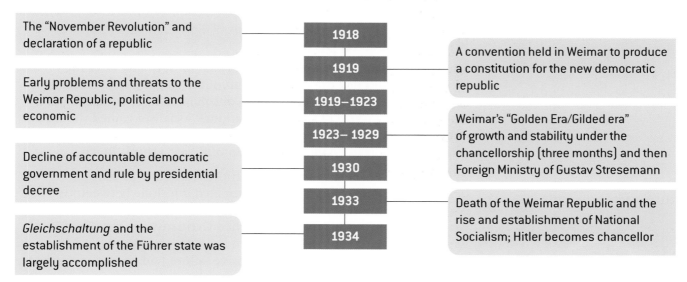

The "November Revolution" and declaration of a republic — **1918**

1919 — A convention held in Weimar to produce a constitution for the new democratic republic

Early problems and threats to the Weimar Republic, political and economic — **1919–1923**

1923– 1929 — Weimar's "Golden Era/Gilded era" of growth and stability under the chancellorship (three months) and then Foreign Ministry of Gustav Stresemann

Decline of accountable democratic government and rule by presidential decree — **1930**

1933 — Death of the Weimar Republic and the rise and establishment of National Socialism; Hitler becomes chancellor

Gleichschaltung and the establishment of the Führer state was largely accomplished — **1934**

4.1 The emergence of the authoritarian state in Germany, 1919–1934

Conceptual understanding

Key questions

→ Was democracy desperately desired in Germany in 1918, or was its implementation part of a scheme by Germany's wartime leaders (Field Marshals Hindenburg and Ludendorff) to avoid a punitive settlement after Germany's surrender?

→ Was the constitution established in 1919 a hindrance to successful democratic practice?

→ What role did economic distress play in polarizing and brutalizing German political life during the period? How valid is AJP Taylor's view that "only the Great Depression put the wind into the sails of National Socialism"?

→ What elements in Germany after 1918 were either actively hostile or simply apathetic towards the new system?

→ Was the rise to power of a party committed to a totalitarian system a story of the "irresistible rise" of National Socialism?

Key concepts

→ Change

→ Causes

→ Consequences

→ Significance

Hitler's rise to power

The Weimar democratic system, established in Germany after the First World War, preceded the establishment of the single-party National Socialist state, which was effectively consolidated in 1934 when Adolf Hitler became Führer of Germany. National Socialism gained the support of the military, which eliminated domestically the last major obstacle to Hitler's ambition to establish his "Thousand Year (Third) Reich".

In explaining the emergence of the "Hitler state", it was common to describe the Weimar Republic "as a troubled interlude between two eras of greater and more sinister importance: the *Wilhelminian Kaiserreich*, which saw the consolidation of a unified Germany, and the Third Reich, which destroyed it". Weimar was seen as "a desperate and grudging experiment in democracy whose decisive failure had consequences not only for Germany but the world".

Such interpretations are linked to a pessimistic view of German history, in which the triumph of National Socialism is accepted as an inevitable and irresistible force welcomed by most Germans. However, at no point prior to the establishment of the one-party state in Germany did the National Socialist German Workers' Party (NSDAP) achieve support from the majority of the electorate. The highest percentage of votes achieved in March 1933 was 43.9 per cent – impressive, but short of

an absolute majority. The Nazis achieved power not because most Germans actively desired it but because of a combination of circumstances, which calls into question the claim that the NSDAP "seized power", as Nazis later claimed. More recent interpretations emphasize the "*Stabübergabe*" – the "passing of the baton" or handover of power – by **vested interests** in Germany that tried to use the Nazis to counter the rise of the Communist Party (KPD) in the period 1932–1933.

Pessimists and catastrophists see the years 1919–1934 as little more than a prelude to Hitler's rise to power. The British historian AJP Taylor later claimed that "if there had been a strong democratic sentiment in Germany, Hitler would never have come to power … (Germans) deserved what they got when they went round crying for a hero." Germanophobes willingly accepted a simplistic argument that the emergence and coming to power of National Socialism was the result of an inherent inability in the German character to appreciate and accept democratic principles. Such a view adds little to an understanding of the complexity of the period: the problems (internal and external) facing the democratic experiment and mistakes made by political parties and individuals that brought about Nazi success. As Ian Kershaw pointed out, "Hitler was no inexorable product of a German 'special path' (*Sonderweg*), no logical culmination of long-term trends in specifically German culture and ideology."

▲ The caption to this postcard from 1933 reads: "What the king conquered, the prince formed, the field marshal defended and the soldier saved and united."

Conditions in which the authoritarian state emerged

1 A discredited parliamentary system that, due to instability and policy errors, produced a high level of disillusionment and frustration

2 The dislocation produced by the First World War of 1914–1918 and the subsequent Paris Peace Settlement, which produced **revisionism**, nationalism, and **revanchism**

3 Economic crises that produced social and economic conditions causing panic among the population, that is, political extremism resulting from economic instability

4 Fear of the Left, which was increased by the existence of the new Soviet state and the growth of socialist/communist movements in western Europe

5 The collaboration/capitulation of the existing political establishment or institutions – when **vested interests** underestimated the Fascists/Nazis in a tragedy of miscalculation

6 Semi-legal assumption of power, despite subsequent fascist/Nazi claims of a "seizure of power"

Research and thinking skills

The figures shown on the postcard above are, from left to right, Frederick the Great of Prussia, Otto von Bismarck, Paul von Hindenburg, and Adolf Hitler.

1 With reference to the personalities shown on the postcard, what was the intended message of this card issued by the National?

2 Find out the meaning of the phrase "Janus-faced". In what way does the postcard illustrate this characteristic of National Socialism?

revisionism
The desire to alter the terms of what was perceived as the unjust treaty settlement after the First World War.

revanchism
The desire for revenge.

vested interests
Groups or individuals (such as political leaders, businessmen, and landowners) with an interest in resisting changes they felt would be to their disadvantage.

pragmatism

A willingness to be flexible and adapt to circumstances instead of sticking rigidly (dogmatically) to principles.

millenarianism

From "millennium"; literally a thousand years, and generally taken to mean the promise of a future period of prosperity under the regime.

Left and Right

During this period "the Left" was a term commonly used to describe political parties that were left of centre, tending towards communist/socialist beliefs. By contrast, parties such as the German Nationalists (DNVP) and the NSDAP were referred to as the Right and Extreme Right respectively. While the IB does not use the terms in exam questions, many textbooks do use these terms to describe political stances, in the inter-war period especially.

Spartacists

A group of radical socialists, led by Rosa Luxemburg and Karl Liebknecht, who made a futile attempt in January 1919 to establish a Bolshevik-type state in Germany.

ATL Research skills

Look back over the factors that promoted fascism/National Socialism, noted above, and find specific details of the rise of Mussolini's fascism in the period 1919–1926.

Compare the relative significance of the factors promoting the growth of the two extremist movements. Alternatively, compare and contrast the factors behind the emergence of the Bolshevik state in Russia, 1917–1924.

7 The appeal of the movements/leaders and the skills of these leaders, in terms of:

- **pragmatism**
- **millenarianism** (also referred to as "chiliastic" programmes/promises)
- propaganda
- paramilitary forces and the use of violence to control the streets and destroy opponents.

The emergence of the Nazi regime cannot be reduced to one simple cause: the rise of authoritarian regimes is the result of circumstances leading to popular disillusionment with a preceding governmental system. In Germany this disillusionment led to popular demand for change in uncertain times, and to the unwillingness of the population to defend the preceding regime from overthrow by extremist groups.

The Weimar Republic, 1918–1933/34

In Germany the "November Revolution" of 1918 occurred on 9 November, although Kaiser Wilhelm II, by then in exile in Holland, did not officially abdicate until 28 November. The declaration of a republic by Philip Scheidemann, an SPD (Social Democratic Party) leader, was followed two days later by the signing of an armistice with the Allied powers.

The removal of the dynasty and the German defeat produced a vacuum in political life that extremists sought to exploit. Only in January 1919 – following an unsuccessful revolt in Berlin led by the **Spartacists** – was a convention elected to produce a constitution for the new democratic republic. The holding of the convention in Weimar (at a safe distance from troubled Berlin) gave the republic its name and a constitution designed to replace autocratic and dynastic rule with one based on popular sovereignty.

Below is an overview of the six stages in the life of the short-lived democratic republic, linked to the question of why it failed and was replaced by the National Socialist state. Weimar's existence was plagued by domestic and external problems that allowed outright enemies of democratic principles – and those who had never provided more than lip service to such principles – to subvert the republic.

Stage 1: 1918–1919

German military leaders later claimed that Germany's defeat in 1918 was a result of a "stab in the back" by internal enemies. While it was true that no Allied armies occupied German soil at the time of the armistice, both Hindenburg and Ludendorff, the military leaders of Germany, realized that defeat loomed. Weakened by blockade, by its own allies' collapse, by the superior resources of a reinvigorated Allied enemy after the USA entered the war in April 1917, and by worrying incidents of the breakdown of military discipline in Germany itself, surrender was necessary by late 1918.

The peace settlement that followed was likely to prove punitive (given the severity of Germany's treatment of Russia at Brest–Litovsk in March 1918 and the desire for revenge against the Central Powers generally, and Berlin specifically). The military leaders' acceptance of both Wilhelm II's

abdication and a democratic form of government could thus be seen as a means of trying to reduce the damage that might be inflicted on Germany in the treaty to come. It was hoped that Germany, as a "democratic state", would avoid the wrath of the victorious Allies or, if not, that blame for any punitive or "Carthaginian" peace would fall on the new democratic system rather than the High Command. It has been claimed that Hindenburg and Ludendorff's "last great manoeuvre on the battlefield" was an attempt to soften punishment rather than a commitment to democratic principles, then or for the future. In this sense the radical change that occurred in German political life was essentially a "revolution from above" rather than the result of popular groundswell.

Peter Gay wrote:

> *Germans had little practice in politics… When the democratic Weimar constitution opened the door to real politics, the Germans stood at the door, gaping, like peasants bidden to a palace.*

Commentators have seen the lack of familiarity with the practice of democracy as a factor inhibiting the success of the Weimar system. Hugo Preuss, a principal author of the new constitution, was aware early on of the need for the rapid adoption of a new attitude to a system that came unexpectedly for most Germans, stating:

> *One finds suspicions everywhere. Germans cannot shake off their old political timidity and their deference to the authoritarian state. They do not understand that the new government must be blood of their blood, flesh of their flesh.*

The lack of a "revolution from below" contrasted significantly with that of the older western European democracies such as Britain or France, where democracy was the outcome of popular pressures over a long period to end authoritarian systems represented by absolute monarchy. The democratic era in 20th-century German history was ushered in by the same individuals and interests that were later to preside over its decline and dissolution. While this did not necessarily mean that the system was doomed to failure, it provided a fragile base for development, especially combined with the fact the democratic government became linked, in the eyes of many, to the betrayal, defeat, and national humiliation of Versailles in 1919.

The Versailles Treaty (or "Diktat") produced bitterness because of the perceived injustice of the punishments inflicted upon Germany. Article 231 – the "War Guilt Clause" – was deeply resented and referred to as the *Kriegsschuldlüge* (the War Guilt Lie). Article 231 paved the way for the Allies to strip Germany of territory in Europe, of its colonial empire and military capacity, and to enforce the payment of reparations for war damages.

While Germany felt itself the victim of a callous Allied peace settlement, the country still retained the potential for recovery – not only economically but also geopolitically, since it was now girdled to the east by new states of dubious economic and military strength and a weakened Soviet Union focused on domestic reconstruction and development. As the Austrian playwright Hans Weigel later wrote in relation to the impact of the Paris Peace Settlement on Austria-Hungary, "Germany lost an empire, we lost a world."

ATL Research and thinking skills

1 What "price", in economic and territorial terms, was Bolshevik Russia forced to pay in the Treaty of Brest–Litovsk in order to quit the war with Germany?

2 In what ways could this be considered a punitive peace?

At the time, relatively few Germans accepted that the "dictated peace" was anything but a national shame. Nationalists held the governmental system responsible for signing the armistice and the Versailles Treaty.

Summary of the terms of the Treaty of Versailles

Article 231: The "War Guilt Clause" (or the "War Guilt Lie") by which Germany and its allies were held responsible for the war of 1914– 1918; Germany was named but not held solely responsible, as many students believe.

Territorial provisions:

- Germany lost 13 per cent of its European territory, 12 per cent of its population and all its colonies, which were distributed to other powers. This meant the loss of 16 per cent of coal production, 48 per cent of iron production, 15 per cent of agricultural production, and 10 per cent of manufacturing capacity. (Many of these assets had only been acquired by Prussia in the 19th century, in a series of wars during the unification of the nation.)

- Alsace-Lorraine was returned to France, Eupen and Malmedy to Belgium, and Posen and West Prussia to the new state of Poland; Danzig was to become an international city under the supervision of the League of Nations, and Memel was returned to Lithuania.

- Northern Schleswig became part of Denmark and Upper Silesia became part of Poland. The Saar was put under control of the League of Nations; a plebiscite was to be held in 1935 to determine its future.

- *Anschluss* (or union) with Austria was forbidden.

Financial penalties: Reparations of £6600 million sterling were to be paid in restitution for the "loss and damage" caused by the war.

Military provisions:

- Demilitarization of the Rhineland area and its left bank to be occupied by Allied forces for 15 years.

- Germany's army to be restricted to 100 000 men; no conscription, tanks or heavy artillery.

- Navy restricted to 15 000 men, no submarines and the fleet limited to six battleships, six cruisers and 12 destroyers.

- Germany not permitted to have an air force.

Stage 2: 1919–1923

Even before the republican constitution was adopted in August 1919, the new government, under Friedrich Ebert (SPD), found itself faced with threats to its survival. On 10 November Ebert concluded a pact with Wilhelm Groener, Chief of Staff of the German military. In return for military support against enemies of the new Republic, Ebert agreed to allow the army to remain a virtual "imperium in imperio" ("state within a state"). Until 1934 – when it took an oath of allegiance to Hitler – the military, rather than being the servant of the people and its elected representatives, acted in its own interests. Military support proved *conditional* throughout the life of the Republic – the army chose when it would act in defence of the government, and when it would not. In the case of the Spartacist uprising of 1918–1919, the army was ready to suppress the "Bolsheviks" with alacrity, but at the time of the Kapp putsch in 1920 – a move by those on the opposite side of the political spectrum from the Spartacists – the military declined to act in defence of the state. With the statement *"Reichswehr* does not fire upon *Reichswehr"*, the army made it clear that it would not act against forces it considered good German nationalists, many of whom were ex-soldiers. Only a socialist-inspired general strike ended the putsch.

Key provisions in the constitution are often blamed for the failure of Weimar democracy. Although Article 17 introduced universal and secret suffrage, it also the stated the principle of proportional representation, identified as a major weakness of the system. Proportional representation

meant that the plethora of political parties were often unable to form long-term stable governments, either on their own or in coalition. To blame the system is simplistic: no system could succeed without a willingness to work in the spirit of democracy. Some political parties of Weimar were either actively hostile or ambivalent towards democratic government, accepting it but often looking back fondly to the pre-Weimar Wilhelminian era.

Political parties committed to democracy included the Social Democrats (SPD), the Democratic Party (DDP), the German People's Party (DVP) and the Centre/Zentrum and its sister party, the Bavarian People's Party (BVP), although by the early 1930s the latter two began to veer towards support of movements with non-democratic programmes.

The main political parties of the Weimar era	
Party	**Ideology**
KPD (Communist Party)	Hostile to democracy, committed to a Soviet- (Moscow-)style regime and taking instructions from Moscow throughout most of the Weimar period Paramilitary organization: Red Veterans' League
SPD (Social Democrats)	Often spouted Marxist rhetoric but essentially dedicated to socialism through the ballot box – that is, non-revolutionary socialists in comparison to the KPD Paramilitary organization: Reichsbanner
DDP (Democratic Party)	Committed to the Weimar democratic system
DVP (German People's Party)	To the right of centre of the political spectrum but largely committed to a democratic system
DNVP (German National People's Party or Nationalists)	Well-funded party linked to "big business" and landowners. At best a reluctant supporter of Weimar and, as late as 1931, "committed to the renewal of the German empire as established under the Hohenzollerns", noting that the "monarchical form of government corresponds to the uniqueness and historical development of Germany" Paramilitary organization: Stahlhelm
NSDAP (National Socialist German Workers' Party)	Hostile to democracy and favouring the establishment of a single-party state on the extreme right of the political spectrum, stressing ultra-nationalistic, militaristic and racist views Paramilitary organization: Sturmabteilung (SA)
Centre/Zentrum and **BVP** (Bavarian People's Party)	Ambivalent towards Weimar. Initially a significant contributor to coalition government, along with the SPD and DDP. As the parties of "political Catholicism", by the early 1930s (and fearful of the rise of communism in Germany) willing to collaborate with parties and individuals not sympathetic to democracy

Article 48 has also been identified as a constitutional weakness. It stated that the president was entitled to suspend basic principles of the constitution and rule by emergency decree "in the event that the public order and security are seriously disturbed or endangered". Given the turmoil in Germany in late 1918 and early 1919, this provision was a practical one if rapid action had to be taken to defend the democratic government. While it is accurate to claim that Germany after March 1930 was run by emergency decree, and in an increasingly authoritarian manner, was it the fault of the constitution or the misuse (or abuse) of the constitutional provision by individuals or interests acting according to their own agenda?

The constitution was a construct of principles adopted from existing systems in Western states and one of the most progressive documents of its time. Did it fail, or was it failed, because groups deliberately undermined it and used the very freedoms permitted to destroy accountable government?

Weimar laboured from the beginning under economic and political burdens not of its own making: the defeat in war, the signing of an ignominious peace treaty, reparations, apathy from those steeped in nostalgia for the pre-1914 authoritarian structure, and political extremism and putschism. As Gay noted:

> *… from the beginning (of the Republic) there were many who saw its travail with superb indifference or with that unholy delight in the suffering of others for which the Germans have coined that evocative term Schadenfreude.*

One thing that totalitarian regimes did focus on, when consolidating power in the USSR and in Nazi Germany, was the need to ensure that basic governmental structures and apparatus were purged of elements disloyal or potentially opposed to the new system. Weimar, due to its hasty establishment, inherited many administrators, bureaucrats, judges, and army officers from the time of the Kaiser. The Wilhelminian structure was thus basically left intact after 1918–1919 and the democratic system was left to work with people who were, at best, "reluctant Republicans" (*Vernunftrepublikaner*) and, at worst, downright obstructionist and defiant. Neither Lenin nor Hitler made that mistake when they established their single-party regimes. In both cases a rapid "cleansing" of the state apparatus resulted in a loyal machine to deliver and implement single-party policies.

Vernunftrepublikaner
Republicans not from conviction but from necessity – for example, because of the lack of practical alternatives at that time.

The polarization and brutalization of political life in the early stages of the Republic was witnessed not only in the Spartacist and Kapp threats but also by communist uprisings in Munich, the Ruhr, and Hamburg (1919–1923) and the attempt by Hitler to copy (unsuccessfully) Mussolini's "March on Rome" in November 1923.

The economic crisis of 1923

The "currency delirium" that convulsed Germany by late November 1923 was the result of events initiated by the Franco-Belgian occupation of the Ruhr area, Germany's industrial heartland. France especially, infuriated by a default in reparations payments and determined to enforce the Versailles Treaty provisions, appeared determined to teach Germany a lesson – and possibly hold on to the area for the longer term to weaken any possibility of German recovery. The reactions to the occupation were passive resistance and non-cooperation by the workers of the Ruhr, along with government support for the workers in terms of wage payments, regardless of the fact that production had collapsed. By resorting to the printing press, inflation, which had been occurring since the end of the war, accelerated to levels that destroyed confidence in Germany's currency and also in Weimar's ability to defend the territorial and economic interests of the nation.

For the longer term, the inability of Weimar to cope with the crisis of 1923 helped undermine confidence in the system and contributed to anti-republicanism. This would provide the basis for the growth of support for authoritarian and totalitarian movements when a second economic crisis struck in 1929.

By November 1923 one US dollar was worth 4.2 trillion German marks. For many, savings accumulated over years were wiped out. Those on fixed incomes or pensions were ruined and a barter economy emerged.

While there were beneficiaries (those with access to foreign currency and those with outstanding loans that could be paid off easily, for example, the German industrialist Hugo Stinnes), for most citizens the experience was one of misery. The government of Chancellor Cuno resigned in August 1923, to be replaced by a new coalition of the DDP, SPD, Zentrum and DVP under Gustav Stresemann. Under Stresemann, recovery from the economic disaster, aided by the USA in the shape of the **Dawes Plan** of 1924, ushered in a period known as the Golden Era (1924–1929).

But before the recovery, extremists in Hamburg (Communist Party of Germany or KPD) and in Munich (Nazi Party or NSDAP) had seized the opportunity to exploit the situation by staging unsuccessful uprisings against the government. In the case of the National Socialists, Hitler's "Beerhall Putsch" (also known as the November, or Munich, Putsch) proved an inglorious failure, although the subsequent trial and sentencing allowed the Nazis to articulate their ideology nationally for the first time. In *Mein Kampf*, written during his brief period of imprisonment, Hitler stated:

> *All great movements are popular sentiments, volcanic eruptions of human passions and emotional sentiments, stirred either by the cruel Goddess of Distress or by the firebrand of the world hurled amongst the masses…*

This climate of economic and social distress encouraged his gamble to seize power, but the fact that it took him another decade or more to gain power suggests that such distress did abate, at least temporarily. If, as Frank McDonough claimed, Hitler's "utopian dream could only have prospered in the dark of a very black night", the achievements of the Golden Era of Weimar from 1924–1929 deprived extremism of the opportunity to flourish. Only by 1929 was recovery of National Socialist fortunes made possible with the onset of the Great Depression. The rise of Hitler provides a classic example of the generally accepted view that political extremism arises out of economic misery.

The NSDAP's 25-point programme

The NSDAP was officially founded in 1920, a renamed version of Anton Drexler's German Workers' Party (DAP) established in Munich in 1919. Originally tasked by military intelligence to attend and report upon the activities of such groups, Hitler joined the party, helping in the drafting of a 25-point programme, and became leader of the NSDAP in 1921.

The programme contained a mixture of points that could be pitched to a wide audience. Mussolini claimed, in relation to Italian fascism, that, "We play the lyre on all its strings" – setting out a range of offerings designed to appeal to as many as possible. The NSDAP, by its very change of name from the original DAP, suggests a similar approach to targeting the population.

If the intention of such a programme was to ensure mass support, it failed in the short term. Policies in the programme that were aimed at various constituencies in Germany – whether aggrieved nationalists, the industrial working class, farmers, and small proprietors/businessmen, for example – were already on offer by other parties. Attempts to wean the population from existing party allegiances proved unsuccessful until the economic crisis of 1929 onwards.

Dawes Plan (1924)

This measure (undertaken by the US to prop up the German and thus the European economies, which had also suffered from Germany's collapse) allowed Germany to make economic improvements as well as reducing their annual reparations payments that had precipitated their default and the 1923 occupation of the Ruhr. The aid ensured that America's export-driven economy would benefit – and prevented the growth of communism in Germany. A new currency (the Rentenmark) replaced the worthless mark in November 1923 and the American loans helped restore confidence in this new currency, renamed the Reichsmark in 1924.

ATL Thinking skills

Find the specific points of the 25-point programme at: avalon.law.yale.edu/imt/nsdappro.asp

Given the circumstances in Germany in the early post-war years, and with reference to the 25 points, answer the following:

1 Identify and explain what groups or individuals (for example, social/economic/professional) might be attracted by specific points of the programme and which might not.

2 To what extent was the programme "nationalist" and "socialist" in its offerings?

3 Which elements of the programme suggested strong authoritarian and anti-democratic tendencies?

Lack of support for National Socialism was illustrated by the abortive putsch in November 1923. The treason trial of the putschists that followed provided Hitler not only with the opportunity to justify his actions to a national audience but also reinforced the extent to which the judicial system was unsympathetic to the democratic principles it was constitutionally bound to uphold. Hitler and Ludendorff (one of the military leaders who presided over the establishment of Weimar) were dealt with leniently. Ludendorff was acquitted and Hitler received a five-year sentence, of which he served only nine months in Landsberg prison.

The lack of sympathy for the Republic exhibited by important elements of the state apparatus underlined the fact that Weimar remained, for many, both unwelcome and unloved.

Stage 3: the Golden Age, 1924–1929

The years of Gustav Stresemann's leadership, first as chancellor for three months in 1923 and then as Foreign Minister till his death in October 1929, ushered in a period of remarkable recovery in terms of economic growth after the crisis of hyperinflation and a period of political stability that contrasted greatly with the violence of the earlier years.

Approximate % of vote for political parties			
Party	May 1924	December 1924	1928
KPD	12	9	11
SPD	21	26	30
DDP	6	6	5
Zentrum/BVP	17	18	15
DVP	9	10	9
DNVP	19	21	14
NSDAP	7	3	2
Others*	9	7	14

*"Others" refers to parties often based on individual states or regional interests or the Independent Socialists (USPD), who had been a significant force before 1924 but which had split by 1922, with most members finding new homes within the KPD or SPD

Faith in the system under Stresemann was reflected in the voting patterns in the three Reichstag elections of 1924–1928, to the left. Parties actively hostile to the Republic over the period made little progress (the KPD) or lost heavily in terms of electoral support (the NSDAP). Conversely, the SPD, which was committed to the parliamentary system, made significant gains. While this does not prove that attitudes to the Republic had undergone a profound change among German voters as a whole, it did appear to offer hope that the challenges to Weimar were over. Just as political extremism thrived in conditions of social and economic suffering, the Stresemann era, during which a raft of economic and foreign policy measures were enacted, helped remove the reservoir of misery from which opponents of democracy drew their inspiration and support.

The image of Germany during these years was of a nation recovering not only from the ravages of war but also one enjoying a respite from its problems. Forces hostile to democracy were either in retreat or quiescent. Yet the period was also one where less attractive developments were obvious, and these threw into question how solid the achievements of the period were.

The achievements of the Stresemann era

- Resolution of the Ruhr problem (the basis of hyperinflation)

  Germany committed itself to making future reparations payments. This promise, backed in combination with the loans made to Germany by the USA, allowed French and Belgian forces to withdraw from the occupied Ruhr area and the resumption of production of Germany's industrial heartland.

- Restoration of Germany's finances with US aid under the Dawes Plan of 1924

- Suppression of physical threats from extremist movements in Hamburg and Munich in October and November 1923

- Reconciliation with France in the Locarno Pact of 1925

  In this pact, Germany stated its acceptance of its western borders. All parties (France, Germany, and Belgium) renounced the use of force, with Britain and Italy acting as guarantors of the pact. Significantly, eastern frontiers did not form part of the agreements of the pact.

- Recognition of Germany's new status by the Great Powers

  Germany, originally excluded from the League of Nations, was admitted in 1926. It now appeared as if the nation was being welcomed back into the European family of Great Powers with its Council member position.

- The **Kellogg-Briand Pact** of 1928

  Signatory states renounced the use of force in the settlement of international disputes. Stresemann's signing on Germany's behalf helped to convince states that Germany was committed to peace and to establish a possible basis for diplomatic revision of the Versailles Treaty.

The failures of the Stresemann era

- The outcome of the trial of the putschists in November 1923

  This reinforced the fact that enemies of the Republic were treated leniently, as long as they were of the nationalist persuasion. This continued the earlier trend of treating the perpetrators of political assassinations differently according to their political affiliation. Left-wing murderers on average served a 15-year sentence; right-wing murderers served four months. No right-wing murderer was given the death sentence (out of 354 committed); 10 left-wing murderers were executed (out of 22 committed).

- The outcome of elections for a successor to President Ebert after his death in February 1925

  In April, the 78-year-old Hindenburg was elected. Kolb noted that this "began … a silent change in the constitution, whereby – gradually and at first barely perceptibly – the balance shifted in favour of presidential power". Hindenburg, claimed Gay, "smelled of the old order; he had been sold to the public in a demagogic campaign as the great man above parties". As Stresemann himself noted in 1925, "The truth is, the Germans do not want a president in a top hat… He has to wear a uniform and a chestful of medals".

- The end of accountable government, 1930

  Under Hindenburg, accountable government was replaced, by March 1930, with a process of rule through Article 48 and a series of presidential cabinets, culminating with the appointment of Hitler as chancellor in January 1933.

- Germany's reliance on US loans, which made it vulnerable to problems should they be withdrawn

  Nationalist groups saw the Young Plan (proposed in 1929, just before the death of Stresemann and the Wall Street Crash) to reduce the reparation payments set by the Dawes Plan of 1924 and extend the period of repayment as a sign of the Republic's continued weakness. It was seen as pandering to the Allied powers and the Versailles Diktat.

- Coalition governments

  Continuing coalition governments were unlikely to provide a firm foundation to deal effectively with major economic or political problems.

- Agrarian distress

  Farmers' debts accumulated as a result of decreasing food prices, leading to agrarian distress even before the depression of 1929.

- Low industrial production

  While improving, this was still behind other developed European states. Unemployment figures hovered around the million mark even before the crisis of 1929.

- The reorganization of NSDAP

  While extremist parties made little electoral progress throughout the period, the NSDAP worked to reorganize itself as a national movement. The establishment of a strong leadership principle (*Führerprinzip*) under Hitler, the appointment of Gauleiters (local area leaders subordinate to Hitler), the promotion of the *Volksgemeinschaft* (the concept of the People's Community based on blood rather than class), the establishment of youth and professional associations with party links (for example, associations for German physicians, teachers, jurists, craftsmen, and small traders) and the use of propaganda aimed at exploiting the grievances of those in distress allowed the Nazis to exploit the crisis of 1929 onwards and garner support.

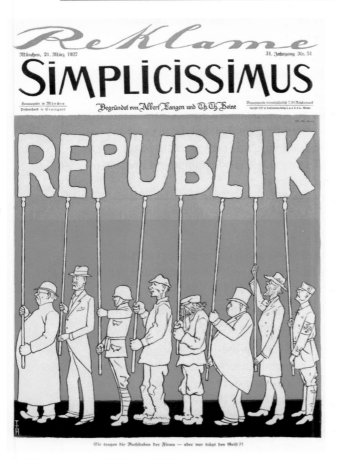

▲ *Simplicissimus*, 21 March 1927: the caption at the bottom reads, "They carry the initials of the institution, but who exhibits the spirit?"

The movement's decision to reject any more putsch attempts and pursue a parliamentary road to power was stated by Hitler when he pronounced, "If outvoting them takes longer than outshooting them, at least the result will be guaranteed by their own constitution." This period of preparation proved vital for Nazi success in the aftermath of Wall Street's collapse, as did the appointment of Alfred Hugenberg as leader of the German National People's Party (DNVP) in 1928. Hugenberg, "among the crowd of self-appointed grave-diggers to the Republic", had "made overtures to Hitler, still the pariah of German politics". Even before the Depression, the move towards authoritarian and anti-democratic government increased its pace. Hitler, the rebel, was able to cloak himself in the respectability that Hugenberg's support would provide.

Stage 4: decline (1930–1933)

The "Golden Years" of the Stresemann era might more accurately be described as "Gilded Years". Foreign aid from the USA, which did so much in the "Golden Years" to rescue the economy, proved a double-edged sword. When America's economy collapsed, the fragile nature of Weimar's economic structure was revealed – along with the abandonment of any glimmers of growing faith in the Weimar system.

On 3 October 1929, Stresemann, "the political cement which bound together the coalition ministries of those years", died. Later that month, the stock market on Wall Street collapsed. The impact on Germany was huge: the country plunged rapidly into depression, as short-term credits from the US were recalled. Unemployment figures (high even before the crisis) soared, from 1.3 million in September 1929 to more than 3 million in September 1930, peaking at just over 6 million – a third of all German workers – by early 1933.

The growth in support for extremism

The economic and psychological impacts of the Great Depression were not unique to Germany but it was in Germany that the political system buckled under pressure. Anti-republican elements mobilized against the parliamentary system, which appeared unable to deal with the catastrophe that enveloped the nation.

Not only did frustration with the Republic produce a move to extremes in voting returns (1930–1933) but, as Kolb pointed out, it became "the primary object of the industrial leaders (after 1929–30) to deprive

the Reichstag of power and establish an authoritarian system of government", which would allow them to wage "a ruthless fight against parliamentarianism and the 'party state', social democracy and the trade unions." The actions of these vested interests and the growth in support for extremist parties were aided by the implementation of rule by presidential decree after March 1930, when the last truly accountable government of Weimar collapsed over the issue of unemployment insurance payments.

From then on, Weimar experienced a shift of power from the elected representatives of the people to "presidential cabinets", in which decision-making was in the hands of a select few, an increasingly senile President Hindenburg was entrusted with the power to rule in the interests of the constitution during the period of distress. In practice, his appointment of chancellors was determined by a circle of interests surrounding him with a common outlook unsympathetic to democratic government.

The day after the collapse of the Müller cabinet (27 March 1930), Hindenburg appointed Heinrich Brüning, who became known as the "Hunger Chancellor" because of his deflationary economic policies which, with their emphasis on increased taxation and reduced welfare benefits, antagonized the parties of the Left and provided fuel for Nazi propaganda in the period of economic distress that followed. Election results for the Reichstag in September 1930 revealed the growth of support for extremist parties in these new circumstances of misery.

Brüning governed until May 1932 with the aid of emergency decrees issued by Hindenburg. He was dismissed when Hindenburg, under advice from those surrounding him and worried by Brüning's plan to implement agrarian changes that would adversely affect the large landowners, brought in Franz von Papen as the new chancellor. Von Papen's cabinet was referred to as the "Barons' Cabinet" (the *Almanach de Gotha* Cabinet – a reference to the directory of European royalty and higher nobility) because of the preponderance of aristocrats it contained. The failure of von Papen's cabinet to deal with the economic and political unrest was responsible for continued electoral gains for extreme parties in the Reichstag elections of July 1932.

New elections in November 1932 witnessed a decline in votes for extremism of the Right, but a growth of electoral support for the KPD. Von Papen resigned, to be replaced by von Schleicher, who himself resigned in January 1933. It was on von Papen's advice to Hindenburg – along with the urging of pro-Nazis such as Hindenburg's secretary Otto Meissner and the president's son Oskar – that Hitler was offered the position of chancellor (of a coalition cabinet) on 30 January, at a point when the elections of the previous November had revealed declining popular support for the NSDAP.

As Bracher commented:

> Hitler made his way into the government… through the authoritarian gap in the Weimar constitution (i.e. the misuse of Article 48), and immediately set about destroying the constitution he had taken an oath to defend.

Von Papen's belief that Hitler could be controlled proved false. As early as 1928, Goebbels, in relation to Weimar parliamentary government, had written in the Nazi newspaper *Der Angriff*, "We come as enemies; as the wolf bursts into the flock, so we come."

Research and thinking skills

1 Find out what type of publication *Simplicissimus* was – its origins and political outlook before and after 1933.

2 Bearing in mind the date of the above front-page illustration and that economic recovery was under way, what point was being made about support for Weimar?

While it was not yet obvious in January 1933, with hindsight Peter Gay claimed that, with Hitler's appointment, "The Republic was dead in all but name, the victim of structural flaws, reluctant defenders, unscrupulous aristocrats and industrialists, a historic legacy of authoritarianism, a disastrous world situation and deliberate murder."

Weimar foundered, not because of any major change in Nazi policy (which remained remarkably consistent) but because of:

- the collaboration of elites that sought to use Hitler against a perceived greater threat (communism)

- the failure of parties on the Left to combine in the interests of self-preservation against an ideological enemy

- the reorganization of the Nazi movement in its expansion from a South German regional organization to a national one by 1929, which allowed it to exploit opportunities with the onset of the depression

- the propaganda campaign waged by the Nazis to promote National Socialism and portray Hitler as the saviour of Germany in its time of trouble.

Source skills

Below are a series of sources, primary and secondary, focusing on the last years of democracy and Hitler's coming to office.

Source A

Reichstag election results: September 1930–November 1932 (showing number of deputies and % of national vote)			
Party	September 1930	July 1932	November 1932
KPD	77 (13.1%)	89 (14.3%)	100 (16.9%)
SPD	143 (24.5%)	133 (21.6%)	121 (20.4%)
DDP (known as Deutsche Staatspartei after 1930)	20 (3.8%)	4 (1.0%)	2 (1%)
Zentrum/BVP	87 (14.8%)	97 (15.7%)	90 (15%)
DVP	30 (4.5%)	7 (1.2%)	11 (1.9%)
DNVP	41 (7%)	37 (5.9%)	52 (8.3%)
NSDAP	107 (18.3%)	230 (37.3%)	196 (33.1%)

NB: 'Other parties' have not been included as they make up only a very small percentage of seats and percentages. For a more complete table see Eberhard Kolb's *The Weimar Republic* (Routledge, 2004).

Source B

Analysing the November and December 1932 election results, [the latter were communal elections held in Thuringia where the Nazi vote had dropped by 35 per cent], the liberal Vössische Zeitung saw grounds for hope: the 'nimbus of constant success has vanished, mass propaganda has lost its sensational appeal, the most superlative promises fall on deaf ears. The recovery of health can commence.' Optimism returned abroad, too. Harold Laski, the Left-wing British scholar-seer of the London School of Economics, thought that Nazism was a spent force. Exhibiting an unerring capacity to get the major issues hopelessly wrong, Laski predicted that Hitler was destined to spend the evening of his life in a Bavarian village, reminiscing in a beer garden about how he had nearly ruled the Reich.

Burleigh, M. 2000. *The Third Reich: A New History.*

Source C

Kurt Lüdecke, in his 1938 publication *I knew Hitler*, described the gloom that had descended on the NSDAP by December 1932, citing excerpts from the diary of Joseph Goebbels, Hitler's propaganda chief, which indicated the despair within the party:

December 6: The (Nazi) situation in the Reich is catastrophic.

December 8: Severe depression prevails… Financial worries render all systematic work impossible… The danger now exists of the whole Party's going to pieces… For hours on end the Führer walks anxiously up and down the hotel room… Once he stops and merely says:

"If the Party should ever break up, I'll make an end of things in three minutes with a revolver."

December 17: We decide to work with all our means on the Party organization… and see if we cannot lift the organization up again, in spite of all.

December 20: We must summon all our strength to rally the Party once more.

December 21: Altercation and discord… The financial crisis continues.

December 29: It is possible that in a few days the Führer will have a conference with Papen. There a new chance opens.

Lüdecke joined the Nazi movement in 1922 and helped in the organization of the SA paramilitary force as well as being given responsibility for fundraising for the Party. He was a close friend of Ernst Röhm, the SA leader killed in the purge of the SA leadership in June 1934. Lüdecke survived the purge and was permitted to go into political exile in Switzerland where, in 1938, the book was produced.

Source D

The decisive factor (which substantially facilitated 30 January 1933) was the careless playing with further-reaching projects and the associated activity of the Papen-Hugenberg-Hindenburg group. Believing with ambitious self-assurance that it was taming and exploiting the totalitarian mass movement, this tiny minority in fact helped the National Socialist leadership into positions of power they had not been able to achieve of their own accord.

Karl Dietrich Bracher. 1955. *Die Auflösung der Weimarer Republik.*

Source E

Hitler's broad-based totalitarian movement was not capable of toppling the Republic on its own, despite the fact that it had attained an astonishing level of political dynamism and had become the voice of a good one-third of Germans as the crisis deepened…. By the end of 1932 the NSDAP had plainly reached the limits of its electoral potential and was showing signs of falling back once again… After 1930 the presidential regimes destroyed what was left of the republican constitution and created a power vacuum which their own moves towards authoritarianism proved unable to fill… In 1933, finally the new governing elite consortium, in partnership with the National Socialist movement,

released the destructive energies of the Third Reich. The German crisis had become the German catastrophe; its result was to be the devastation of Europe.

Detlev Peukert 1991. *The Weimar Republic: The Crisis of Classical Modernity.*

Source F

Looked at politically, the result of the election is so fearful because it seems clear that the present election will be the last normal Reichstag election for a long time to come… The elected Reichstag is totally incapable of functioning, even if the Zentrum goes in with the National Socialists, which it will do without hesitation if it seems in the interests of the party. Genuine middle-class parties no longer exist.

The one consolation could be the recognition that the National Socialists have passed their peak… but against this stands the fact that the radicalism of the Right has unleashed a strong radicalism on the Left. The communists have made gains everywhere and thus internal political disturbances have become exceptionally bitter. If things are faced squarely and soberly the situation is such that more than half the German people have declared themselves against the present state, but have not said what sort of state they would accept. As the lesser of many evils to be feared, I think, would be the open assumption of dictatorship by the present government.

Wilhelm Külz (DDP /Staatspartei), former Weimar Interior Minister and Mayor of Dresden, writing of the November 1932 Reichstag election.

Source G

In January 1933 the German upper classes imagined that they had taken Hitler prisoner. They were mistaken. They soon found that they were in the position of a factory owner who employs a gang of roughs to break up a strike: he deplores the violence, is sorry for his workpeople who are being beaten up, and intensely dislikes the bad manners of the gangster leader whom he has called in. All the same, he pays the price and discovers, soon enough, that if he does not pay the price (later, even if he does) he will be shot in the back. The gangster chief sits in the managing director's office, smokes his cigars, finally takes over the concern himself. Such was the experience of the owning classes in Germany after 1933.

AJP Taylor. 1945. *The Course of German History.*

Source H

Hitler was the last chance, not the first choice or the preferred solution for the overwhelming majority of the traditional elites. Despite their anti-democratic consensus the elites themselves were too fragmented and too diverse in their alternative visions to be able to mount a deliberate conspiracy… In fact the willingness of the elites to embark upon the risk of 30 January 1933 represents the bankruptcy of their strategies and of the goal of an essentially traditional, typically reactionary "counter-revolution". The behaviour of the different power groups was characterized by an overestimation of their own strength and an underestimation of the modalities of the new mass politics.

Ian Kershaw, *Der 30 Januar 1933: Ausweg aus der Krise und Anfang des Staatsverfalls.*

Source I

▲ *A-I-Z*, 16 October 1932. The main caption reads, "The meaning of the Hitler salute", followed by "Millions stand behind me" and, at the bottom, "Little man asks for big gifts".

Questions

1 How does the performance of the KPD (1930–1932) differ from that of the NSDAP according to source A?

2 Given that the economy was beginning to show signs of recovery by autumn 1932, why might businessmen and conservative politicians find the result of the November 1932 election worrying?

3 What could explain the relatively consistent performance of the Zentrum/BVP in this period of economic turmoil (1930–1932)?

4 With reference to sources B and C, explain why those hostile to National Socialism might believe that the danger of right-wing extremism had passed by late 1932.

5 What motive could von Papen have for approaching Adolf Hitler at this stage?

6 Explain the reference in source D to 30 January 1933.

7 According to Bracher, what was the aim of the Papen-Hugenberg-Hindenburg group in their dealings with the Nazi leadership?

8 What phrase does Bracher use to describe the misguided attitude of this "group" in their plans for "taming and exploiting the totalitarian mass movement"?

9 In what ways does Peukert's view of the strength of National Socialism by late 1932 echo those shown in sources B, C and D?

10 According to Peukert, when had democratic government in Germany ceased to exist effectively?

11 What is meant by the phrase "governing elite consortium", which Peukert claims entered a "partnership" with National Socialism in 1933?

12 According to Külz, what was the most revealing fact about the attitude of German voters towards the "present state" in Germany in November 1932?

13 For Külz, what welcome development had the November election produced and what dangers faced the Republic in November 1932?

14 What does the phrase "lesser of two evils" mean, and what did Külz see as a possible solution to continued political uncertainty?

15 According to sources G and H, where does the blame lie for the coming to power of National Socialism by 1933?

16 What impression is given in sources G and H of the motives of the "owning classes"/

"traditional elites" for their actions in late 1932 and early 1933?

17 With which political party was the *A-I-Z* (*Arbeiter-Illustrierte-Zeitung*) closely linked?

18 What was the purpose of this photomontage (source I) produced by John Heartfield in October 1932?

19 Who, or what, were the 'millions' to which Heartfield was referring?

20 What values and limitations does such a source have in explaining the rise of Hitler and the NSDAP at this time?

Stage 5: from democracy to dictatorship (January–March 1933)

Whether National Socialist beliefs, wholly or in part, were attractive to a majority of Germans before or after 1933 is difficult to ascertain. Certainly there was never an absolute electoral majority for the Nazis even after the manipulation, bribery, and intimidation that marked the last election in Germany (March 1933) before Weimar was wound up.

When Hitler was appointed chancellor by Hindenburg (he was *not* elected by the majority of German voters), it was as chancellor of a mixed cabinet. Von Papen was appointed vice-chancellor and only three National Socialists were represented in the cabinet (Hitler, Goering, and Frick). While von Papen was reported as stating that "Within two months we will have pushed Hitler so far into a corner that he'll squeak", the events of the following months illustrated how Hitler had been misjudged as he used his position as chancellor (and Goering's role as Minister of the Interior) to manoeuvre himself into the role of semi-legal dictator.

Hitler's appointment may have been largely due to intrigue or "political jobbery" on the part of the vested interests (or the traditional elite), but responsibility for the meteoric rise of Nazi fortunes was not attributable to economic turmoil and elite plots alone. The failure of the Left to unite in defence of the Republic (and in the interests of their own future security) and the skilful manipulation of circumstances by the Nazis (from January to March 1933) set the scene for a totalitarian state in Germany. While democracy might have been in a state of suspension since 1930, the developments of 1933 and 1934 led to its complete liquidation.

Inside the Left, the unwillingness of the SPD and KPD to recognize the danger of Hitler's movement allowed the Nazis to consolidate power. Relations between the SPD and KPD (both of which Hitler considered "Marxist") had become embittered as early as 1918/1919 with the crushing of the

▲ SPD election poster, 1932

communist-inspired Spartacus uprising by the SPD-led Weimar government of Friedrich Ebert. The SPD manifesto of January 1919 declared:

> *We refuse any longer to allow ourselves to be terrorized by lunatics and criminals. Order must be at long last established in Berlin and the tranquil erection of the new ... Germany must be safeguarded.*

The crushing of the Spartacus uprising and the murder of its leaders led to accusations by the KPD that the SPD were traitors to the workers' movement and supporters of a bourgeois, capitalist democracy. In the following years, with Moscow's encouragement, the KPD openly vilified the SPD as "social fascists" – a party which distracted the working class from Marxist goals – that by default aided the growth of capitalism and what the KPD believed to be capitalism's hired thugs: the NSDAP.

In 1929, the Communist International (Comintern) railed against parties such as the SPD whose "principal function at the present time is to disrupt the essential militant unity of the proletariat ... against capital". The programme maintained that "social democracy of all shades" had become "the last reserve of bourgeois society and its most reliable support". The hostility between these two parties of the Left was not resolved until it was too late. By March 1933, Hitler was in a powerful position as chancellor and, by August 1934, as Führer.

Stage 6: the establishment of the Führer state, August 1934

After 1933–1934, Germans found themselves subjected to the beliefs of Adolf Hitler's movement, until 1945. Ascribing the rise of Hitler to the position of chancellor to the errors of others is only partly accurate. The NSDAP, since 1923, had worked steadily to build up its organization and establish links with other movements of the Right that would enable them to seize opportunities offered by the years of despair after 1929.

In 1937 G. Ward Price commented on the contribution to Nazi success of the steps taken after the release of Hitler from Landsberg prison:

> *Never has any Party prepared for power more thoroughly than the Nazis during the eight years between Hitler's release from Landsberg and his arrival at the Chancellorship. Their campaign was by no means confined to speeches and propaganda. With German zest for organization the framework of the Nazi movement was expanded and departmentalized until it had virtually became a "shadow government".*
>
> *It had its "Cabinet", consisting of Hitler and his intimate advisers; a political department, with sub-divisions gradually extending throughout the country; a Press and propaganda organization; and bureaux for dealing with labour questions, agricultural interests, financial matters.*
>
> *There were technical corps for the Party's motor and aerial transport; supply-services which passed large contracts for uniforms, banners and Party equipment; an insurance fund for the dependents of members killed*

ATL Thinking skills

In what way does the SPD election poster support the view that the relationship between the Social Democrats and the KPD was, at this critical time, very poor?

or injured in clashes with the communists. A legal branch conducted the lawsuits in which the Party was frequently involved, and lastly the defence departments of an actual Government were represented by the Storm Troopers (SA) and the "Protection Guards" (SS) organized on military lines under their commanding officers, Ernst Röhm and Heinrich Himmler.

Such impressive organization required financing a Evidence indicates that magnates such as Fritz Thyssen, Friederich Flick and the IG Farben chemical group made contributions towards the NSDAP, although they also contributed to other non-socialist parties. As HA Turner pointed out, industrialists, by the crisis years, were investing the money as "political insurance premiums" in the sense that they sought to "buy political insurance against the eventuality of a capture of the government".

Funding of other parties, especially the DNVP, was just as significant and the "alliance" of the DNVP leader Hugenberg, with whom Hitler had made common cause over opposition to the Young Plan in 1929, provided the Nazis with access to Hugenberg's communications empire (both press and film in the form of the UFA cinema chain). Hugenberg, "animated by insatiable political passions and hatreds masquerading as convictions", provided a vehicle for Nazi propaganda and a link to conservative and other right-wing movements as seen in the meeting of Nazis, military leaders, and industrialists in Harzburg in October 1931, where Hitler was able to portray himself as potential leader against the dangers of communism.

The popularity of the NSDAP by late 1932, despite the drop in electoral support, should not be underestimated. While reasons for Hitler's accession to the position of chancellor can be attributed to other factors, many German voters (although not a majority) found the message of National Socialism attractive in the post-1929 depression years. Not all who voted for the Nazis were committed to all points of the Nazi package but, having cast their vote, they enabled the National Socialists to portray themselves as the choice of a significant part of Germany's population. This was what convinced important groups to collaborate with them by 1933.

The ability to remain consistent in policy, combined with the fear factor of 1930–1933, allowed Hitler to put himself forward as a national saviour. It also convinced the political elite to "hire" him to rescue Germany from further descent into political and economic chaos, from which only the KPD seemed to be benefiting.

David Schoenbaum described these ideas, set out in *Mein Kampf,* as "the jail-born reflections of a frustrated revolutionary", but in the hothouse of discontent after 1929, they struck a chord with many Germans. Whether Germans who voted for the NSDAP agreed with all the ideas is debatable, but a vote for National Socialism was a vote in a sense for the package. Nationalists, anti-Semites, and anti-communists may have been attracted to individual elements but the National Socialist state and Hitler proved consistent in its pursuit of all the elements once in power.

ATL Research and communication skills

1. Read the article "Who voted for the Nazis?" by Dick Geary (*History Today*, Vol. 48 (10), October 1998 available at http://www.johndclare.net/Weimar6_Geary.htm).

2. Identify the particular appeal to voters (by gender and social class) of the NSDAP, 1928–1932.

3. In groups, discuss the particular appeal of the NSDAP to specific sectors of German society, and why other sectors appear to have been relatively immune to the Nazi appeal.

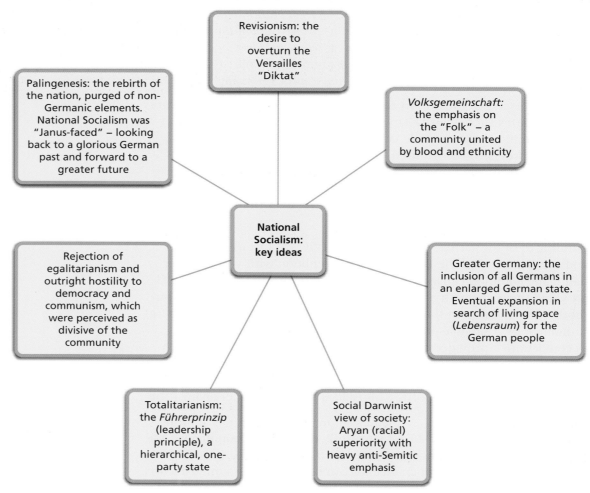

Revisionism: the desire to overturn the Versailles "Diktat"

Palingenesis: the rebirth of the nation, purged of non-Germanic elements. National Socialism was "Janus-faced" – looking back to a glorious German past and forward to a greater future

Volksgemeinschaft: the emphasis on the "Folk" – a community united by blood and ethnicity

National Socialism: key ideas

Rejection of egalitarianism and outright hostility to democracy and communism, which were perceived as divisive of the community

Greater Germany: the inclusion of all Germans in an enlarged German state. Eventual expansion in search of living space (*Lebensraum*) for the German people

Totalitarianism: the *Führerprinzip* (leadership principle), a hierarchical, one-party state

Social Darwinist view of society: Aryan (racial) superiority with heavy anti-Semitic emphasis

▲ The ideas of National Socialism

In early 1933 the Nazis were still part of a coalition government. Only in the following months did the Party convert itself into a virtual dictatorship, confirmed by August 1934 on the death of Hindenburg and the adoption, by Hitler, of the position of Führer (combining the office of chancellor and president).

Roger Griffin wrote:

> *For those who came under its spell, the Hitler movement alchemically transformed a generalized despair at the present order of society, a sense of being a foreigner in one's own country, into hope for the future, a sense of belonging. This, rather than anti-Semitism or middle-class reaction as such accounts for the build-up of the party and the SA before 1928, despite the pathetic showing at the ballot box. … the slogan "Germany awake", the omnipresent Swastika with its connotations of mystic regeneration and the appearance of Hitler as the embodiment of a new order could symbolize the hopes and certainties which the Weimar state could no longer provide.*

4.2 Hitler's consolidation of power, 1934–1935

Nazis used the term *"Machtergreifung"* (seizure of power) to describe the appointment of Hitler as chancellor in January 1933 although, as Eatwell points out, "at first, this was more a statement of hope than a description of political reality". From January 1933 to August 1934 Hitler focused on converting his position to one of complete control by eliminating obstacles to Nazi rule. He was able to do this by using intimidation and bribery and both the political elite and the Left opposition failed to combat his moves.

Hitler as Chancellor

The decision to call new elections in March 1933 was Hitler's attempt to seek to improve Nazi election figures, which had declined in the November 1932 Reichstag vote. Given that he was now able to use his position as chancellor and take advantage of the roles of Göring as Prussian Ministry of the Interior (Prussia being the largest by far of the German states) and Frick as National Minister of the Interior, it was believed that the NSDAP was capable of achieving an absolute majority for the first time in Weimar's troubled history.

The burning of the Reichstag

The burning down of the Reichstag on 27 February, a week or so before the March election, has been interpreted as a Nazi ploy to frighten voters into giving their support for the NSDAP as a bulwark against a supposed KPD uprising. There is little doubt that Marinus van der Lubbe was responsible for the fire but whether he was acting alone, was a victim of National Socialist subterfuge, or part of a larger communist conspiracy remains unclear. It appears that the NSDAP stood to gain most from the fire. Hitler, according to Hermann

Rauschning (who later fell out of favour with the regime), remarked: "The Reichstag Fire gives me the opportunity to intervene. And I shall intervene." Rauschning reported later, from exile, that "Göring described how 'his boys' had entered the Reichstag building by a subterranean passage from the President's palace, and how they had only a few minutes at their disposal and were nearly discovered".

Van der Lubbe was tried and executed. Rauschning and anti-Nazi contemporaries such as Willi Münzenberg (author of *The Brown Book of the Hitler Terror*) blamed the NSDAP for the fire, viewing it as a Nazi attempt to portray the incident as the beginning of a KPD insurrection. According to Münzenberg, the KPD were the victims of a Nazi conspiracy. Given the subsequent ease with which the KPD were dealt with, it appears that they were woefully unprepared to defend themselves, far less spark a revolution. For Hitler, it allowed him, as chancellor, to carry out his dream of "crushing … the murderous pest with an iron fist".

Using the excuse that Germany was endangered by a communist *coup d'état*, Hitler persuaded Hindenburg to issue an emergency decree that temporarily suspended basic rights and "thus was laid one of the legal cornerstones of the Nazi dictatorship".

The March 1933 election

The election of March 1933 resulted in a leap in votes for the NSDAP, which gained 288 out of 647 seats in the Reichstag (43.9 per cent) – still not an absolute majority despite the propaganda campaign and anti-communist hysteria that characterized the Nazi pre-election campaigning. Only with the collaboration of the DNVP and their 8 per cent of the vote was Hitler able to form a majority coalition. Even at this stage, and despite the propaganda value of the Reichstag fire, the majority of German voters were unwilling to deliver an outright majority for the Nazis.

What was significant, as Richard Evans has pointed out, was that

> … *nearly two-thirds of the voters had lent their support to parties – the Nazis, the nationalists, and the communists – who were open enemies of Weimar democracy. Many more had voted for parties, principally the Centre party (Zentrum) and its southern associate the Bavarian People's Party, whose allegiance to the Republic had all but vanished.*

Street violence preceded and followed the March elections as Nazi SA members (brownshirts) attacked KPD and SPD paramilitary organizations, Reichstag deputies and offices. The breakdown of law and order initiated by the Nazis was the excuse used by Hitler for tighter measures to save Germany from a chaos largely manufactured by the Nazis themselves.

The KPD, whose leaders had been arrested after the Reichstag fire, found itself a forbidden organization. While the names of communist candidates had not been removed from the election lists and the party itself gained 81 deputies, none was permitted to sit in the newly elected parliament or vote on legislation.

Election results of the main parties, March 1933	
Party	**Result (in approximate % terms)**
KPD	12 (81 deputies)
SPD	18
DDP	1
Zentrum/BVP	14
DVP	1
DNVP	8
NSDAP	44
Others	2

The Enabling Act and the end of democratic government

Hitler introduced an Enabling Bill that would allow him to rule by decree for four years, essentially making him dictator. His coalition with the DNVP gave him 52 per cent. By eliminating the 12 per cent of the KPD, by intimidating many of the SPD deputies from attending the meeting in the Kroll Opera House (the new venue for the Reichstag after the fire), and by offering the Zentrum/BVP guarantees for the protection of rights of the Catholic Church, the two-thirds majority he needed was surpassed. All deputies who attended the session, except those of the SPD, voted in favour of the Bill – thus making it into the Enabling Act (444 to 94 deputies voting in favour).

Through bullying, banning, and "buying" the support of the Catholic parties (with approval from the Vatican, which in 1929 had already made an agreement with the fascist regime in Italy), democratic government was buried in Germany. Hindenburg signed the Bill, more or less transferring his constitutional powers to the chancellor. Whether Weimar's death was the result of political murder or political suicide remains an area of debate.

Otto Wels, the SPD leader in the session, delivered the epitaph for democracy and for his doomed party when he declared:

> In this historic hour, we German Social Democrats solemnly profess our allegiance to the basic principles of humanity and justice, freedom and socialism. No Enabling Act gives you the right to annihilate ideas that are eternal and indestructible.

The fact that he attended the meeting with a concealed cyanide capsule in case he were to be arrested and tortured for his opposition, revealed the level of brutalization political and parliamentary life had reached.

The passage of the Act in March 1933 was the prelude to a raft of legislation as the Nazis implemented the process of *Gleichschaltung.* The Enabling Act alone was no guarantee that all institutions within Germany were committed to National Socialist rule. Institutions such as the Churches and the military, the labour movement, and the civil service had to be brought under control in order to make Nazi power a reality.

The purge of the civil service

The Law for the Re-establishment of the Civil Service of April 1933 was enacted to avoid the difficulties that had plagued Weimar. It constituted a purge of the civil service, allowing the government to remove elements it considered anti-Nazi. "Officials who are not of Aryan descent" were to be dismissed, as were "officials whose political activities hitherto do not offer a guarantee that they will at all times support the national state without reserve".

The intention was to remove anyone hostile to National Socialism as well as those of Jewish descent in public service – employees in the fields of the judiciary, diplomacy, and education. This "cleansing" was also an opportunity to reward loyal Nazis (the "Old Fighters" or *Alte Kämpfer* – those who had joined the party before September 1930) as well as to attract what became known as the "March Violets": those who joined the Party after March 1933 to further their careers.

Gleichschaltung
Literally, "coordination": the means whereby Hitler intended to consolidate Nazi power over Germany. Described by Sir Horace Rumbold (British Ambassador to Berlin) as the attempt to "press forward with the greatest energy the creation of uniformity throughout every department of German life", the process aimed to identify and eliminate all anti-Nazi elements.

Socialism and National Socialism

"Socialism" in the Marxist sense was not what was meant in the context of National Socialism. Whereas the former was a political philosophy dedicated to the complete overthrow of capitalism and which stressed the primacy of the working class, Hitler's use of the term was based on the idea of community – the *Volksgemeinschaft* (characterized by blood and ethnicity) rather than class, which was held to be divisive. The original 25-point programme contained anti-capitalist elements, but the concept of private property and protection of small businesses was emphasized.

Some Nazis did reject the power of big business (the Strasser brothers, for example) but Hitler was willing to accommodate the major industrialists during his rise to power (an example of his pragmatism) in order to gain financial and political support – much to the irritation of these more radical elements who, after 1933, expected more attention to the material needs of the workers.

The abolition of trade unions and political parties

The labour movement was associated with Leftist influence, and the Nazis sought to break the trade unions and the power of organized labour. In May 1933 such organizations were abolished and replaced by a Nazi-run organization known as the German Labour Front (DAF). Collective bargaining and the power to strike were forbidden as Hitler announced his plan to re-establish "social peace in the world of labour" and replace "discord" with "harmony" in the interests of the "people's community".

The single-party state was technically established by July 1933, when all political parties except the NSDAP were abolished. The Zentrum/BVP voluntarily dissolved (on 5 July) with the prospect of the signing of a Concordat between the National Socialist state and the Vatican (signed 20 July 1933). Similarly, the DVP and the DNVP bowed to pressure or the promise of guarantees of job security in the new Germany (under the Law for the Re-establishment of the Civil Service) and accepted self-dissolution.

The Night of the Long Knives (1934)

The purge of Germany's civil service was followed on 30 June by a purge of the Sturmabteilung (SA) through a series of murders the Night of the Long Knives. This purge was carried out for a variety of reasons:

- rivalry between its leader Ernst Röhm and leading Nazis such as Heinrich Himmler (chief of the SS) and Göring

- the claim that Röhm was planning a "second revolution" to redistribute wealth (Hitler had failed to distance himself from industrialists and big landowners)

- the fear that Röhm's ambitions to amalgamate the SA and the armed forces under his control would antagonize the army.

Berliners joked about the SA, referring to many of the ordinary members as "beefsteaks" – "brown on the outside but Red on the inside" – but there was little evidence that an SA-led putsch, far less a "socialist" one in terms of more radical members of the NSDAP, was on the cards. By eliminating Röhm and his supporters Hitler was able to assuage the army leadership's fears (and those of big business) and pave the way for an accommodation with the one institution which by 1934 still had the ability (physically) to oppose the regime. On 3 July 1934, the government retroactively passed the Law Relating to National Emergency Defence Measures justifying the murder of the victims of 30 June as having been necessary "to suppress attempts at treason and high treason".

The radical elements in the Party, alongside the rumours of a "second revolution", threatened not only established groups but also Hitler's control of the Party – hence the need to placate these groups, establish the *Führerprinzip* and eliminate a perceived rival. The "blood purge" of

the Night of the Long Knives was used not only to bring the SA under control but also to settle scores with what had become known as the Left wing of the Party – the radicals such as Gregor Strasser (murdered) and his brother Otto, who was forced into exile. Old enemies from the days of the Beerhall Putsch were also removed on the pretext of once more "rescuing" Germany from chaos.

The administrative structures of the new Reich

Political control of the NSDAP increased with the adoption of new administrative structures for the new Reich based on Nazi Party structures that had existed before 1933. By 1934 the state governments of Germany no longer existed and were replaced by a scheme intended to enforce central control and the hierarchical system of a totalitarian state. The country was divided into *Gaue* (regions essentially the same as the old states or Länder) under a *Gauleiter* appointed by, and answerable to, Hitler. There were 32 such *Gaue* in 1934 and 42 by 1945. Each *Gaue* was subdivided into *Kreis* (district), *Ort* (town or city), *Zell* (street) and *Block* (building). The purpose of the structure was to coordinate Nazi control throughout the state and not only administer but also, in conjunction with the Gestapo, supervise the population of the Reich at all levels to enforce obedience and conformity.

▲ The cover of *Kladderadatsch* magazine, published 2 April 1933. The caption reads "Spring cleaning".

On 10 August 1934 Hindenburg died. Hitler announced himself Führer and the army (*Reichswehr*), grateful for the removal of Röhm whose ambition had been to merge the SA and the army under his leadership, swore a personal oath of loyalty to Adolf Hitler:

> I swear by God this sacred oath, that I will render unconditional obedience to Adolf Hitler, the Führer of the German Reich and people, supreme commander of the armed forces, and will be ready as a brave soldier to risk my life at any time for this oath. ...

The institution that had been so grudging in its acceptance of the Weimar government and constitution was seduced by the possibility of rearmament and increase of numbers. Satisfied by the "blood purge" it now surrendered to the National Socialist state and became a servant of the regime.

Between January 1933 to August 1934, Hitler successfully transformed his position from that of leader of a coalition government to ruler of a single-party state. Coordination or *Gleichschaltung* had been rapidly applied to consolidate Nazi rule and the process of control was to expand thereafter to maintain it.

Thinking skills

What process is being referred to in the illustration? What elements are being swept away by the housewife?

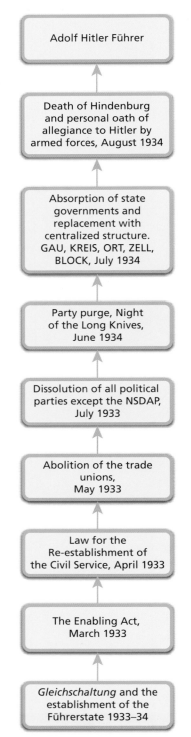

Adolf Hitler Führer

↑

Death of Hindenburg and personal oath of allegiance to Hitler by armed forces, August 1934

↑

Absorption of state governments and replacement with centralized structure. GAU, KREIS, ORT, ZELL, BLOCK, July 1934

↑

Party purge, Night of the Long Knives, June 1934

↑

Dissolution of all political parties except the NSDAP, July 1933

↑

Abolition of the trade unions, May 1933

↑

Law for the Re-establishment of the Civil Service, April 1933

↑

The Enabling Act, March 1933

↑

Gleichschaltung and the establishment of the Führerstate 1933–34

▲ Hitler's consolidation of power, 1933–1934

Hitler's methods

Here is a summary of the methods Hitler used in his rise to power.

Demonization

Groups and individuals were identified as hate symbols and used to rally support from different groups within the German population. Groups were encouraged to unite behind the Nazis' policy of "negative cohesion" against the supposed enemies of Germany:

- Jews
- the Marxist threat posed by the KPD, and, in Hitler's eyes, the SPD
- the "November Criminals" – those who signed the Armistice of 11 November 1918
- Weimar "traitors" who signed the Versailles "Diktat" of June 1919.

Violence, intimidation and murder

- The Beerhall Putsch of 1923

  This imitation of Mussolini's March on Rome of October 1922 was unsuccessful, but it permitted a national platform for Hitler at the ensuing trial.

▲ The caption on this poster reads: "The National Assembly, by its signature, is in agreement with the peace treaty."

- Paramilitary organizations (the Sturmabteilung/SA and later the Schutzstaffel/SS)

  These organizations protected Party meetings, disrupted the meetings of other parties, and won control of the streets of Germany during the Weimar era.

- Intimidation of SPD deputies

  Hitler used intimidatory tactics in his attempt to gain the two-thirds majority to pass the Enabling Bill in March 1933; street violence increased before and after the Reichstag fire in February.

- Murder

  According to Rudolf Diels, head of the Gestapo in Prussia, 500–700 political murders of Nazi opponents were carried out between March and October 1933, many by the SA forces appointed as auxiliary police after Hitler's appointment as chancellor in January 1933.

Abuse of the democratic system

After 1923–1924, Hitler followed a dual path: intimidation of enemies and the pursuit of power through the ballot box, "outvoting" his opponents rather than simply "outshooting" them.

Goebbels made no secret of the nature of Nazi tactics in pursuing votes in the Reichstag. In 1928 he made clear:

> …We are an anti-parliamentarian party that for good reasons rejects the Weimar constitution and its republican institutions. …We see in the present system of majorities and organized irresponsibility the main cause of our steadily increasing miseries.
>
> Do not believe that parliament is our goal. … We are coming neither as friends or neutrals. We come as enemies. As the wolf attacks the sheep, so come we.

- Transformation of the NSDAP from a largely Bavarian/Munich-based party to a national organization. Membership growth of the party was significant. In 1925 there were 25 000 members, by 1927 there were 72 000, and by 1931 there were 800 000. The party was organized into geographical sections and separate departments for youth, women, campaigning, policymaking, SA and propaganda. This allowed the party to be well positioned for elections and campaigns by 1930 onwards.

- Collaboration with existing interest groups (big business/industrialists) and political parties such as the Zentrum/BVP and DNVP by late 1932, early 1933.

- Appointment of Hitler as chancellor by Hindenburg: perfectly legal according to the provisions of the constitution.

- Passing of the Enabling Bill by more than the required two-thirds majority.

Propaganda

Joseph Goebbels was responsible for the Nazi propaganda campaign from 1929 when he was appointed Reich Propaganda Leader of the NSDAP. Prior to that he had published *Der Angriff* (*The Attack*), a weekly newspaper dedicated to promoting Nazi ideas. Goebbels has been credited with the stage-managing of Nazi propaganda that helped capture the attention of potential supporters in the period before 1933. Techniques used to "advertise" the party and the leader ranged from radio broadcasts, film shows, torchlight processions, mass meetings, and the use of loudspeakers, banners and the innovative "Hitler over Germany" campaign of 1932. In the presidential election campaign of 1932 – during which Hitler ran against Hindenburg – Nazi "dynamism" was characterized by Hitler's literal use of flying visits across the nation to address audiences.

By the late 1920s and early 1930s the propaganda machine was greatly aided by the link to Hugenberg, who provided access to the press and film theatres of UFA as well as introductions to leading businessmen whose funding could be used to pay for impressively coordinated Nazi campaigns.

Charisma and powers of oratory

Connected to the issue of propaganda is that of Hitler's charisma. Many accounts emphasize his hypnotic attraction for audiences. This is a difficult aspect to evaluate. Was the appeal of his speeches due to their content (often repetitive and with little detailed information about solutions to complex problems) or the performance?

Otto Strasser, writing from exile in 1940, remarked:

▲ The caption on this 1932 campaign pamphlet reads, "Hitler over Germany"

Hitler responds to the vibrations of the human heart with the delicacy of a seismograph, or perhaps a wireless receiving set, enabling him, with a certainty with which no conscious gift could endow him, to act as a loudspeaker proclaiming the most secret desires, the least admissible instincts, the sufferings and personal revolts of a whole nation… I have been asked many times what is the secret of Hitler's extraordinary power as a speaker. I can only attribute it to his uncanny intuition, which infallibly diagnoses the ills from which his audience is suffering…

Albert Speer, who joined the NSDAP in 1931 and later rose to become Minister of Armaments, commented:

Goebbels and Hitler knew how to penetrate through to the instincts of their audiences; but in the deeper sense they derived their whole existence from these audiences. Certainly the masses roared to the beat set by Hitler's and Goebbels's baton; yet they were not the true conductors. The mob determined the theme. To compensate for misery, insecurity, unemployment, and hopelessness, this anonymous assemblage wallowed for hours at a time in obsessions, savagery, licence… for a few short hours the personal unhappiness caused by the breakdown of the economy was replaced by a frenzy that demanded victims. And Hitler and Goebbels threw them the victims. By lashing out at their opponents and vilifying the Jews they gave direction to fierce, primal passions.

For Speer, his joining the party was not due to the offerings of any party programme. As he declared: "I was not choosing the NSDAP but becoming a follower of Hitler, whose magnetic force had reached out to me."

The programme offering of National Socialism

This was the mix of features such as **palingenesis**, ultra-nationalism, racism, revisionism, appeals to a *Volksgemeinschaft*, anti-Marxism, German expansionism, and anti-Semitism, which was targeted at the disillusioned, the frustrated, and the fearful. The "catch-all" nature of the programme would never win over significant elements of the Left but it acted as a "life raft" for those seeking safety from unemployment and political uncertainty.

> **palingenesis**
> National rebirth, a core idea of National Socialism.

Pragmatism

Hitler's views were dogmatic in many respects but his willingness to adapt to circumstances, to play down or drop parts of the original Nazi programme, enabled him to advance the cause of the NSDAP. Notable here was the abandoning of the anti-capitalist stance permeating the 25 points and the cooperation Hitler sought with industrialists and businessmen such as Hugenberg. This was illustrated by his appearance before the Industry Club in Dusseldorf in January 1932, where his speech was greeted by the assembled businessmen with "long and tumultuous applause" when he stated:

> *Today we stand at the turning point of Germany's destiny. If the present development continues, Germany will one day of necessity land in Bolshevist chaos, but if this development is broken off, then our people will have to be taken into a school of iron discipline. … Either we shall succeed in working out a body-politic hard as iron from this conglomerate of parties, associations, unions, and conceptions of the world, from this pride of rank and madness of class, or else, lacking this internal consolidation, Germany will fall into final ruin…*

Later, in February 1933, to another meeting of industrialists, he declared:

> *Private enterprise cannot be maintained in the age of democracy; it is conceivable only if the people have a sound idea of authority and personality…*

Similarly, despite earlier hostility towards other parties such as the DNVP and the Zentrum/BVP, Hitler was able by the early 1930s to work with them, whether through the Harzburg Front of October 1931 with the DNVP (to "protect our country from the chaos of Bolshevism and to save our polity from the maelstrom of economic bankruptcy") or through collaboration with the Catholic parties to secure the Enabling Act in March 1933.

Opportunism

The NSDAP recognized the opportunities presented by circumstances. AJP Taylor claimed that "only the Great Depression put the wind into the sails of National Socialism", but the sails were already there in 1929 as a result of Hitler's organization of the party in previous years. Slogans about "Work and bread" in a time of desperation played well to many.

Similarly, the Reichstag fire, whether caused by the Nazis or not, played into Hitler's hands at a critical time – just before the March 1933 election. The party was able to benefit from conjuring up the threat of an alleged revolution, and to eliminate the KPD as an effective opposition, inside or outside the Reichstag.

▲ *Der Wahre Jacob*, 14 February 1931

Die Lebens-Stationen Adolf Hitlers

▲ *Der Wahre Jacob*, 14 January 1933. The caption reads: "Stages in the life of Adolf Hitler"

Bribery

Where force proved ineffective, the NSDAP was able to "buy" support in the period up to August 1934. Acts of bribery led to:

- the NSDAP/DNVP alliance of March 1933, to give an absolute Reichstag majority

- the collusion of the Zentrum/BVP in burying Weimar when they voted in favour of the Enabling Act

- the "deal" with the army following the elimination of Röhm, whose SA had once sung of "the grey rock" (the army) being drowned in a "brown flood" (the SA) and the death of Hindenburg.

Other factors

Hitler's rise to power (and consolidation up to August 1934) was also made possible by acts of commission or omission by other groups or parties:

- The lack of a solid base for the democratic experiment in Germany; Weimar's legitimacy was never sufficiently accepted throughout the period

- The abuse of constitutional provisions such as Article 48 that undermined the functioning of accountable democratic government by March 1930

- The failure of political parties to work the system of proportional representation in the spirit in which it had been designed – too many parties proved unwilling and unable to work for the success of parliamentary rule

- Disillusionment with Weimar policies and actions from 1919 and the inability to deal with economic crises in the early 1920s and 1930s; the brief period of respite under Stresemann was not enough to anchor the system on a solid foundation

- The failure of the army to support democracy, a system it regarded with distaste and outright hostility

- The schism (division) on the Left during the life of Weimar, which hindered any real attempt to unite against extremist parties of the Right – what the Marxist historian Eric Hobsbawm in 2002 referred to as the "suicidal idiocy" of Moscow's failure to promote an anti-Nazi front until too late

- Fear of the Left by important sections of society (big business, the Catholic Church, and so on), which led to support for National Socialism, or to an unwillingness to confront it before 1933/1934

- Political intrigue (jobbery) on the part of figures such as Hindenburg and von Papen and the fatal underestimation of Hitler who it was believed could be controlled.

External factors also had a role in weakening the chances of democracy flourishing, from the imposition of what most Germans perceived as a humiliating and punitive peace treaty to the Franco-Belgian invasion of the Ruhr in 1923 (following Germany's defaulting on reparations payments) and the US stock market crash in October 1929.

Winston Churchill later referred to the reparations issue as a "sad story of complicated idiocy". And five months before the outbreak of war in Europe, Robert Vansittart (Chief Diplomatic Adviser to the British government in 1939) reflected wistfully:

> *How different things would have been if we had all provided the Republican regime in Germany with greater concessions and with greater authority and credit. We might have all lived happily ever afterwards.*

The opposition during the Third Reich, 1934–1945

The Nazi state's objective was to exercise a monopoly of power over all aspects of the lives of the population. The party and its leader were exalted as infallible, omniscient and omnipotent. The essence of totalitarian government, as Hannah Arendt remarked, was "total terror" – the instrument used to enforce conformity and eliminate opposition to the will of the leader and the party. As Bracher noted, the totalitarian goals of 20th-century single-party states, whether they were "Russian Bolshevism, Italian fascism or National Socialism" shared "common techniques of omnipresent surveillance (secret police), persecution (concentration camps), and massive influencing or monopolizing of public opinion".

Both "stick and carrot methods" were used to achieve the Nazi goal. As well as brute force, propaganda (through radio, print, and film), control over education, and economic and social policies designed to alleviate the suffering of the masses were used to "seduce" the population into accepting the new regime. Bribery and patronage had helped bring the Nazis into power and were also used to maintain that power.

The nature of the opposition

Most Germans remained loyal to the regime. McDonough estimated that less than 1 per cent engaged in active opposition, and most Germans accommodated themselves to domestic and foreign policies that proved popular, certainly up to 1942. Fear of punishment was partly responsible for an attitude of "tepid neutrality" among potential resisters.

Hans Rothfels, commented: "no one has the right to pass facile judgment on conflicts of conscience and the possibility of unqualified resistance who has not himself fully experienced the trials of life under a totalitarian system". Rothfels was critical of the view that German "submissiveness" permeated the Nazi period and that too many Germans "pursued the policy of the ostrich".

Opposition ranged from "silent opposition" (refusing to offer the Nazi salute, telling jokes about Hitler and the regime) to more active opposition such as sabotage in the workplace, the circulation of anti-Nazi propaganda and plots to assassinate Hitler (the most well known being

▲ *Der Wahre Jacob*, 7 January 1933. The caption reads: "Darn it, the paint is peeling off everywhere." The paint tin is labelled "brown".

ATL Research and thinking skills

What point is the cartoonist making regarding Nazi political progress in early January 1933, and why?

the 20 July 1944 bomb plot). Motives of the opponents of the regime varied – from a desire to morally and ethically resist Nazi policy, to a desire to salvage what was possible in the last phase of the Second World War, when defeat by the Allies appeared certain.

Rudolph Herzog in 2006 published *Heil Hitler, Das Schwein is tot* (*Heil Hitler, the pig is dead*), a collection of jokes told during the Nazi regime. Such humour was no laughing matter, as noted in the review of Herzog's book in the German magazine *Der Spiegel*:

> ... by the end of the war, a joke could get you killed. A Berlin munitions worker, identified only as Marianne Elise K., was convicted of undermining the war effort "through spiteful remarks" and executed in 1944 for telling this one:
>
> "Hitler and Göring are standing on top of Berlin's radio tower. Hitler says he wants to do something to cheer up the people of Berlin. 'Why don't you just jump?' suggests Göring."
>
> A fellow worker overheard her telling the joke and reported her to the authorities.

The treatment of the opposition

Whether active or "silent", opposition to National Socialism faced an apparatus of terror that was effective in repressing dissent. In April 1933 Göring established the police state of the Gestapo (*Geheime Staatspolitzei*) when he transformed the existing Prussian political police service, with its new headquarters in Berlin. Reitlinger pointed out the irony that "The Gestapo ... was the successor of the political police" which was in fact "a product of the Weimar constitution of 1919 conceived in the double fear of Bolshevism and Freikorps anarchy ... an instrument waiting for a dictator to come to power". This element of continuity was also witnessed in the remarkable number of former Weimar police who continued in the service of the Gestapo after 1933 when, for example, referring to figures in late 1938, "it was found that all but ten or fifteen out of a hundred Gestapo men in Coblenz had joined the police under the Weimar Republic".

This outwardly formidable structure of repression was the instrument used to maintain order within Germany, although much recent scholarship has stressed the level of collaboration with the secret police among ordinary citizens, who informed upon "enemies of the state". With 30 000 officers at its peak, the Gestapo relied on the aid of a "culture of denunciation" among many who sought to benefit from the turning in of supposed enemies of the regime. The image of a monolithic and all-seeing secret police was fostered by the system itself, as part of its tactics of inducing an atmosphere of fear to dissuade resistance. This combination of fear of the apparatus of repression and the cooperation of informants was capable of stifling opposition throughout the period of Nazi rule.

The Gestapo

The official secret police of Germany and Nazi-occupied Europe. In 1933 Heinrich Himmler, leader of the SS (*Schutzstaffel*) – originally formed as Hitler's personal bodyguard in 1925 but greatly expanded by 1933 – was appointed leader of the Gestapo. Hence the Gestapo fell under the control of the SS, much to the annoyance of Göring. By 1936 Himmler's appointment as Chief of Police as well as SS leader led to a bewildering overlapping of police services and intelligence-gathering offices under Himmler and his second-in-command Reinhard Heydrich. In 1939 the various police functions and forces were combined under the control of the RHSA (*Reichssicherheitshauptamt*, or Reich Central Security Office), which wielded authority over the Gestapo, the SS, the SD (the intelligence service of the SS), and the Kriminalpolizei (Kripo). From its formation until his assassination in Czechoslovakia in 1942, Heydrich headed it.

The main forms of resistance

Failure of opposition from the Left contributed towards the rise to power of Hitler. The failure of the KPD in particular to change strategy until 1935 enabled the Nazis to consolidate power. The legacy of distrust between the KPD and SPD remained, even in the face of the brutal repression of both parties after 1933. Two other major institutions had the power to oppose (both before and after 1933) but also failed to do so: the military and the Churches. While groups within each institution attempted to challenge the Nazi state, they, like the Left, proved incapable of undermining the regime.

A despairing report from SOPADE, the executive committee of the SPD in exile, from 1937 perhaps summarizes the general situation concerning resistance to the Nazi state, whether from religious or Leftist political principles:

> *The number of those who consciously criticize the political objectives of the regime is very small, quite apart from the fact that they cannot give expression to this criticism. …They do not want to return to the past and if anyone told them that their complaints about this or that aspect threaten the foundations of the Third Reich they would probably be very astonished and horrified.*

From North Germany, an SPD agent reported in 1938:

> *The general mood is characterized by a widespread political indifference. The great mass of the people is completely dulled and does not want to hear anything more about politics…*

Opposition from the Left

Both the KPD and SPD were early victims of the Nazi attack on Marxism. As early as January 1933, the Left found itself the target of physical violence from the SA street fighters who were incorporated as auxiliary police by Göring in Prussia. The Reichstag fire led to the banning of the KPD and the threats and intimidation of SPD deputies in March 1933 indicated what lay ahead for anti-Nazi opponents.

In late March 1933, Dachau concentration camp near Munich was set up to intern and re-educate political prisoners. Many of the inmates in Dachau and later camps in Sachsenhausen (1936) and Buchenwald (1937) were under "protective custody", which meant no trial was necessary under emergency regulations introduced by the regime. In later years these main camps bred satellite camps that fell under the supervision of the SS. Originally they were detention centres; only later did they become extermination centres.

Opposition from the KPD

By late 1932 the KPD had gained significant electoral support, with almost 6 million votes in the November 1932 Reichstag election, and a party membership of 360 000. The rapidity with which the KPD was broken was astonishing. The arrest of the KPD leader Ernst Thälmann and leading party cadres in March, followed by further waves of arrests, rendered the party's organizational structure on a national level ineffective.

Some leaders who evaded capture (Wilhelm Pieck, Franz Dahlem, and Wilhelm Florin) removed themselves to Paris to build up opposition, while others remained in Berlin to organize some form of resistance (one of whom, Walter Ulbricht, later became leader of the GDR). Leaflets, the issuing of underground newspapers, the raising of red banners, and the continued circulation of the official Party newspaper *Die Rote Fahne* were the main activities undertaken – yet no serious consideration was given to an armed insurrection. The KPD still held to the belief that the Hitler regime was the last kick of desperate capitalism and would soon collapse.

This ideological stance played into Nazi hands. The increased printing of anti-Nazi propaganda and its clandestine distribution in Germany was meant to keep spirits of party members high but did little to threaten the developing Hitler state. Continued arrests of party members sapped morale and open protest was minimal.

The ideological misinterpretation of the nature and strength of the emerging Nazi state and the loss of initiative led to radical rethinking by August 1935, when Moscow, through the Comintern (the Communist International) dropped its hostility to the "social fascism" of the Social Democratic Party and advocated the policy of a "popular front" of all forces that had suffered from the rise of fascism. It was a case of relatively little, too late. By this point the KPD's centralized structure was in tatters – and what cooperation in a "popular front" did exist was undertaken by émigrés at interminable meetings in foreign capitals: internal opposition of any substance did not materialize.

The outbreak of civil war in Spain in 1936 and the opportunity to fight fascism on foreign soil distracted many German communists from the lack of success in Germany. In August 1939, when Moscow and Berlin signed a non-aggression pact, KPD members found themselves faced with a dilemma: the National Socialist enemy had suddenly become involved in a friendship agreement with the USSR. Confusion and disillusionment followed in Germany. Only after Hitler's attack on the Soviet Union in June 1941 (Operation Barbarossa) did the "German comrades", under Stalin's orders, renew resistance. But Moscow's directives on the need to work towards the defence of the USSR were of little consequence inside Germany. While KPD communist exiles in Moscow urged industrial sabotage to halt the Nazi war effort, such attempts were on a small scale and often unsuccessful. The SPD remained sceptical of the "popular front" idea, given its previous experience with the KPD and the fact it appeared to be a policy more to defend Moscow's interests and Soviet security than to liberate Germany from National Socialism.

Opposition from communist groups

Groups of communists – or communist sympathizers – such as the Uhrig Group in Berlin were small, both in number and in terms of impact. Support of the USSR during the Second World War was an unpopular and unattractive prospect. The group's attempts to disrupt war production were small scale and, like the Home Front and the Baum Group whose actions were focused on producing anti-Nazi leaflets, their life and effectiveness were limited by the ability of the Gestapo to identify and eliminate their threat to the regime in 1942. Similarly, the attempts of the Red Orchestra (*Rote Kapelle*), members of which were employed in government ministries and who sought to pass on details of Nazi economic and war effort capabilities to the USSR, were short-lived.

Round-ups by the Gestapo of communists involved in industrial disruption, illustrated the extent to which the party was incapable of organizing any effective opposition. By 1944 the remnants of KPD domestic resistance were swept up. The myth of "heroic resistance" by the KPD, which was to form the basis of future historical writing in the GDR, was simply that. The party, a tool of Moscow's policies throughout the Weimar and Nazi eras, failed to provide an alternative to the rise or rule of the extreme Right.

Opposition from the SPD

With a party membership of approximately a million and a sound performance in the elections of 1932 and March 1933, the SPD was well placed to organize resistance to the encroaching totalitarian system. Those SPD deputies able to attend the Reichstag meeting during the debate on the Enabling Bill were the only ones to vote against its passage. By June, the party was officially banned by the regime, its funds confiscated and the leadership removed itself first to Prague, then Paris and later, from 1940–1945, to London.

In exile, the SPD undertook similar actions to the KPD: distributing news-sheets and posting anti-Nazi leaflets. While specific groups emerged inside Germany to carry out anti-Nazi propaganda (for example, Red Shock Troop/*Der Rote Stosstrupp* and New Beginning), the numbers involved were small and by 1938 these groups and their activities, which proved little more than irritants to the Hitler regime, were arrested.

Alongside Gestapo efficienct, economic conditions in Germany by the mid to later 1930s also undermined Social Democratic efforts to maintain contact with industrial workers. As Hartmut Mehringer noted, "full employment and increasing demands for production and working hours left less time for (clandestine) meetings that had previously benefited from unemployment and temporary employment". Arguably, material improvement in the lives of former supporters of the SPD sapped their commitment to the SPD underground programme. Isolated meetings in bars, homes, and restaurants of SPD sympathizers were not a major challenge to the Reich. SOPADE was unable to mobilize mass opposition and, while some small socialist opposition groups remained below the radar of the Gestapo, the very nature of their low-level activities and secrecy of meetings to ensure safety was not conducive to promoting serious resistance.

Opposition by the military

During the Weimar era the army had not committed itself to the Republic wholeheartedly. It stood largely on the sidelines in the critical period 1930–1933 but in August 1934 submitted to the Hitler state with an oath of personal loyalty to Adolf Hitler as Führer. While its support was "bought" by visions of a Nazi foreign policy that rejected the military restrictions of Versailles and by the removal of the Röhm threat, it became the victim of a process of "death by dilution". As numbers increased, so did the number of commissioned and non-commissioned officers who were committed Nazis. As the armed forces grew, the influence of the professional officer class diminished.

By the later 1930s, however, elements of the army leadership questioned the relationship that had been established with the Nazis in 1934. As the influence of the professional officer class weakened and Nazi foreign policy became more adventurous, groups within the military entered an alliance with conservative German politicians who rejected the repressive nature of the regime – its persecution of the Churches and its rabid anti-Semitism. The fear that Hitler's policies could spark a major war that would destroy Germany strengthened the resolve of such groups to rid Germany of the Hitler regime.

Individual army leaders who dared question Hitler's foreign policy or his interference in the affairs of the military at the highest levels were dealt with in 1938, when Field Marshals Blomberg and Fritsch were forced to resign. Revelations by the Berlin police that Blomberg's new wife had links to prostitution was sufficient for Hitler to demand his resignation, and for Blomberg to agree as a matter of honour and to save the honour of the officer corps. Fritsch became the victim of charges that he had committed acts of homosexuality. While a subsequent trial found no substance to the charge, Fritsch, his honour impugned by the publicity, also resigned. Both had challenged Hitler's concept of *Lebensraum* in 1937, which they felt would lead to disaster. Both were destroyed by intrigue and scandal organized by the Nazis.

With Blomberg's departure as Minister of Defence and Supreme Commander of the armed forces and Fritsch's stepping down as Commander in Chief of the army, Hitler assumed supreme command of the armed forces. The nazification of the army officer corps continued and many, but not all, of the professional officer corps remained bound by their personal oath and were reluctant to actively challenge Hitler. Exceptions included General Ludwig Beck, who in 1938 plotted a coup against the regime. Worried by the possibility of war over the Sudetenland issue, Beck assembled a group of conspirators who made contact with British Prime Minister Neville Chamberlain, but Chamberlain's policy of active appeasement and lack of support rendered any coup impractical. Beck, disappointed but not discovered as a plotter against Hitler, continued to work to oppose the Nazi state alongside Friederich Goerdeler, a leading conservative politician disillusioned with the regime's repressive nature.

By 1941 the Beck–Goerdeler group had begun to organize a network of military and conservative nationalist supporters with the intention of ending the Hitler state. But in the midst of war – a successful war until 1942, at least – mobilizing support proved difficult. Military success bred support for the regime – or at least a lack of will to actively undermine the nation during such a critical period. When the tide turned against Germany with major losses on the eastern front by 1943, the group was able to attract more support in Germany and establish contact with British and US officials.

What would replace the Hitler state, though, remained an obstacle for Britain and the USA, which viewed the Beck–Goerdeler group with suspicion, interpreting their motives as being not so much anti-Nazi as an attempt to avoid the possibility of defeat and invasion by the Soviet Union. Additionally, plans put forward by the group for a post-Hitler state smacked of an authoritarian system not in keeping with democratic principles – in a sense a reactionary system, looking back to monarchical and Wilhelminian Germany and reflecting the conservative beliefs of the politicians and officers involved.

In loose collaboration with the Beck–Goerdeler group were leading members of the **Abwehr** led by Admiral Canaris and Hans Oster. Both had been involved in anti-Hitler activities since 1938 and the Sudetenland crisis. In association with others in what was known as the Kreisau Circle, led by Helmuth James von Moltke, plans were laid throughout 1942–1944 to physically remove Hitler. An estimated six assassination attempts were made unsuccessfully in 1943 but Operation Valkyrie, the July bomb plot of 1944, has remained most prominent (although also unsuccessful) in accounts of the military–conservative resistance to Hitler.

> **Abwehr**
> The intelligence service of the German Foreign Office.

Operation Valkyrie, 1944

The Beck–Goerdeler group produced Operation Valkyrie, the plan to kill Hitler, in July 1944, a month after the Normandy Landings in France and just after the beginning of Operation Bagration on the Eastern Front, which was to produce, by August, a crushing defeat of German forces in Belorussia and Eastern Poland as Soviet armies headed towards Germany. The timing of Valkyrie has led to claims that the motives of the conspirators were based not just on moral qualms about National Socialism but on the necessity to remove Hitler, negotiate a rapid peace with the British and French, and prevent an invasion of German soil by the advancing Red Army. Less cynically perhaps, General Henning von Tresckow, who played a central role in the planning of the coup, stated:

> *The attempt on Hitler's life must take place at any cost. If it does not succeed, the coup d'état must nevertheless be attempted. For what matters is no longer the practical object, but that before the world and history the German Resistance movement should have staked its life on risking the decisive throw. Compared with this nothing else matters.*

Similarly, another plotter, Erwin Planck declared:

> *The attempt … must be made, if only for the moral rehabilitation of Germany … even if thereby no direct improvement of Germany's international prospects is achieved.*

The planned assassination was to be carried out by Claus von Stauffenberg, although an impressive range of military leaders was also involved and knowledgeable about what was to happen – including Field Marshal Erwin Rommel, who approved of the coup but who preferred the prospect of arresting and putting Hitler in the dock on charges of war crimes.

Hitler survived the explosion and the retribution carried out against the plotters was swift and terrible. Some conspirators chose suicide, many were sentenced to death and the military–conservative opposition was wiped out after Gestapo round-ups. Executions of opposition elements continued up to early 1945. Under *Sippenhaft* laws, the principle of collective guilt was applied and led to the punishment of family members of the accused, even though there was no proof of their complicity in the plot.

Opposition from the Catholic Church

If, as Ernst Nolte argued, "The origin of the Right (in Europe in the interwar years) lies always in the challenge of the Left", the actions of the Catholic Church in abetting the rise of the Nazis can be understood in the light of its anxiety about Bolshevism. The papacy had already, in 1929, signed a series of agreements with the Italian leader Mussolini (the Lateran Treaties), which helped provide legitimacy for Mussolini's single-party state. The growth of the KPD in Germany by 1932 frightened not only the existing political elite but also the Catholic Church and its political representatives (Zentrum and BVP).

The Zentrum and BVP, frequently part of democratic coalition governments during the period, abandoned any commitment to the restoration of accountable democratic government after March 1933 when they helped to pass the Enabling Act. By July 1933 voluntary dissolution of the party occurred following Hitler's signing of a Concordat with the Catholic Church, in which he promised not to interfere in Church affairs (including the right of the Church to retain and establish Catholic schools and promote Catholic youth groups) in exchange for a guarantee that the Church would abstain from interference in political life. Such an agreement had been sought with the Weimar government previously, but without success. The Papal Nuncio (representative) in Germany who negotiated the settlement was Cardinal Pacelli (later Pope Pius XII), a keen admirer of Hitler's anti-Marxist beliefs.

Political Catholicism, in the form of organized parties that had played a role in German political life from the time of Bismarck, ceased to exist. Its disappearance was achieved through false promises on the part of Hitler and short-sightedness on the part of the Catholic Church – but it shared this myopia with other political figures and Christian religious groupings at the time. If the Catholic Church had assumed it was to be "a loyal dialogue partner", in van Norden's words, it was to be disappointed. *Gleichschaltung* envisaged not only the elimination of political opponents but also the taming and subjugation of religious institutions. "Coordination" meant that *all* aspects of life were to be controlled and channelled towards meeting the will of the Führer. When Catholic bishops, in a pastoral letter in August 1935, publicly protested against what was described as a "new paganism" sweeping the state, it was already too late. The repressive apparatus of the totalitarian state found no major difficulties confronting a religious institution that had effectively dismantled its political parties in 1933 at the same time as giving respectability to the Nazi regime when it appeared to have Vatican approval.

The promises made in the Concordat were, for Hitler, expedients: *Gleichschaltung* was about winning over Catholic (and Protestant) Churches at the outset of Nazi rule until the force of the totalitarian state could be organized. A gradual erosion of Catholic rights followed as legislation was enacted to limit Catholic religious education, press, and youth groups. At no time did the Vatican actively challenge the increasing brutality of the regime in its persecution of minorities such as the Jews, or of political groups of the Left.

Individual clerics did take a stand on policies such as euthanasia and sterilization – the most prominent being Bishop Graf von Galen – but the one major critique by the papacy in March 1937 by Pope Pius XI, an

encyclical (a papal letter sent to all bishops of the Catholic Church) entitled "With Burning Anxiety", was less an attack on the policies of National Socialism towards minorities and persecution of political enemies than a criticism of Nazi breaches of the Concordat in relation to the Catholic religion in Germany. Pius's main emphasis, as Stackelberg and Winkle pointed out, was on "spiritual and doctrinal matters". To the credit of individual priests (many of whom were interned in Dachau), dissenting messages were delivered from some pulpits, but as an institution the Catholic Church failed to provide any organized resistance to the state.

Opposition from the Protestant Churches

Catholicism was particularly strong in southern Germany and the Rhineland but Protestantism, for example, in the form of the Protestant Evangelical Church, was the largest Christian Church in Prussia. As early as September 1933 Ludwig Müller was elected Reich Bishop by a national synod (council) of the Evangelical Church when the 28 regional Protestant Church organizations, with the backing of a group known as the "German Christians", attempted to transform the Church into one preaching a specifically German national religion in the service of the Nazi state – a Christianity stripped of study of the Old Testament (described as a Jewish book and therefore unfit for study by Aryans). This *Reichskirche* (Reich Church) was short-lived: Evangelical ministers resented and resisted the political machinations used to elect Müller and formed the Confessing Church under the leadership of Martin Niemöller. In 1934 they held a synod of the Confessional Church in Barmen, and the resulting Barmen Declaration rejected the "false doctrine" of the Reich Church.

Resistance to the Nazi-sponsored Reich Church was largely resistance to interference in Church affairs rather than outright condemnation of the political principles of National Socialism. Most clergy remained silent on the increasing persecution of the Jewish population and the aggressive nature of Nazi expansionism. Those who did speak out were interned in concentration camps (Niemöller was arrested in 1937 and detained until 1945) but the majority of pastors and their congregations did not organize themselves and challenge the political basis of a single-party state that extinguished civil liberties. Interestingly, Niemöller offered to fight for Germany during the Second World War – an offer which was not taken up but which perhaps revealed the dilemma facing many Christians, torn between resistance to government attempts to control the Church and feelings of patriotism.

Opposition from Jehovah's Witnesses

Although very much a minority religious group (approximately 25 000–30 000 members), Jehovah's Witnesses stood out as steadfast opponents of the Nazi state. Banned soon after the Nazis came to power, they continued to challenge the state by their refusal to give the Hitler salute or join Nazi organizations (including the armed forces) and they were accordingly ruthlessly persecuted. As Detlev Garbe noted:

> *…the courage of conviction and the (under the circumstances) recklessness of the numerically rather insignificant religious community occupied surprisingly large circles: at times, the highest legal, police, and SS organs were occupied with the "Bible Students' Question".*

ATL	**Thinking skills**

For the full text of the Barmen Declaration, see Stackelberg and Winkle, *The Nazi Germany Sourcebook* (Routledge, 2002), pages 168–9.

To what extent did it resist the policies of the National Socialists?

Despite such bravery, the comparatively small numbers involved limited the impact of their dissent. It is estimated that 10 000 were imprisoned and 250 executed for their refusal to serve in the military.

Youth/student opposition

Much has been made of youth/student opposition to the Hitler regime but, despite the best efforts of authors and film studios to glorify the brave efforts of these relatively few individuals, it appears they had little effect. The Edelweiss Pirates and its regional variations (the Essen Gallivanters, the Viennese Shufflers, the Stäuber gangs in Danzig) were resistant to the officially sanctioned Hitler Youth, but their activities (occasional leafleting, adopting nonconformist dress and listening to "non-Aryan" music) were more examples of "youthful disobedience" than political resistance. While their impact was limited, several of them did pay the ultimate price for their unwillingness to conform.

In the summer of 1942 through to early spring 1943, the Munich-based "White Rose" group began circulating flyers calling for passive resistance to the state. Motivated partly by the experience of some of their members who had witnessed the horrors of the campaign against civilians in the Soviet Union – and also by Christian religious beliefs – the flyers, especially after the German army's disastrous defeat at Stalingrad, emphasized the need for peace. The Allies used the subsequent arrests, trials, and executions for treason of the members of the group for propaganda purposes, but the impact of the group on the Nazi war effort was minimal. Arguably, for many Germans, whether staunch supporters of Nazi ideology or not, the thought of betraying the nation by harming the war effort at a critical stage was unacceptable.

As Ian Kershaw argued:

> *The mere presence of a ruthless repressive apparatus is usually sufficient to intimidate the mass of the population into not actively supporting the resistance… large proportions of the population did not even passively support the resistance, but actually widely condemned it.*

Propaganda and its role

Joseph Goebbels, was appointed Reich Minister of Popular Enlightenment and Propaganda after March 1933. In a press conference soon after his appointment, he emphasized the fact that:

> *It is not enough for people to be more or less reconciled to our regime, to be persuaded to adopt a neutral attitude towards us, rather we want to work on people until they have capitulated to us.*

In a subsequent meeting with radio officials, he stressed the need to achieve "a mobilization of mind and spirit in Germany". To that end he recruited talented, well-educated party loyalists to staff the new departments of his ministry: Budget and Administration; Propaganda; Radio; Press; Film; Theatre; and Popular Enlightenment.

To promote the Nazi *Weltanschauung* among the population, the state established a monopoly over all media, eliminated all materials hostile to the spirit of National Socialism ("alien elements"), and promoted a cult of the Führer to bind the people together. Methods used varied but, as Goebbels admitted, "I consider the radio to be the most modern and the most crucial instrument that exists for influencing the masses." His instruction to Nazi officials placed in charge of radio broadcasting to, "At all costs avoid being boring. I put that before everything…" illustrates his approach to spreading the Nazi message: that propaganda should be dynamic, like the movement itself, and use methods that were "modern, up to date, interesting, and appealing: interesting, instructive but not schoolmasterish".

Broadcasting and the press

Cheap radios – the *Volksempfänger* or "people's receiver" – were mass-produced, ensuring that the message of National Socialism was broadcast to the population. By late 1939 an estimated 70 per cent of German households possessed a radio that was deliberately manufactured with a limited range of reception to block foreign broadcasts. Such radios and loudspeakers were also installed on the factory floor, in public areas, and in bars and cafes. Goebbels established large-scale transmitters to broadcast propaganda to foreign states. By 1938 short-wave stations were transmitting in 12 languages to countries as far away as the USA, South Africa and the Far East.

Even during the Weimar period, radio was a state monopoly, which made it easy to establish control over the airwaves. It proved more difficult to implement a monopoly over the press, but the process of *Gleichschaltung* used to remove obstacles in the political and religious spheres was also used to "coordinate" Germany's press. Socialist and communist newspapers were banned early on in the regime (as were the parties themselves) and in 1934 the Reich Press Law imposed "racially clean" journalism. Jewish and liberal journalists were sacked and Jewish owners of newspapers such as the Ullstein publishing house were forced to sell out to the Eher Verlag, the official Nazi publishing house. While their ownership changed, Goebbels did allow existing newspapers to keep their names and layout – although daily directives from the Ministry dictated the line they had to follow.

At an early press conference delivered in March 1933, Goebbels made it clear what the role of the press in Nazi Germany would be:

> I see in the task of the press conference held here daily something other than what has been going on up to now. You will of course be receiving information here but also instructions. You are to know not only what is happening but also the Government's view of it and how you can convey that to the people most effectively. We want to have a press which cooperates with the Government just as the Government wants to cooperate with the press.

Reporters and editors had to prove their "racial and political loyalty". The Hitler state thus controlled "ownership, authorship and content of the newspapers", as Noakes and Pridham observed in their documentary analysis, *Propaganda and Indoctrination in Germany, 1933–9*.

Weltanschauung
A particular philosophy or view of life of an individual or group.

Propaganda and the deification of Hitler

The deification of Hitler in the media generally was a main plank of Nazi propaganda. His "infallibility" and "omniscience" were repeatedly alluded to in feature films, weekly newsreels shown in cinemas, over the airwaves, and in officially approved literature. Such "Führer worship" was also present in the annual "public rituals" introduced by the regime to mark significant dates in the development of the Hitler state: 30 January, to remember the appointment of Hitler as chancellor; 20 April to celebrate Hitler's birthday; 1 May, a "National Day of Labour"; September rallies in Nuremburg; and 9 November, to commemorate those who died in the 1923 Beerhall Putsch. These occasions reminded the people and the party faithful of Nazi tribulations and how they had been overcome under Hitler's leadership. Speechmaking, parades, and public shows of support were expected on these occasions. Failure to enter into the National Socialist spirit could be noted and reported.

Literature, music, and film

The Propaganda Ministry also influenced the fields of literature, music, and film. The task of propaganda was not only to promote Nazi ideology but also to attack and eliminate alternative views to the Nazi "world view". Writers not aligned to the ideals of the party were unable to publish or circulate their works after 1933, and driven into exile. An early indication of the treatment of what was considered "non-German" literature occurred on 10 May 1933 in Berlin where Goebbels presided over the burning of books considered poisonous to "the soul of the German people". The works included not only those of German writers, past and present, but foreign authors.

Department VII of Goebbels Ministry was entrusted with controlling the output of literature available to the population. Rigorous control over publishing houses, authors, bookshops and libraries ensured that only writing acceptable to the Nazi party was printed and available for public consumption. Writers were permitted to produce work and publish it (subject to scrutiny by Department VII) as long as it conformed to one of four main categories:

- *Fronterlebnis* (front experience), which emphasized German heroism in battle and the bonds established by the common experience

- works promoting the Nationalist Socialist *Weltanschauung*, as reflected in the outpourings of the Führer

- *Heimatroman* (regional novels stressing the uniqueness of the German spirit)

- *Rassenkunde* (ethnology), which stressed the superiority of the German/Aryan race over all others.

Above all, *Mein Kampf* was actively promoted as the model for German writing. Censorship was justified on the basis that the banned works were a threat to "National Socialist cultural aspirations" and too often reflected the increasing "Jewish cultural infiltration" of the Weimar era.

In music, the state lauded the works of Wagner (Hitler's favourite composer), but German orchestras were not allowed to play music by composers from a Jewish background (such as Mendelssohn). "Modern" experimental music works by composers such as Paul Hindemith were banned from public performance, being considered "degenerate" and atonal (not written in any key or mode) by Hitler. Like writers, musicians left for foreign states because of the restrictions placed on them.

Germany's film industry fell under the control of the Ministry of Propaganda and Public Enlightenment. Weimar's cinema was considered a stronghold of Jewish influence and purges of producers, actors, and film music composers of Jewish background took place soon after 1933. That same year the Nazi propaganda films *SA-Mann Brand*, *Hitlerjunge Quex*, and *Hans Westmar* were released, to celebrate the role of the SA, a murdered Nazi youth, and an SA martyr (Horst Wessel) killed by communists, respectively.

In 1935 Leni Riefenstahl produced her film documentary *Triumph of the Will*, based on the 1934 Nuremburg rally. Party rallies were meant to stress not only unity of the party but to build the cult of the Führer, which through the medium of film could be screened throughout the nation.

In 1938 Riefenstahl went on to produce *Olympia* based on the 1936 Berlin Olympic Games, once more a cinematographic celebration focused less on the competition and the competitors but on portraying the monolithic nature of the National Socialist state and its leader.

By the Second World War, films with an anti-Semitic bias were being produced (*The Rothschilds' Shares in Waterloo, The Jew Süss*) and wartime production was geared to sustaining morale – as was the case in the Allied nations. While an estimated 1363 feature films were produced during the regime, not all – or even the majority – were overtly propagandistic. Even Goebbels realized that the population required more than simply a film diet of Nazi ideology.

The theatre

Goebbels was in charge of supervising theatre productions, the result being the purging of actors and producers with Jewish and leftist sympathies. The flight of playwrights to foreign countries echoed the situation in the fields of literature, film, and music. Berthold Brecht fled first to Denmark and then to the USA, where his output included anti-Nazi works such as *The Resistible Rise of Arturo Ui*, parodying the process of the Nazi rise to power. In the Reich itself, theatre was controlled through the Reich Theatre Chamber under Hanns Johst, who sponsored propaganda pieces such as *Schlageter* – a play based on an early Nazi martyr killed in 1923 during the Franco-Belgian occupation of the Ruhr. While plays by Shakespeare and renowned German playwrights such as Goethe and Schiller were permitted, increasingly the theatre became a vehicle for performances that exalted the virtues of German nationalism, past and present, and the evils of communism and democracy.

Art

The Nazi state sought to eliminate the "Bolshevization" of art, which they claimed, had characterized the Weimar era – the *Judenrepublik* (the "Jewish Republic"). To combat what Hitler perceived as sickness and decadence in the arts, a Reich Chamber of Culture and a Chamber of Visual Arts were established. Artists had to join the latter and were vetted for their political reliability. Again, many artists unable to work in such conditions left the country (Klee, Kandinsky, Grosz, and Kokoschka, for example) as the government mounted exhibitions of "degenerate art" (*Entartete Kunst*) and sponsored exhibitions of art by approved artists.

Museums and galleries were subject to raids by Nazi officials to remove anything considered not in the spirit of National Socialism, the product of "Jewish decadence" or modern art forms such as expressionism or cubism, which Hitler disapproved of. The message of Nazi art in visual form was the projection of what Snyder referred to as paintings that "stressed heroism … rustic family scenes, Storm Troopers marching with their banners, and fruit harvesting by bare-bosomed Amazons", in other words art "purged of pretentiousness and crazy rubbish". Artists in the Third Reich – as in the USSR under Stalin – were seen as what Stalin referred to as "engineers of the soul" – tasked with spreading the messages of the regime.

Triumph of the Will

Piers Brendon described this film as "brilliant and repulsive" and one that "elevated propaganda into an art form". In it, according to Brendon, "Hitler descends from the clouds, his plane casting the shadow of a cross over marching stormtroopers" in a scene "heavy with messianic symbolism… [in which] Hitler tried to inspire the devotion of the people by presenting himself as the incarnation of their destiny".

The effects of propaganda

The constant information flow of adulation of the ideology and the leader at the same time as constant negative portrayals of alternatives through print, the screen, the stage, or through approved visual arts provide a heavy diet of indoctrination even among a well-educated population.

Estimates of how successful propaganda was in Germany are notoriously difficult to make with any accuracy. Those who already believed eagerly accepted. Those who did not learned not to question. A combination of repression, fear of denunciation, the constant barrage of party doctrine, *and* successes in economic and foreign policy meant that active opposition was exceedingly limited.

One of the most literate societies of the 20th century succumbed to the regime, partly as a product of "atomization" caused by a fear of being reported and punished and partly through a grudging acceptance that Germany's pride and economic fortunes were being restored under the Nazis. Nazi supporters already idolized the state and Hitler and those who were not Jews, card-carrying communists/socialists or dedicated outspoken democrats had little to fear as long as they conformed. Propaganda in its widest sense did not necessarily produce an atmosphere of consent among all Germans, although the mixture of force and indoctrination diminished the urge to participate in any popular dissent.

The impact of foreign policy

National Socialism's rise was largely a product of economic despair and its promises to solve Germany's economic problems. While appealing to many, its promises remained vague. Paul Johnson claimed that Hitler "had no economic policy. But he did have a very specific national policy", which was rearming Germany in preparation for possible conflict that might arise in the pursuit of expansionist goals (the *Wehrwirtschaft*, or "defence economy").

Hitler's foreign policy moves before 1939 – in conjunction with the policy of appeasement by Britain and France – allowed for the expansion of Germany and its re-emergence as a European great power 20 years after Versailles. The military campaigns of 1939–1941 resulted in impressive victories in Europe. It was not until the "crusade" against Bolshevism from June 1941 that National Socialist fortunes declined, following a massive underestimation of the Soviet Union's ability to absorb and then repel German armies over the next three to four years.

The destruction of National Socialism in 1945 was the consequence of foreign policy decisions made by Hitler. These decisions led to the formation of a hostile grand alliance that, in economic, demographic and military terms, the Third Reich and its Axis partners (principally Italy and Japan) could not defeat.

The Nazi regime's foreign policy, 1933–1939

In the Nazis' rise to power, foreign policy objectives were in some ways little different from those of other German nationalist politicians, principally in the desire to revise the "Diktat" of Versailles. Resentment against the post-war treaty was not exclusive to Hitler's party but what did differentiate the Nazis were the calls for a Greater Germany (the inclusion of all ethnic Germans in central Europe within the borders of an enlarged state) and the acquisition of **Lebensraum** in the east – the conquest of land and resources as the basis for German world power. Hitler's interpretation was based on gaining land in Poland and the USSR. Not only would this provide guaranteed material resources for the regime and its population, but war would also ensure the elimination of the Soviet state – also a mainstay of Hitler's foreign policy before and after 1933.

Fritz Fischer commented on the continuity of German foreign policy "directions", seeing Hitler in some respects as a continuer of trends observable in German foreign policy from the eras of Wilhelm II and Stresemann. Pre-Weimar Germany's plans for German economic and political dominance (hegemony) were seen in the idea of a "Mitteleuropa" as described by Chancellor Bethmann-Hollweg after the outbreak of the First World War. This would entail the reduction of French and Russian power, annexing parts of eastern Europe, and establishing spheres of influence over territory such as the Ukraine, valued especially for its fertile land.

While Stresemann achieved great respect internationally for his diplomatic achievements in the interests of peace in Europe, he too was pursuing a foreign policy geared to winning concessions and preparing the ground for the revision of Versailles – but in a peaceful manner. He stated in a private letter to the former Crown Prince in September 1925:

> *In my opinion there are three great tasks that confront German foreign policy in the more immediate future… the solution of the reparations question, the protection of Germans abroad, those ten to twelve millions of our kindred who now live under a foreign yoke in foreign lands, the readjustment of our eastern frontiers; the recovery of Danzig, the Polish corridor, and a correction of the frontier in Upper Silesia.*

As he stressed, though, in relation to the use of military force to achieve these goals, "That, alas, we do not possess". Hence a case can be made that Hitler was *in some ways* pursuing goals that had been present under previous government systems – but in a far more ambitious and brutal manner.

In a speech to the Reichstag on 28 April 1939, Hitler declared:

> *I have further tried to liquidate that Treaty sheet by sheet, whose 448 Articles contain the vilest rape that nations and human beings have ever been expected to submit to. I have restored to the Reich the provinces grabbed from us in 1919; I have led millions of deeply unhappy Germans, who have been snatched away from us, back into the Fatherland; I have restored the thousand-year-old historical unity of German living space; and I have attempted to accomplish all that without shedding blood and without inflicting the sufferings of war on my people or any other. I have accomplished all this, as one who 21 years ago was still an unknown worker and soldier of my people, by my own efforts…*

Lebensraum

"Living space": the idea that Germany needed more land in order to survive. A concept used even before the First World War, when it had been used basically in reference to colonial ambitions, *Lebensraum* became an important element of Nazi ideology and foreign policy.

ATL **Research and thinking skills**

1 Why did the regime adopt its foreign policy aims: for example, to overturn grievances caused by perceived injustices inflicted upon the state; to bolster the prestige of the regime by appealing to nationalistic instincts; to distract the attention of the population from a failing or lacklustre domestic programme?

2 With specific reference to actions, discuss in what ways, and with what success, foreign policy objectives were achieved in the short and longer term.

3 In both cases, was there any evidence to suggest that the regime's foreign policy was a continuation of the policy of previous governments, or did it exhibit a contrast – in aims and methods?

Willi Brandt (1913–1992)

The future chancellor (SPD) of the Federal Republic of Germany (1969–1974), Brandt was at this time a member of the Socialist Workers' Party, having left the SPD in 1931. He rejoined the SPD in 1948.

Thinking and communication skills

Discuss the following questions:

1 Were German foreign policy moves in the period 1933–1935:

   a) reckless, and a threat to general European peace?

   OR

   b) shrewdly planned, cautious moves largely acceptable to other European great powers, which were either consumed by their own internal problems or a feeling of **meaculpism**?

2 What factors during the above period prevented Hitler's pursuit of a forceful expansionist Nazi foreign policy?

3 What factors explain the adoption of a significantly more adventurous foreign policy after 1935/36?

meaculpism

A feeling of guilt or responsibility for past actions provoking German nationalism and bitterness due to the "unjust suffering" inflicted on Germany in 1919 at Versailles

Research and thinking skills

With reference to the origin and purpose of SOPADE reports, assess the values and limitations of such reports for historians studying the effect of Hitler's foreign policy moves up to 1939.

As early as March 1935, when the Nazi government announced military conscription in defiance of the restrictions of the Treaty of Versailles, a SOPADE report stated:

> *Enormous enthusiasm on 17 March. All of Munich was out on the streets. You can force a people to sing, but you can't force them to sing with that kind of enthusiasm … The trust in Hitler's political talent and honest will is becoming greater, as Hitler has increasingly gained ground among the people. He is loved by many.*

As Kershaw points out:

> *The bold moves in foreign policy that Hitler undertook to overthrow the shackles of Versailles and reassert Germany's national strength and prestige were, therefore, guaranteed massive popular support as long as they could be accomplished without bloodshed.*

Between 1933 and the outbreak of war in Europe in 1939, Nazi foreign policy successes in righting the wrongs of 1919 ensured that, when war did occur, the population accepted the conflict with resignation, if not widespread fervour. A successful revisionist attack on the "Diktat", allied to domestic policies linked to economic recovery and full employment, meant that most Germans not targeted as enemies of the state (and punished accordingly) gave their support to the regime in the war effort – not because of belief in Hitler's racist or anti-Semitic beliefs but because he had restored German pride. The manufactured cult of the Führer, became even stronger as the state monopoly of the media worked ceaselessly to promote adulation of the "leader" and his role in the national salvation of Germany. Again, as Kershaw indicated:

> *On a clandestine visit to Germany from his Norwegian exile in the second half of 1936, Willi Brandt, no less, admitted much the same: that providing work had won the regime support even among those who had once voted for the Left.*

From 1936 to early 1939, with the growth of German military power and in conjunction with the reluctance of great powers to physically resist breaches of the Treaty of Versailles, German foreign policy gains were impressive – and popular. A SOPADE report on Hitler's uncontested remilitarization of the Rhineland remarked upon the "universally impressive" response of the German population and the fact that many were "convinced that Germany's foreign policy demands are justified and cannot be passed over. The last few days have been marked by big fresh advances in the Führer's personal reputation, including among the workers".

Similarly, the union with Austria in March 1938 was noted in another SOPADE report as having produced "enormous personal gains in credibility and prestige" for Hitler and the regime. Any doubts among the majority of Germans about the wisdom of challenging the Versailles settlement and the potential risks involved had evaporated as the "wrongs" of 1919 were corrected.

Territorial acquisition and successful revision of the humiliations imposed upon Germany produced, as Kershaw noted, an image of Hitler and the National Socialist state as "a defender of German rights"

and Hitler as an accomplished statesman who had achieved "triumphs without bloodshed". By 1938 he had presided over:

- the restoration of the rich industrial Saarland to Germany (although this was really the result of a League-supervised plebiscite of the population and in keeping with the Versailles Treaty)

- the restoration of military sovereignty

- the recovery of the Rhineland

- Anschluss with Austria and the incorporation of the Sudetenland into the Reich, in partial fulfilment of the goal of building a "Greater Germany".

The result, according to Kershaw, was the winning by the regime of "support in all sections of the German people and unparalleled popularity, prestige and acclaim".

Whether the gains of the regime's foreign policy before the Second World War were the product of a carefully planned and executed blueprint or the result of a series of pragmatic and opportunistic moves (the intentionalist versus structuralist/functionalist debate) is less relevant than the fact that successes in foreign policy generated support for the National Socialist state. Edgar Feuchtwanger stressed that, "While living in Germany, I became aware that Hitler's apparently sensationally effective coups in foreign policy were fundamental to his hold on the German people".

The Nazi regime's foreign policy, 1939–1945

Feuchtwanger, who with his family went into exile in Britain in 1938, pointed out the problem associated with Hitler's "success": that Hitler, as a "high-risk gambler" with no interest in listening to advice, was liable to falter eventually since he became "a prisoner of his own myth and imagined infallibility". The errors in foreign policy made from March 1939 ultimately led to the breaking of "the chain of success". Despite Germany's military victories, the decisions made by Hitler meant that, after 1941–1942, overextension of German forces and lack of resources in comparison to the grand alliance – between Moscow, Washington, and a previously isolated London – would ensure Allied victory. The formation of this grand alliance did not occur until late 1941, after Hitler's June invasion of the USSR (Operation Barbarossa) and declaration of war on the United States after Japan's attack on Pearl Harbor.

Significantly, just as foreign policy success had gained the regime popular backing, foreign policy failure was to provoke not only stirrings of internal opposition but overwhelming external opposition, which would destroy the Reich.

Hitler's domestic policies, 1933–1945

Having gained power, the Nazis were expected to produce solutions to economic ills that they had blamed the previous system for neglecting or incompetently addressing. Of the pressing economic problems, unemployment was by far the most prominent.

Employment

When Hitler came to office as chancellor, unemployment stood at around 6 million; by 1939 Germany was experiencing a labour shortage. Impressive as this sounds, it is important to note that economic recovery was already evident by late 1932. In addition, much of the reduction in unemployment was linked to the establishment of an economy based on production for possible war after 1936 (and the Four-Year Plan); and employment statistics were manipulated by a series of measures that removed large sections of the population from unemployment tables.

Victims of purges of the civil service did not count as jobless. Disincentives for married women to remain in employment, plus the offering of incentives for single women to give up employment in order to qualify for marriage loans, were followed by the introduction of a labour service for young, unemployed men and compulsory military conscription by 1935. Technically these measures removed large numbers from official statistics.

This "massaging" of unemployment figures did not detract from the fact that job opportunities arose from various government-inspired public works projects and placements in heavy industry as Germany announced its intention to breach the arms restrictions of Versailles by 1935. In pursuit of a policy of economic self-sufficiency, in defiance of the "Diktat" and to honour previous promises of *"Arbeit und Brot"* ("Work and bread"), National Socialism embarked on job creation programmes to help rebuild the economy.

Economic recovery

Hitler viewed economic reconstruction as vital for future expansionist plans. The lessons of the Allied Blockade of the First World War, which had crippled Germany's war effort and contributed hugely to defeat, showed the necessity for building an economy that would avoid dependence on other states. He was also aware that economic crisis had destabilized the Weimar Republic and given opponents (such as the Nazis themselves) a chance to capitalize on the failure to relieve the misery of the depression years. Maintaining power meant finding rapid solutions to immediate problems.

Historians have tended to see the measures adopted by National Socialism as a series of ad hoc programmes rather than a well-thought-out blueprint of economic planning. Big business and private enterprise were entrusted with carrying out the general aims of German economic recovery under guidance from the regime. Hitler declared that the job of the Ministry of Economics was "to present the tasks of the national economy" which "the private economy will have to fulfil". Government contracts placed with German companies ensured a partnership between the regime and industry – with the senior partner in this relationship being the government. Under National Socialism, German industry thrived in a period of enforced political "stability", a trade-union-free environment with lucrative government orders that provided profits for business.

Under Hjalmar Schacht (as president of the Reichsbank, from March 1933, and then as Minister of Economics, 1934–1937), priorities were set to deal with the unemployed and then to plan the financing of rearmament. Both issues were partly linked, in that public works programmes such as railway and *Autobahn* (motorway) construction would provide the communications infrastructure necessary for war. It was no coincidence that the majority of motorways ran east-west, although, as Burleigh pointed out, "Actually the military preferred trains and thought tracked vehicles would rip up the road surface and fracture bridges, whose load-bearing tolerances were only ascertained in spring 1939". Nevertheless, as a highly visible prestige project, similar to fascist Italy's *autostrada*, it did capture the imagination of many German and foreign observers, as well as providing work.

Schacht's "New Plan" witnessed the use of "Mefo" bills to prime heavy industry and production of armaments. These bills (a form of government-sponsored promissory note issued via a dummy company) were a way of the Reichsbank covertly financing arms production. The bills acted as a new form of currency as well as a way of hiding the involvement of the government in promoting arms production, at a time when Germany was still not strong enough to publicly challenge the arms restrictions of Versailles.

Public works projects

Labour-intensive public works projects, for building houses, schools, hospitals, canals, bridges and railways, and the motorway scheme, offered employment and a sense of purpose to many Germans. For the regime, the establishment of the *Reichsarbeitdienst* (RAD: State Labour Service) meant that cheap and regimented labour could be used to promote German recovery. At first voluntary, service in the RAD became compulsory in 1935 for all Germans aged between 19 and 25. Labour battalions and work camps ensured authoritarian control over the recruits, who worked mainly on the land but also on building projects and were subject to Party political indoctrination in the camps. William Shirer, attending the 1934 Nuremberg Party Rally, described how 50 000 members of the RAD, "a highly trained, semi-military group of fanatical Nazi youths… Standing in the early morning sunlight which sparkled on their shiny spades suddenly made the German spectators go mad with joy when, without warning, they broke into a perfect goose-step." It was the government's expectation that the spirit of these 1934 volunteers would be adopted after the service became compulsory in 1935.

Göring's Four-Year Plan

In October 1936, under Göring's leadership, a "Four-Year Plan" was introduced. The plan heralded a major expansion in war-related industrial production. Hitler proclaimed that "there is only one interest, the interest of the nation; only one view, the bringing of Germany to the point of political and economic self-sufficiency". He declared his intention that, within four years, two main tasks had to be achieved: that Germany's armed forces were operational and that the economy "must be fit for war within four years".

Under Göring the projected goals of the plan were not reached, although in specific areas such as aluminium production, explosives, coal, and mineral oil the increases were impressive. Richard Overy claimed that the failure to produce a strong war economy capable of withstanding any long-term conflict helped shape the *Blitzkrieg* military tactics of 1939 onwards, which relied on quick victories in the hope of gaining much-needed resources before committing to subsequent campaigns, rather than a war of attrition for which Germany was unprepared. Noakes and Pridham estimate that by 1939 Germany was still reliant on external sources for around one-third of its raw materials. An exiled Social Democrat observer in 1938 argued that "Under the lash of the dictatorship the level of economic activity has been greatly increased" but that a fundamental problem arose:

> One cannot simultaneously … increase armaments for the land and air forces ad infinitum, to build up a massive battle fleet, to fortify new extended borders, to build gigantic installations for the production of ersatz [substitute] materials, to construct megalomaniacal grandiose buildings, and to tear down large parts of cities in order to build them somewhere else. On the basis of the living standards of the German people hitherto, one can either do one or the other or a little bit of everything, but not everything at the same time and in unlimited dimensions.

The revival of the economy in the field of war production took place at the expense of consumer goods production. Real wages (actual purchasing power) of German workers were less impressive than the statistics the regime publicized concerning Germany's production of pig iron, steel, machinery, chemicals, and other commodities for rearmament purposes. Shortages of consumer products and wages frozen at 1933 levels, however, were compensated for by the fact that there was employment – in comparison with the dark days of the depression years. David Crew summed up the attitude of many workers when he cited the opinion of a socialist worker in the heavily industrialized Ruhr area who commented,

> They [the worker] had four, five, even six years of unemployment behind them – they would have hired on with Satan himself.

Cultural and social policies

Stripped of trade unions with which to engage in collective bargaining for wages and working conditions and forbidden to strike, German workers were provided by the government with the alternative of organizations such as the "Strength through Joy" movement under the supervision of the German Labour Front (*Deutsche Arbeitsfront*/DAF), which the Nazis introduced after the prohibition of independent trade unions in 1933. Harmony in the workplace was meant to produce social peace and increased production in the national interest.

In 1949 in the Federal Republic of Germany, a survey conducted by the Institute für Demoskopie (Public Opinion Institute) entitled "Consequences of National Socialism" reported many of the respondents looked back on the Nazi regime with some fondness in relation to the social and economic provisions it offered, claiming:

> *The guaranteed pay packet, order, KdF and the smooth running of the political machinery… Thus National Socialism makes them think merely of work, adequate nourishment… and the absence of disarray in political life.*

Nazi terror and the destruction produced by Hitler's foreign policy, while obviously acknowledged, formed only a subsidiary part of the reminiscences of those polled. Loss of personal freedom under the regime was compensated for by perceived material benefits that were enjoyed in comparison to the last years of Weimar.

For Schoenbaum, this type of selective appraisal of the National Socialist state by those who lived through it (and who were not targeted) was an example of "interpreted social reality" as opposed to the grimness of "objective social reality" – a process in which the era of National Socialism was remembered as:

> *… a society united like no other in recent German history, a society of opportunities for young and old, classes and masses, a society that was New Deal and good old days at the same time … a world of … authoritarian paternalism … of national purpose and achievement …*

The Nazi wartime economy

The performance of the Nazi economy during the war years was bound up with the question of the extent to which Hitler's Germany could be considered a "polycratic state" – whether it was a centralized, efficient, monolithic 'Führer state' or whether it contained a bewildering variety of overlapping authorities – what Geary refers to as "personal fiefdoms" which interfered with the smooth running of not only political decision-making but, in this context, the organization of the wartime economy.

Whether Nazi policies arose from **intentionalism** or **structuralism**, there was a high degree of overlap within the regime structure which blurred clear lines of authority in specific areas and led to Nazi officials implementing fragmented policies as they interpreted what they believed was the Führer's will. Gauleiters of the occupied states acted without central coordination and pursued policies, both political and economic, which were not harnessed effectively to promote the war effort.

The Strength through Joy (*Kraft durch Freude*/KdF) movement

The DAF established the KdF to offer incentives to the working population in the form of leisure facilities at heavily subsidized rates, under the watchful eye of the Nazi state. On the surface a recreational organization meant to raise worker morale and production levels, the KdF offered a wide variety of activities, such as theatre visits, sports, hiking, folk dancing, excursions by train to foreign countries, and even cruises on purpose-built ocean liners. Such "carrots" would, according to Robert Ley, head of the DAF, allow the worker to "lose the last traces of inferiority feelings he may have inherited from the past" and fulfil the plan not only to boost output but also contribute towards the sense of solidarity required in the new *Volksgemeinschaft*.

intentionalists
Historians who argue that Hitler encouraged deliberate chaos in the National Socialist state in order to create competing power centres that would allow him to be the final arbiter.

structuralists
People who stress the nature of the development of the NSDAP that moved rapidly from an opposition party to the party of administration in 1933–1934.

Nazi failure to establish a central wartime administration from the outset hampered successful mobilization of the nation's resources and war effort. Competing authorities, as Overy pointed out, hampered efficiency – for example, Fritz Todt as Minister of Munitions (1940–1942) had no control over the production of aircraft "which constituted two-fifths of all war production" – and this remained the case until 1944. The army was unwilling to sacrifice the production of "vanguard technologies" (high-quality weapons that were expensive in terms of labour costs and materials) for the large-scale production of standardized weaponry adopted by the USA and the USSR.

While great strides in rearmament had been made by 1939, the goals of the Four-Year Plan were not attained and the series of *Blitzkrieg* successes in 1939–1941 masked the fact that a long, drawn-out war would be difficult for Germany to sustain after the expansion of the conflict in the Soviet Union. The "New Order" that Hitler sought in Europe through military conquest was partly a political move but also an attempt to ensure Germany's economic future through ruthless exploitation of the resources of the occupied territories. Hitler's forces arrived not as liberators of the people of the USSR, for example, but as conquerors whose intention was to subjugate the population. Racial war in Eastern Europe produced resistance and an expansion of the conflict that the Reich was unable to deal with. Expansion of Germany's war effort to the Balkans, North Africa, and the Soviet Union, combined with the decision to declare war on the USA, resulted in the emergence of a united military and economic opposition that far outweighed Germany's resources.

Gordon Wright argued that the Nazis could, in the occupied territories of eastern and western Europe, have chosen to collaborate with the conquered people but, instead, their "simpler" policy of smash and grab alienated the occupied populations and led to failure to benefit from the vast resources of a militarily underestimated Soviet state. The scorched earth policy of the Soviets, which denied resources to the Nazis, and the inability to replenish the loss of military material to meet the increasing demands of an ever-broadening conflict all worked to hinder the war effort.

By 1942, Todt had informed Hitler that the result of expansion of the war against the USA rendered victory impossible. His death in February 1942 saw his replacement by Albert Speer. While Speer was credited with significantly improving the efficiency of arms production (three times more weaponry was produced in 1944 than in 1941), in combination with a massive programme of labour conscription from occupied states (headed by Fritz Sauckel), the massive Allied bombing raids on Germany by 1944 and the advance of the Red Army meant that Germany, lacking "the resources of geopolitical supremacy" faced military defeat.

Youth and education policies

By necessity, the "Thousand Year Reich" envisaged by Hitler required future generations committed to the world view of the Nazi movement. Youth was to act as the standard bearer of the NSDAP vision of the future.

The conditioning of youth in school and through extracurricular activities and organizations was a regime priority. In November 1933 Hitler stated:

> ...when an opponent says, "I will not come over to your side", I calmly say, "Your child belongs to us already... You will pass on. Your descendants however, now stand in the new camp. In a short time they will know nothing but this new community."

In November 1933 this was certainly an exaggeration of the extent to which German youth had been indoctrinated, but the Nazi state made strenuous efforts to make the claim a reality in the following years.

The education system

Just as *Gleichschaltung* had been implemented in political and religious life, the Nazis sought to Nazify the school system. In April 1934 Bernhard Rust was appointed Reich Minister for Science, Education and Culture and tasked with establishing the educational system as a bulwark of the Nazi state, then and for the future.

Schools and universities were cleansed of teachers held to be unsympathetic to the aims of National Socialism or considered, because of their Jewish background, unfit to be in charge of the instruction of Aryan youth. Membership of the National Socialist Teachers' League (NSLB or *NS Lehrerbund*) became essential for teachers wishing to work in education. The intention was to ensure conformity in the presentation of the Nazi message to youth, by ensuring that those working in schools were subject to party control. From primary through to tertiary education, indoctrination of the young was undertaken in order to produce end products imbued with the race consciousness of the movement and absolute loyalty to the regime. In schools, curriculum changes placed emphasis on sports, biology, history, and "Germanics".

Sport was meant to produce, according to Hitler, "bodies which are healthy to the core" and capable of physical contribution to the nation – whether in the field of reproduction or military service. The teaching of history was used to promote the greatness of Germany's past, the struggles of the National Socialist movement in its efforts to destroy the "evil legacy" of a degenerate and incompetent Weimar republic, and the dangers of Bolshevism (and its "Jewish backers"). In 1938 the German Central Institute of Education stressed that:

> The German nation, in its essence and greatness, in its fateful struggle for internal and external identity, is the subject of the teaching of history... (it) has the task of educating young people to respect the great German past and to have faith in the mission and future of their own nation...

Interestingly, as Noakes and Pridham pointed out, even in Weimar, Germany history teaching had been much influenced by a "nationalist bias", largely a reflection of the fact that teachers had themselves "passed through a school and university system dominated by the *völkisch* nationalist ethos" of the pre-Weimar era. In this sense, National Socialist guidelines on the teaching of history supplemented (albeit to greater extremes) existing approaches to teaching in many institutions.

Biology teaching included heavy emphasis on race and eugenics (the science of improving a population through controlled breeding), inculcating the need for racial purity in the Reich by adhering to "principles" of "natural selection" and elimination of "inferiors" whose existence threatened the Aryan bloodline. Hermann Gauch's *New Foundations of Racial Science* (1934) typified the manner in which pseudo-biological teaching, masquerading as fact, was delivered in the guise of "race science". Replete with comments about the "unmanliness and barbarous feelings" of the non-Nordic, the dangers of the admixture of races, the lack of hygiene of non-Nordics and the failure of such non-Nordics to clearly enunciate ("The various sounds flow into each other and tend to resemble the sounds of animals, such as barking, snoring, sniffling, and squealing"), this widely used text went on to claim that:

> *The Nordic and the non-Nordic races have not a single characteristic in common. We are not justified, therefore, in speaking of a "human race". Nordic man is ... the creator of all culture and civilization. The salvation and preservation of the Nordic man alone will save and preserve culture and civilization...*

Similarly, "Germanics" included the study of language and literature with the aim of proving the superiority of Germans as a "culture-producing" race as opposed to "culture-destroying" races such as Jews. What this meant was the rejection of any works considered hostile in spirit, or message, to National Socialist ideology and the promotion of works glorifying nationalism, militarism, sacrifice for the Nazi cause and devotion to Adolf Hitler, the Übervater (Supreme Father).

The regime made special provision for the education of future leaders. *Adolf-Hitler-Schulen* reinforced the values of physical exercise, race purity and obedience to the Führer in selected cadets. The *Nationalpolitische Erziehungsanstalten* (the Napolas, or National Political Training Institutes) focused on military discipline and duty to the leader, the party, and the nation, while the *Ordensburgen* (Order Castles) were reserved for the future ruling elite who undertook a four-year course studying racial science, athletics, and political and military instruction and indoctrination. Many students in this last category were selected from the already selective Adolf Hitler schools and Napolas, which chose potential recruits from Hitler Youth following a check on their racial background and Aryan appearance.

Youth groups

Outside the formal institutions of education, the regime attempted to encourage conformity and apply techniques of indoctrination by establishing youth groups. Schools themselves were not considered capable of creating Hitler's declared goal for German youth, as enunciated in late 1938 – a German youth "slim and slender, swift as the greyhound, tough as leather, and hard as Krupp steel ... a new type of man so that our people is not ruined by the symptoms of degeneracy of our day". Absent from the description was any reference to intellectualism or academic excellence. Such qualities were not prioritized by a regime whose leadership was deeply suspicious of academic achievement. "I will have no intellectual training. Knowledge is ruin to my young men", asserted Hitler, who equated such intellectualism with the cultural decadence which he claimed intellectuals had inflicted on Germany in the Weimar years.

Youth movements with affiliations to Churches or political movements were exceedingly popular in Germany before 1933 and the Nazi youth organization formed in the early 1920s was only one, relatively small part, of this youth movement, accounting for approximately 50–55 000 members by the time Hitler became chancellor. That same year (1933), Hitler set up two organizations to educate Germany's young in the spirit of National Socialism: the Hitlerjugend (HJ/Hitler Youth) for boys and the *Bund Deutscher Mädel* (BDM/League of German Maidens) for girls. Accompanying their establishment was the banning of existing youth movements (aside from Catholic youth organizations, whose autonomy was guaranteed by the Concordat Hitler had signed with the Catholic Church) and the absorption of many of their members into the Nazi movement.

By 1935 the Nazi youth movement accounted for approximately 60 per cent of young Germans and on 1 December 1936 all young Germans were expected to join. Schoolteachers were instructed to promote membership of the organization. Originally the HJ and BDM catered for the age range 14–18 but efforts were made to expand the movements for 10–14-year-old girls and boys (the *Deutsches Jungvolk*/DJ and *Jungmädelbund*/JM respectively). In March 1939 membership became compulsory. As Knopp declared, "Never before in German history had the young been so courted … seduced by the feeling of being something special". Membership gave access to a variety of activities: for boys, camping and hiking expeditions, sport, music, attendance at rallies, and military training provided via specialized air and naval sections; for girls, physical fitness and domestic science in preparation for marriage and childbearing. A SOPADE report of 1934 lamented that, early in the regime, "Youth is … in favour of the system: the novelty, the drill, the uniform, the camp life, the fact that school and the parental home take a back seat compared to the community of young people – all that is marvellous".

Increasingly, as the spare time between school and attendance at HJ/BDM meetings and activities diminished, parents became reduced to a "bed and breakfast service" and parental control over offspring weakened in many cases, as parents found that their children became "strangers, contemptuous of … religion, and perpetually barking and shouting like pint-sized Prussian sergeant-majors".

The NSDAP sought to monopolize the life of the young, to wean them from parental to party control in order to maximize the opportunities for indoctrination. Retrospective accounts by members of youth organizations vary widely in the nature of their reminiscences – some looking back fondly to the comradeship experienced in the youth movements, others highly critical. Not all youth were seduced by or willing to join the movement, despite the regime's regulations, but the great majority of young Germans were recruited into youth organizations that in theory promised to:

- liberate them from the "evils" of democracy, Marxism and the supposed stranglehold of the Jews

- restore German pride and honour

- revise the Diktat of 1919.

However, in reality, they were imprisoned in a huge bureaucratic organization that stultified creative thought, producing a generation of what, according to Sax and Kuntz, "were duller and stupider, though healthier, individuals".

The impact of policies on women

Hitler's view of the role of women in the Nazi state is often referred to as the attempt to subjugate women – to limit their participation in German life to "*Kinder, Küche, Kirche*" (Children, Kitchen, Church). In 1934 at the annual Nuremberg rally, he declared: "Man and woman must ... mutually value and respect each other when they see that each performs the task which Nature and Providence have ordained". The intention was not to make women into second-class citizens, but to rescue them from "the false paths of the democratic-liberal-international women's movement" of the Weimar era, which had "denigrated" and attempted to destroy the dignity and honour of women through moral corruption. For the regime, although the "world of a woman is a smaller world ... her husband, her family, her children, and her house", it complemented the man's world, which consisted of "the state, his struggle, his readiness to devote his powers to the service of the community". The relationship between male and female, according to public speeches, was that of a partnership in the service of the nation.

Cleansed of the immorality that Nazis argued pervaded the Weimar years, Hitler claimed that his task was to renew the traditional role of women as mothers, the basis of the family unit and the bearer of children who would ensure the "national future" in an age of declining birth rates. Indeed, Germany's birth rate was, with the exception of Austria, the lowest in Europe. For an ideology committed to expansion and anxious at the prospect of being "swamped by fecund hordes of Slavs from the East", in Noakes's words, the necessity of reversing the decline in the birth rate was obvious. As Burleigh noted, in the Nazi state:

> *Out went Weimar tolerance of a plurality of lifestyles, in which no official stigmas [were] attached to being single, childless or homosexual, and in came state-driven pro-natalist policies designed to produce "child-rich"... families.*

Anti-feminism, in the sense of rejection of liberties for females (including, for example, legal abortion and easy access to contraception) enshrined in the Weimar Constitution, was not peculiar to the Nazis. It was shared by traditionalists, the Churches and the DNVP before 1933. Hitler capitalized on the misgivings of such groups, with his plans to implement what critics have claimed to be a reactionary policy based on male supremacy, despite Nazi claims to the contrary.

Pro-natalist policies

Pro-natalist policies (policies to encourage growth in the birth rate) were pursued through a mixture of incentives and disincentives. As an incentive, monetary rewards were offered in the form of low-interest loans, introduced in June 1933 as Section 5 of the Law for the Reduction of Unemployment. Married couples would receive a marriage loan of 1000 Reichsmarks, to be repaid at 1 per cent per month, with the amount to be repaid reduced by a quarter for every child produced (provided it was a racially pure child). A condition of the loan was that the woman had to give up employment – leaving positions open for males. An estimated 700 000 couples received such a loan between 1933 and 1937 (a third of all marriages). By 1939, 42 per cent of all marriages received such loans. Marriage rates increased from 516 800 in 1932 (the pre-Nazi period) to 740 200 by 1934, although the birth rate did not increase significantly. Burleigh noted:

> Although there was an appreciable short-lived increase in the birth of third or fourth children, the absence of a commensurate public housing policy did little to affect the secular drift towards modest nuclear families, with SS members especially distinguished by their failure to go forth and multiply.

As commentators pointed out, couples preferred to have one or two children, since the expense of having more "would outweigh the advantage of the cancellation of the remainder of the loan".

Further incentives included income-tax reductions for married couples with children (and higher rates of taxation for single people or married couples without children), family allowance (child support) payments, maternity benefits, reduced school fees and railway fares for larger families and the provision of facilities such as birth clinics, advice centres, home help provision, postnatal recuperation homes, and courses on household management, childrearing, and motherhood. As Emilie Müller-Zadow, an official in the National Socialist Women's Organization, wrote in her article "Mothers who give us the future" in 1936:

> There is a growing recognition that mothers carry the destiny of their people in their hands and that success or ruin of the nation depends on their attitude towards the vocation of motherhood … The place that Adolf Hitler assigns to woman in the Third Reich corresponds to her natural and divine destiny. Limits are being set for her, which earlier she had frequently violated in a barren desire to adopt masculine traits … due respect is now being offered to her vocation as mother of the people, in which she can and should develop her rich emotions and spiritual strengths according to eternal laws.

In May 1939 the regime introduced the "Mother's Cross" award: gold for women who had given birth to eight children, silver for six and bronze for four – as long as parent and children were of Aryan blood, free from congenital disease, politically reliable and not classed as "**asocial**" in their attitudes or behaviour by the Party. The programme was reminiscent of that implemented by the French Superior Council for Natality since 1920.

Disincentives, in the sense of denying women control over their own bodies in terms of reproduction, took the form of the illegalization of abortion and the closing down of birth control centres and access to contraceptive devices. Breaches of these regulations resulted in convictions.

Women in the workplace and the public sphere

Laws initially restricted the number of females in higher education and employment in the civil service after the age of 35. Nazi pronouncements and propaganda aimed at discouraging females in the workplace were made partly to fulfil Nazi ideological goals concerning the return to the "idyllic destiny" of women and partly to make jobs available for unemployed males. By 1937, though, the appearan...

▲ A recipient of the Mother's Cross, Berlin 1942. Note the older children in the uniform of the Hitlerjugend and the BDM.

asocial
Anyone regarded by the regime as outside the "national community": habitual criminals, tramps and beggars with no fixed abode, alcoholics, prostitutes, homosexuals, and juvenile delinquents, as well as the "workshy" (those unwilling to commit themselves to labour in the service of the Reich) and religious groups that refused to accept Nazi doctrine.

labour shortages in the economy as rearmament programmes aided rapid recovery, meant that the regime compromised its ideological stance and accepted the necessity of female employment. As Geary observed:

> … *ideological purity still had to give some ground to economic necessity: in 1933 almost 5 million women were in paid employment outside the home, whereas the figure had risen to 7.14 million by 1939.*

The earlier requirement for wives in families who qualified for marriage loans to give up work was dropped. Similarly, women's access to higher education, restricted in 1933, was now permitted because the economy and the regime required increasing numbers of professionals, in the medical and teaching professions especially. Until the end of the regime, however, Hitler continued to insist women be excluded from participation in the judiciary or in jury service, since he believed them unable to "think logically or reason objectively, since they are ruled only by emotion". While National Socialist attitudes did not change in relation to the role and status of women, there was pragmatic acceptance, given the economic demands of the later 1930s and the Second World War, that female labour was essential.

Women's role in the political system was secondary. Although the Party established organizations to promote Nazi-approved values among the female population, such as the German Women's Enterprise (DFW), National Socialist Womanhood (NSF) and the Reich Mothers' Service (RMD), their role was to funnel the decisions and policies of the male-dominated regime rather than to actively help in the formation and articulation of such policies. As Koonz commented:

> *For women, belonging to the "master race" opened the option of collaboration in the very Nazi state that exploited them, that denied them access to political status, deprived them of birth control, underpaid them as wage workers, indoctrinated their children, and finally took their sons and husbands to the front.*

The impact of policies on minorities

For Nazis, asocials were those who did not conform to desired social norms as defined by the regime. As Noakes indicated in his essay "Social Outcasts in the Third Reich", the term asocial was a flexible one used by the government to label those it felt were undeserving of inclusion in the *Volksgemeinschaft*. These asocial groups were classified as *Gemeinschaftsfremde* – "community aliens"– those who in the eyes of the state exhibited "an unusual degree of deficiency of mind or character" according to a draft "Community Alien Law" presented in 1940. According to the state, the primary aim of this legislation was to "protect" the racially healthy community from such elements.

·gars and the homeless

·ts of the regime, these groups were rounded up from
·3. Classified into "orderly" and "disorderly" categories by
·re registered and issued with permits that required
·ulsory work on the state's orders in exchange
·d. Fixed routes were introduced so that their
· In the case of the homeless, detention in

camps such as Dachau and sterilization were imposed on many. By 1938, fearful that "he (the homeless) is in danger of becoming a freedom fanatic who rejects all integration as hated compulsion" (and thus an irritant to a state which stressed community integration), beggars and homeless people were arrested and many were detained in Buchenwald. An estimated 10 000 of the homeless were imprisoned, of whom few survived.

Homosexuals

Homosexuals were persecuted in a move coordinated by the Reich Central Office for the Combat of Homosexuality and Abortion. The linking of these two areas under one department illustrated the view that the treatment of both was a product of "population policy and national health" as much as any National Socialist homophobic prejudice.

Paragraph 175 of the Reich Criminal Code, which made "indecent activity" between adult males illegal, predated both the Weimar government and the Nazi regime. The moral condemnation of homosexuality (and abortion) by many conservative elements in German society was not a creation of the Nazis but, under the regime, homosexuals suffered penalties much more brutal than those previously imposed. Paragraph 175 was revised in 1935 by the regime with the intention of broadening the definition of "indecent activities" as well as increasing terms of imprisonment for "offenders".

In February 1937, Himmler, the SS chief, in a speech to SS officers, explained his reasoning behind Nazi policy towards homosexuals:

> There are those homosexuals who take the view: what I do is my business, a purely private matter. However, all things which take place in the sexual sphere are not the private affair of the individual, but signify the life and death of the nation, signify world power ... A people with many children has the candidature for world power and world domination. A people of good race which has too few children has a one-way ticket to the grave ...

Identification and registration of homosexuals by the Gestapo produced records of approximately 100 000 "criminals" by 1939. Of these, according to Hans-Georg Stümke, a third were investigated and every fourth person successfully convicted by the state. After the outbreak of war, detentions of homosexuals in concentration camps increased. Between 5000 and 15 000 homosexuals were imprisoned, it is believed. Forced to wear the black dot and the numbers 175 on their prison uniform (later replaced by a pink triangle), they were subject to harsh treatment. Survivors of the camps spoke of the particular brutality shown towards homosexuals by SS guards, who regarded them as at the lowest level in the concentration camp hierarchy.

Jehovah's Witnesses

Nazis targeted this religious group because of their conscientious objection to military service and their refusal to use the Hitler greeting or to join compulsory National Socialist organizations. Nazi "special courts", according to Burleigh, regarded them as "lower-class madmen" and the Gestapo accused them of using religion for political purposes – for "the destruction of all existing forms of state and governments and the establishment of the Kingdom of Jehovah, in which the Jews as the chosen people shall be the rulers".

The group was banned in 1933, and around a third of the community served time in custody during the lifetime of the regime; 2000 ended up in concentration camps, of whom 1200 died, either due to poor conditions or execution for conscientious objection. These "Bible students", or "Bible-bugs" as the SS termed them, were marked out in the camps by the violet triangles they wore to distinguish them from homosexuals (pink), politicals (red), criminals (green), and asocials (black). Ernst Fraenkel, in 1941, writing from exile noted in his work *The Dual State* that, "none of the illegal groups rejects National Socialism in a more uncompromising fashion than this obstinate group … whose pacifism allows no compromises". While the group was not numerically a threat to the Nazi state, its public and outspoken rejection of Nazi views meant that it could not be tolerated.

"Biological outsiders"

Even before Nazi rule, many regarded gypsies (or, more correctly, Sinti and Roma) with suspicion. In the 1920s, police departments in Bavaria and Prussia were active in fingerprinting, photographing, and monitoring these communities. There were approximately 30 000 gypsies in Germany in 1933; by 1945 there were just 5000. The communities were doubly disadvantaged under the regime, in that their nomadic lifestyle allowed them to be classed as "workshy" vagrants (of no fixed abode) and of inferior racial status. While the number of gypsies did not constitute, in Nazi eyes, as great a threat of racial pollution as the Jewish population, they were included in legislation such as the Nuremberg Laws of September 1935.

Racial "experts" from the Research Centre for Racial Hygiene and Biological Population Studies examined the communities to determine who was a "pure" gypsy and who was a *Mischling* or part gypsy. *Mischlinge* were considered a threat to be dealt with by their incarceration in camps where they would be "made to work", pending the prevention of the "continual procreation of this half-breed population", according to Dr Robert Ritter, the Nazi "expert" on gypsy affairs. The issuing of Himmler's Decree for the Struggle against the Gypsy Plague in December 1938 marked an attempt to categorize the population more efficiently into pure gypsy and part gypsy.

The occupation of large swathes of eastern Europe during the Second World War meant larger numbers of gypsies being brought under Nazi control. At one point, both Ritter and Himmler considered the possibility of establishing a virtual reservation for "pure" Sinti and Roma – almost as a living museum, or, as Burleigh says, "as a form of ethnic curiosity", but in December 1942 an order was implemented to transfer gypsies to special camps at Auschwitz and elsewhere. Many of those transferred became victims of Nazi medical experimentation, and half a million were murdered in what has been described as the Holocaust of the Sinti and Roma population of Europe in a National Socialist attempt to solve the "Gypsy Question".

The mentally and physically handicapped

Eugenics, the belief in the possibility of improving the racial stock through selective breeding, was not unique to Hitler's Germany, but it was pursued there with enthusiasm. Just as the emphasis of the regime was to produce "the perfect and complete human animal", in the words of Baldur von Schirach, leader of the Hitler Youth in 1938, it was policy that those unable to contribute to such an aim should be considered without value – consumers of state resources that could otherwise be better used.

Programmes of sterilization and euthanasia would eliminate "hereditary defects", held to be an obstacle to the building of a genetically healthy Aryan race. This approach to "racial hygiene" was not unique to the National Socialists. Such theories were propounded in other countries – even in pre-Hitler Germany in 1932, the Prussian state government produced draft legislation for voluntary sterilization. As early as July 1933 the Nazis introduced the Law for the Prevention of Hereditarily Diseased Offspring, which justified compulsory sterilization on the grounds that "countless numbers of inferiors and those suffering from hereditary ailments are reproducing unrestrainedly while their sick and asocial offspring are a burden on the community".

The law listed conditions such as "congenital feeblemindedness, schizophrenia, manic depression, hereditary epilepsy, Huntington's chorea, serious physical deformities and chronic alcoholism" as grounds for sterilization. Whether some of the foregoing were actually hereditary was questionable – and in the case of feeblemindedness the definition was so vague that it could be used to punish those deemed to have exercised poor judgment in their support for, or membership of, the KPD, for example. Between 1934 and 1945 the state carried out between 320 000 and 350 000 sterilizations.

Sterilization, however, was only one part of a scheme to rid the Reich of those considered a "burden on the community" – "worthless life", in the words of eugenists of the 1920s. Those believed to be suffering from incurable and resource-consuming disabilities (mental and physical) were to become victims of a state euthanasia policy. In 1939 the state-sanctioned murders of adults and children began, resulting in over 72 000 deaths before the T-4 programme (named after the address of the organization responsible: Tiergartenstrasse 4, Berlin) was officially halted in 1941 after protests from the public and the Church. Official halting of the killings may have stopped euthanasia but murders continued in concentration camps of those considered "biological outcasts" and these categories were expanded to include Jews, Slavs, Sinti and Roma, through the euphemistically termed *Sonderbehandlung* (special treatment).

The Jewish population

When examining the tragic impact of National Socialism on minorities, it is the treatment of the Jewish population in Germany (and the occupied territories after the outbreak of war) that has attracted most attention from historians and the public. Jews were held to be not only *Gemeinschaftsfremde* but actual dangers to the *Volksgemeinschaft* and its future.

Hitler did not invent anti-Semitism, nor was it an exclusively German phenomenon. "Russia was the land of the pogrom; Paris was the city of the anti-Semitic intelligentsia," as Johnson remarked. Yet "Judophobia" was present in Germany from the late 19th century and during the Weimar era many saw the supposed "cultural decay" and "moral decadence" of the time as a product of a Jewish conspiracy to undermine traditional German values. Claims that the conspiracy extended to attempts to dominate and manipulate international capitalism as well as promote Bolshevism were illogical, but formed part of the anti-Semitic outpourings by conservative German nationalists seeking a scapegoat for

▲ The caption on this poster reads, "This person suffering from hereditary defects costs the community 60 000 Reichsmarks during his lifetime. Fellow citizens, this is your money too. Issued by the Department (Office) of Racial policy".

Germany's post-war ills. This "syphilis of anti-Semitism" was particularly evident in the ideology of National Socialism, which, from the beginning, maintained a consistent policy of hostility towards Germany's Jewish population, which numbered around half a million in 1933 – less than 1 per cent of the total population.

Institutionalized and **eliminationist** anti-Semitism characterized the Nazi state; it was, in Goldhagen's view, "the defining feature of German society during its Nazi period". The state's anti-Semitic programme was implemented rapidly after March 1933, with legislation and government support for measures to exclude Jews from German professional, economic, and social life. Over the period 1933–1939, increasing restrictions imposed on the Jewish population in relation to citizenship, interracial marriage and sexual relationships, educational provision, and ownership of businesses were used to coerce Jews into leaving the Reich – no easy task at a time when the Great Depression resulted in immigration barriers being raised by countries that had previously welcomed immigrants.

Anti-Jewish measures, 1933–1945

- **April 1933** Boycott of Jewish businesses and Jewish doctors and legal professionals.
  Law for the Re-establishment of the Civil Service, excluding Jews (and other "undesirables" such as socialists or those with anti-Nazi views or non-Germans) from government employment.

- **July 1934** Jews not permitted to take legal examinations.

- **December 1934** Jews forbidden to take pharmaceutical examinations

- **September 1935** "The Nuremberg Laws" (the Reich Citizenship Act and the Law for the Protection of German Blood and German Honour) depriving Jews of German citizenship and forbidding intermarriage and sexual contact between Jews and "citizens of German or kindred blood"

- **July 1938** Ban on Jewish doctors

- **August 1938** Male Jews required to add the name "Israel" and females "Sarah" to any non-Jewish first names

- **September 1938** Cancellation of qualifications of Jewish doctors Jewish lawyers banned from practising

- **November 1938** Kristallnacht: following the murder of a German diplomat in Paris by a young Jewish assassin, attacks made on synagogues and Jewish persons and property. Mass arrest of Jews, their release conditional on their agreement to leave the country and for the Jewish community to pay for the damages occurring during this "pogrom"

  Jewish students forbidden to attend German schools and institutes of higher education

  Compulsory sale of Jewish businesses, part of a process of the "Aryanization" of German business

- **February 1939** Jews forced to surrender all items of gold, silver, and jewellery to the state

- **October 1939** Heinrich Himmler and SS given responsibility for Jewish affairs, followed by the expulsion of Jews from Vienna and, by early 1940, West Prussia. Relocated to German-occupied Poland

institutionalized
The programme of state-directed measures, propaganda, and legislation to persecute the Jewish population.

eliminationist
Plan to remove the Jews from German society through actions that escalated from officially sanctioned discrimination designed to pressure them to leave Germany, to the most extreme form of "elimination" of the Holocaust, which aimed at the physical extermination of the Jewish population in Germany and Nazi-occupied Europe during the Second World War.

- **August 1940** The idea of transporting millions of Jews from Germany and the occupied East to Madagascar abandoned

- **July 1941** Beginning of plans for a "Final Solution to the Jewish Question"

- **September 1941** Jews required to wear a yellow "Star of David" Transporting of Jews to concentration camps and the start of experiments on methods to murder Jews en masse

- **January 1942** Detailed plans for the extermination of Jews drawn up at the Wannsee Conference

- **February 1942** Start of mass executions of Jews in Poland

- **September 1942** Jews, together with gypsies, Soviet prisoners of war and "asocials" given over to Himmler for "destruction through labour" in camps such as Auschwitz (originally established in 1940 but now hugely expanded for "processing" those deemed "undesirable" by the Nazi regime). Other camps, such as Maidanek, Treblinka, Chelmno, Belzec and Sobibor, were tasked with the gruesome process of the annihilation of humans considered unworthy of existence by the Nazis.

  The murder of these "undesirables" resulted in the extermination – the physical elimination – of 6 million Jews alone, as well as Slavs, gypsies and other minorities or groups identified as "social outcasts" and political enemies.

The Holocaust, 1941–1945

Institutionalized anti-Semitism in Germany was the basis for the attempted genocide of European Jewry (the **Holocaust**) in areas under Nazi control and the occupied territories: a systematic elimination of Jews from the social and economic life of the nation and its territories. For Hitler, as Burleigh pointed out in *Sacred Causes*:

> *The Aryan's maleficent counterpart was the Jew … the negation of the Aryan's God-given properties … allegedly a materialist rather than an idealist, lacking culture-creating capacities – an anarchic, egoistic and individualistic "destroyer of culture".*

In the National Socialist world view, predatory capitalism and Marxism were "the twin offspring" of "international Jewry" and Jews were seen as dangerous for the nation – and, indeed, the world. In *Mein Kampf*, Hitler fulminated about the peril of Judaism, and declared:

> *Should the Jew, with the aid of his Marxist creed, triumph over the people of this world, his Crown will be the funeral wreath of mankind … I believe today that my conduct is in accordance with the will of the Almighty creator, in standing guard against the Jew I am defending the handiwork of the Lord.*

While his attitude to the Jewish population pre-1933 was extreme, it was only after the establishment of the regime that Germany witnessed an onslaught of discriminatory policies and programmes to rid Germany (and later Nazi-occupied Europe) of Jews. Historians have argued the extent to which the scapegoating of Jews was an attempt to rally Germans to National Socialism through a spirit of "negative cohesion", by using the existing suspicion and hostility towards the Jewish community shown by some sectors of the population since the later 19th century. Portraying

Holocaust
The systematic, state-sanctioned persecution and murder of 6 million Jews by the Nazi regime and its collaborators.

the struggle against "the Jew" as a life-and-death struggle allowed Hitler to appeal to the xenophobic tendencies of some and the materialistic interests of others, who envied the fact that such a small Jewish population was so dominant (in proportional terms) in business, politics, and the professions.

The "intentionalist" school of historians of Hitler's Germany emphasized the extent to which Hitler relentlessly followed a consistent aim of exterminating the Jewish population, noting frequent references in *Mein Kampf* to the destruction of "undesirable" elements in the proposed *Volksgemeinschaft*. Conversely, the "structuralist" or "functionalist" school puts forward the case that the savage treatment of the Jews, by the war years, was largely a product of local initiatives by Nazi officials in occupied eastern European lands, who attempted to solve the problem of the large Jewish numbers under their authority by simply liquidating the population.

Mommsen claimed that a process of "cumulative radicalization" occurred among Nazi leaders, who vied with one another to interpret and carry out what they understood to be Hitler's desire to physically destroy European Jewry. The interpretation that, in the Reich, many Nazis in the regime hierarchy would create "their own orders within the spirit of what was required of them" was questioned originally by Kershaw, who talked of the tendency of officials to "work towards the Führer".

The methods to be used to "cleanse" Germany may be a matter of debate, but the desire to remove Jews from the nation was not. Measures from 1933 to 1935 aimed to pressure German Jews to leave the country, by applying economic and social sanctions to deprive them of business/professional opportunities and rights associated with citizenship (including legal rights of residency, for example). Discriminatory legislation was paused somewhat in 1936, when Germany hosted the Olympics, but the tempo of anti-Semitic measures picked up again by 1938, when state-sponsored violence was combined with new legislation to intensify the pressure on Jews to quit Germany.

Between 1933 and November 1938, approximately 150 000 Jews emigrated. In the period after Kristallnacht up to the outbreak of war, a further 150 000 were estimated to have left, as brute force, the Aryanization of business through compulsory purchase of Jewish concerns (large and small) and the exclusion of Jews from mainstream life were increased. In this sense, the "eliminationist" policy of the regime had removed more than 300 000 of Germany's Jewish population of half a million (as of 1933).

The outbreak of war altered tactics for the worse, as German military victories brought not only impressive territorial gains but also large Jewish populations in eastern Europe. Emigration was no longer a possible solution to the regime's "Jewish problem". In 1940 the Nazis debated the desperate idea of relocating European Jewry to the island of Madagascar in what would become a virtual reservation for Jews, but failure to defeat Britain and destroy British sea power meant that by 1941 the scheme was abandoned. A new solution had to be found. It was – with dire consequences for 6 million Jews by 1945.

The extent of authoritarian control

National Socialism's destruction was the result of external forces. 12 years of rule were ended by the outcome of the Second World War rather than by any significant internal opposition to the Nazi government. Domestic opposition was limited and in some cases its timing – for example, in 1944 – was conditioned not by hatred of the regime but by the fear of defeat and retribution at the hands of the Allied forces, and the USSR in particular.

In this sense, "authoritarian control" can be seen to have been effective in limiting domestic opposition to the regime. While not all Germans wholeheartedly accommodated themselves to the regime, the numbers of denunciations received by the Gestapo show a wide level of compliance with its aim of identifying enemies of the Reich. Germans, among the best-educated people of Western Europe (a "supposedly civilised country", as Geary remarked), submitted to the regime for a variety of motives, including:

- belief in the aims of the Nazis

- fear of the consequences of disobedience

- disillusionment with the previous democratic system and antipathy towards the possible rise of the Left

- gratitude for the material benefits that the Nazis seemed to offer in their social and economic programmes, which offered employment and upward mobility for those who accepted the NSDAP

- pride in Nazi foreign policy which, until 1939 at least, had succeeded in restoring national pride by rejecting the Diktat of Versailles.

For the majority – those not victimized because of their racial, political, mental, or physical status – there was little reason to risk persecution by a system that had "rescued" Germany from economic despair and humiliation.

On 28 April 1939, the focus of a speech that Hitler delivered to the Reichstag was on the achievements of National Socialism under the Führer. For Kershaw and Haffner, such achievements (constantly stressed by Nazi propaganda techniques and through the promotion of a cult of the Führer/Saviour) were appealing not only to convinced Nazis but had "a wide popular resonance" with many sectors of German society. What many Germans did not realize in April 1939 (five months before the outbreak of war in Europe) was that such achievements were not an end in themselves but "merely the platform for the war of racial-imperialist conquest which they were preparing to fight".

Those who did doubt the regime (its ideological basis and practices after 1933) seldom reacted, due to the terroristic nature of the state, and instead entered what has been described as a form of internal exile – remaining silent and detached from any form of political discourse or overt resistance. In this way lay safety. Such compliance produced horrific results not only for the "enemies" of the Nazi ideology, but ultimately for those who subsequently suffered the misery and destruction brought to Germany by a conflict that resulted in German deaths and partition of the nation in the aftermath of defeat.

Exam-style questions

1 To what extent were constitutional flaws responsible for the collapse of democracy in Germany?

2 When and why did German democracy collapse in Germany in the inter-war years?

3 "The main reasons for the failure of democratic government in Germany in the inter-war years were external rather than internal".

   To what extent do you agree with this statement?

4 "Only the Great Depression put the wind into the sails of National Socialism."

   To what extent do you agree with this statement?

5 "Hitler was jobbed into power."

   To what extent do you agree with this statement?

6 Discuss why internal opposition to the single-party state in Germany (1933–1945) was both limited and ineffective.

7 In what ways, and with what success, did Hitler (after 1933) honour the promises he made relating to domestic issues during his rise to power?

8 Assess the role of each of the following in the rise to power of Hitler:

   - the Paris Peace Settlement

   - the actions of Weimar leaders, 1930–1933

   - fear of the Left.

9 "The coming to power of National Socialism was the result of the distress for which others were responsible."

   To what extent do you agree with this statement?

10 Examine the contribution of each of the following to the maintenance of Hitler's single-party state after 1933:

   - control of education

   - propaganda

   - the use of force.

   (If you are unable to deal with all three areas identified in this type of question, avoid such a question and seek an alternative if possible.)

11 "Between 1930–1933 the NSDAP was less the party of first choice than the party of last resort in desperate times."

   Discuss this claim with reference to the rapid rise in support for the NSDAP.

12 "The NSDAP was at once a symptom of, and a solution to, economic and political crisis."

   Discuss with reference to the growth of National Socialism, 1923–1933.

Evaluating sources

Question

With reference to the origin and purpose of John Heartfield's photomontage of October 1932 ('The meaning of the Hitler salute'), assess its value(s) and limitation(s) for an historian interpreting the reasons for the rise of National Socialism.

Analysis

This question asks you to evaluate primary source material. For IA purposes, you will have had an opportunity to research the source before answering this question. In exam conditions (Paper 1) this would not be the case – it would be an unseen source. You should aim to write around 300 words for an IA evaluation question.

Analysing the question means breaking it down into its constituent parts. Key words in the question are "origin", "purpose", "value(s)" and "limitation(s)". You will need to:

- **identify** the author/artist – his political views, academic standing, etc.

- give the **provenance** of the source (publisher, place, date and whether it was meant for private or public distribution)

- **briefly** explain its **origins**: this is the historical context – the significance of the date of publication and the circumstances in which it was produced

- **identify** the audience to which it was addressed and its intended **purpose** (overt and possibly covert)

- comment on why the source has **value** for aiding understanding of the rise of National Socialism and say why the source might have **limitations** as an aid to understanding.

Don't:

- simply **describe** the source content

- deal with the values/limitations of the source in relation to its **utility** (usefulness) – i.e. don't say "This source was/was not useful because it had information which did/did not help my investigation." This is *not* source evaluation.

- claim **"bias"/subjectivity/partiality** unless you can produce specific evidence

- **make generic comments** about age/memory lapse of the author, translation problems, etc., unless you can show how this has affected the source's reliability

- **generalize** – claiming for example that all primary sources are reliable whereas secondary sources are less so.

Sample answer

The photomontage was produced by Heartfield (a KPD member since 1918) in the A-I-Z, a pictorial newspaper and communist publication based in Berlin, with wide circulation, in October 1932 prior to the November Reichstag elections, when Nazi support and membership was falling and that of the KPD rising. The **purpose** of the photomontage was to ridicule National Socialism, its slogans, salutes and claims and to promote anti-Fascism in the chaotic situation before the November election. It intended to link Hitler's rise to the support offered by "Big Business" – in line with the Comintern interpretation of Hitlerism as the "last kick of decaying capitalism" – Hitler being portrayed as the recipient of funds by the industrial magnates of Germany.

The source is **valuable** as an example of the dogmatic and ultimately disastrous communist interpretation of National Socialism's rise and an example of the early use of photomontage for political propagandizing. A-I-Z readership was sympathetic to such a message already, so in this sense the message was arguably "preaching to the converted". As a KPD member producing for a communist journal run by Willi Münzengerg, a KPD activist and propagandist, the source is **limited** in that Heartfield was emphasizing a "party line" rather than examining the wider range of factors behind Hitler's rise, including the failures of the Left. The actual "contributions" (no details being provided) were available to a variety of parties to the right of centre as business sought to insure itself in a troubled political climate against the rise of the KPD in particular. Heartfield, describing himself as an "engineer" rather than an artist despite his work in commercial publishing and theatre-set design, saw his role as influencing opinion in line with current communist interpretations of European fascism. This Moscow-directed view followed by the KPD did not allow for alternative views or factors.

Examiner comments

This evaluation shows a good understanding of the provenance and the significance of the photomontage as an historical source in relation to the question. It has identified the author and where and when it was printed and made a brief and pertinent comment on the circumstances in which the source was produced. It avoids the temptation to simply describe what can be seen in the photomontage and shows a clear understanding of the source's possible purpose – both overt and covert.

Values and limitations of the source are not focused on utility – i.e. comments about how helpful this was because it provided or did not provide details helpful to the student – neither does it spend time talking about problems of translation of the text. Instead, it tries to indicate the source's value and limitations for understanding the rise of National Socialism – which may be less to do with the influence/importance of business support (still a contentious issue for some historians) than on providing us with an insight into the failings of the strategy of the KPD and its adherence to a policy that ultimately consigned the Party and its members to defeat and exile, like Heartfield himself in April 1933.

Further reading

1 Egypt – Nasser

Abdel-Nasser, Gamal (trans. E. S. Farag).1972. *Nasser Speaks: Basic Documents,* Middle East Monographs no. 1. London. Morssett Press. This includes the complete text of the *Philosophy of the Revolution, The Charter* and the 30 March Programme.

Alahmed, A. 12 March 2011. "Voice of the Arabs Radio: Its Effects and Political Power during the Nasser Era (1953–1967)." Indiana University: paper prepared for the Joint Journalism Historians Conference. Electronic copy available at http://papers.ssrn.com/sol3/papers.cfm?abstract_id=2047212

Amin Morsy, Laila. Jan 1989. "Britain's Wartime Policy in Egypt, 1940–42". *Middle Eastern Studies,* Vol. 25, No. 1. Pp 64–94.

Cook, SA. 2012. *The Struggle for Egypt: from Nasser to Tahrir Square.* Oxford. Oxford University Press.

el-Ghonemy, Riad, 4, 8

Gilbar and Winckler, 286?? [see ref p.21]

Gordon, Joel. 1992. *Nasser's Blessed Movement: Egypt's Free Officers and the July Revolution.* New York, Oxford. Oxford University Press.

Gordon, 2004, 309??[ref p.33]

Hansen, B and Nashashibi, K. 1975. *Foreign Trade Regimes and Economic Development: Egypt.* Cambridge, MA, USA. NBER. http://www.nber.org/books/hans75-1

Hopwood, D. 1993. *Egypt 1945–1990: Politics and Society.* London. Routledge.

Kamrava, Mehran. 2005. *The Modern Middle East: A Political History Since the First World War.* Berkeley, Los Angeles, London. University of California Press.

Kassem, M. 2004. *Egyptian Politics: The Dynamics of Authoritarian Rule.* Colorado. Lynne Rienner.

McNamara, R. 2003. *Britain, Nasser and the Balance of Power in the Middle East, 1952–1967.* London. Frank Cass Publishers.

Neguib, Mohammad. 1955. *Egypt's Destiny.* London. Gollancz. http://www.nasser.org/home/main.aspx?lang=en

This site has been established in cooperation with Bibliotheca Alexandrina and the Gamal Abdel-Nasser Foundation. It includes a number of digital audio-visual documents, photos, and transcripts of speeches (mostly in Arabic). It is an excellent tool for further research.

Oweiss, IM. "Egypt's economy; pressing issues". http://faculty.georgetown.edu/imo3/epe/epe.htm

Pappé, I. 2005. *The Modern Middle East.* London. Routledge.

Podeh, E and Winckler, O (eds). 2004. *Rethinking Nasserism: Revolution and Historical Memory in Modern Egypt.* Gainesville, FL. USA. University Press of Florida.

This is a collection of articles, which includes:

- M Riad El-Ghonemy, "An Assessment of Egypt's Development strategy"
- Meir Hatina, "History, Politics, and Collective Memory: the Nasserist legacy in Mubarak's Egypt"
- Gad G Gilbar and Onn Winckler, "Nasser's Family Planning Policy in Perspective"
- Gabriel M Rosenbaum, "Nasser and Nasserism as Perceived in Modern Egyptian Literature through Allusions to Songs"
- Joel Gordon, "The Nightingale and the Ra'is: Abd al Halim Hafiz and Nasserist Longings"

Vatikiotis, PJ. 1991. *The History of Modern Egypt: From Muhammad Ali to Mubarak.* 4th edition. London. Weidenfeld and Nicolson.

Waterbury, J. 2014. *The Egypt of Nasser and Sadat: The Political Economy of Two Regimes.* Princeton, NJ, USA. Princeton University Press.

Woodward, Peter. 1992. *Nasser.* London, New York. Longman.

2 Cuba – Castro

Balfour, S. 2009. *Castro (Profiles in Power)* London. Routledge.

Bonachea, RL and San Martin, M. 1995. *The Cuban Insurrection, 1952–1959.* New Brunswick. NJ. Transaction.

Bravo, E. (director), Fidel: the untold story (documentary) (DVD Pickwick, 2007)

Castro, F. and I. Ramonet, *Fidel Castro: My Life: a Spoken Biography* (Simon and Schuster Ome, 2009)

Chomsky, N. 5 February 2015. "A Brief History of America's Cold-Blooded, Terroristic Treatment of Cuba." *Alternet,* 5 February 2015

Coltman, L. 2003. *The Real Fidel Castro.* New Haven. Yale University Press.

Detzer, D. 1979. *The Brink: The Cuban Missile Crisis, 1962.* New York, NT. TY Cromwell.

Gaddis, JL. 1998. *We Now Know: Rethinking Cold War History.* Oxford. Clarendon Press.

Guevara, E., *Reminiscences of the Cuban Revolutionary War* (Harper Perennial, 2009)

Hampsey, Major Russell J. November–December 2002. "Voices from the Sierra Maestra: Fidel Castro's Revolutionary Propaganda". Military Review. Command & General Staff College, Fort Leavenworth, Kansas. http://www.latinamericanstudies.org/cuban-rebels/voices.htm

Kellner, D. 1989. *Ernesto "Che" Guevara* (World Leaders Past & Present). Chelsea House Publishers.

Paìs, F. February 1957. "The 1956 Uprising in Santiago de Cuba." *Revolución.* Translated and reprinted in *The Militant* magazine. December 2003. Vol 67, number 46.

Schoultz, L. 2009. *That Infernal Little Cuban Republic: The United States and the Cuban Revolution.* Chapel Hill. University of North Carolina Press.

Stone, O., Comandante (documentary) (DVD Optimum Home Releasing, 2004)

Sweig, JE. 2004. *Cuba: Inside the Cuban Revolution: Fidel Castro and the Urban Underground.* Cambridge, MA. Harvard University Press.

Tunzelmann, von, A. 2011. *Red Heat: Conspiracy, Murder, and the Cold War in the Caribbean.* New York, NY. Henry Holt.

BBC News. 2 March 2005. South America's Leftward Sweep. http://news.bbc.co.uk/2/hi/americas/4311957.stm

3 China – Mao

Becker, J. 1998. Hungry Ghosts: Mao's Secret Famine. Holt McDougal

Breslin. M 1998. *Mao.* London. Longman.

Davin, D. 1997. *Mao Zedong.* Stroud. Sutton Publishing.

Dikotter, F. 2013. *The Tragedy of Liberation.* London. Bloomsbury.

Dikotter, F. 2010. *Mao's Great Famine.* London. Walker.

Fairbank, JK. 1992. *China: A New History.* Cambridge, MA, USA. Belknap Press.

Feigon, L. 2002. *Mao: A Reinterpretation.* Lanham, MD, USA. Ivan R. Dee.

Fenby, J. 2008. *The Penguin History of Modern China*. London. Penguin.

Jun, C. 1991. *Wild Swans*. London. Harper Collins.

Jung, C, and Halliday, J. 2005. *Mao: The Unknown Story*. London, Jonathan Cape.

Lynch, M. 2004. *Mao*. London. Routledge.

Mao, Z. 2001. *Selected Works of Mao Tse Tung*. Stockton, CA, USA. University Press of the Pacific. https://www.marxists.org/reference/archive/mao/selected-works/index.htm)

Mitter, Rana. 2005. A Bitter Revolution. China's Struggle with the Modern World. Oxford University Press.

Salisbury, HE. 1993. *The New Emperors Mao and Deng: A Dual Biography*. London. Harper Collins.

Schram, S. 1975. *Mao Tse Tung*. London. Penguin.

Short, P. 1999. *Mao: A Life*. London. Hodder & Stoughton.

Spence, J. 1999. *Mao*. London. Weidenfeld & Nicolson.

Spence, J. 1990. *The Search for Modern China*. New York, NY, USA. W.W. Norton.

Zhisiu, L. 1994. *The Private Life of Chairman Mao*. London. Chatto & Windus.

Articles

Lynch, M. 2002. 'Mao Zedong: Liberator or Oppressor of China?' *History Review*.

Tarr, Russel. March 2011. "Stalin and Mao: Parallel Rise?" *History Review*. Issue 69.

Documentaries

Williams, Sue. 1997. *China: A Century of Revolution*. Zeitgeist Films.

Davidson, Nick. 2005. *Biography: Mao Tse Tung, China's Peasant Emperor*. A and E Television Networks.

4 Germany – Hitler

Benz, W and Pehle, W. 1997. *Encyclopaedia of German Resistance to the Nazi Movement*. New York, NY, USA. Continuum.

Bracher, KD. 1955. "Die Auflösung der Weimarer Republik", in Bracher, Sauer and Schulz, *Stufen der Machtergreifung*. 1962. Westdeutscher Verlag Opladen.

Bracher, KD. 1995. *Turning Points in Modern Times*. Cambridge, MA, USA. Harvard University Press.

Brendon, P. 2000. *The Dark Valley: A Panorama of the 1930s*. London. Jonathan Cape.

Burleigh, M. 2000. *The Third Reich: A New History*. London. Pan.

Burleigh, M. 2006. *Sacred Causes*. London. Harper Perennial.

Communist International. 1929. *Programme*. New York, NY, USA. Workers Library Publishers.

Corkery, JF and Stone, RCJ. 1982. *Weimar Germany and the Third Reich*. London. Heinemann.

Crew, D. (ed.) 1994. *Nazism and German Society 1933–45*. London. Routledge.

Eatwell, R. 1995. *Fascism: A History* London. Vintage.

Evans, R. 2003. *The Coming of the Third Reich*. London. Penguin.

Gay, P. 1968. *Weimar Culture: The Outsider as Insider*. London. Penguin.

Geary, D. 1993. *Hitler and Nazism*. Lancaster Pamphlets. London. Routledge.

Goldhagen, D. 1996. *Hitler's Willing Executioners*. London. Abacus.

Gregor, N. (ed.). 2000. *Nazism* Oxford, UK. Oxford University Press.

Griffin, R. 1991. *The Nature of Fascism*. London. Routledge.

Haffner, S. alphahistory.com/nazigermany/nazi-germany-quotations/

Himmler, H. 2000. Cited in Hite, J and Hinton, C, *Weimar and Nazi Germany*. London. John Murray.

Jenkins, J and Feuchtwanger, E. 2000. *Hitler's Germany*. London. John Murray.

Johnson, P. 1983. *A History of The Modern World*. London. Weidenfeld and Nicolson.

Kaes, J and Dimendberg, E. 1995. *The Weimar Republic Sourcebook*. Oakland, CA, USA. UC Press.

Kershaw, I. 2008. *The Fuhrer Myth: How Hitler Won Over the German People*. http://www.spiegel.de/international/germany/the-fuehrer-myth-how-hitler-won-over-the-german-people-a-531909-2.html

Kershaw, I cited in https://www.marxists.org/history/etol/newspape/isj2/.../ovenden.htm

Kershaw, I. 1993. "Der 30. Januar 1933, Ausweg aus der Krise und Anfang des Staatsverfalls" (from Winkler, HA. *Die deutsche Staatskrise 1930–33*. Munich, Germany. Oldenbourg Verlag.

Knopp, G. 2002. *Hitler's Children*. Stroud, UK. Sutton Publishing.

Kolb, E. 1988. *The Weimar Republic*. London. Unwin Hyman.

Koonz, C. 2000. "Mothers in the Fatherland", cited in Gregor, N, *Nazism*. Oxford, UK. Oxford University Press.

McDonough, F. 2012. *Hitler and the Rise of the Nazi Party*. London. Routledge.

Noakes, J. 1987. In "Social Outcasts in the Third Reich" in Bessel, R, *Life in the Third Reich*. Oxford, UK. Oxford University Press.

Noakes, J and Pridham, G. 1984. *Nazism 1919–45*, 4 vols. Exeter. University of Exeter Press.

Overy, R. 2004. *The Dictators*. London. Penguin.

Peukert, D. 1991. *The Weimar Republic: The Crisis of Classical Modernity*. London. Penguin.

Preuss, H. 1982. Cited in Corkery, JF and Stone, RCJ, *Weimar Germany and the Third Reich*. London. Heinemann.

Rauschning, H. 2000. "The Voice of Destruction, 1940". Cited in Jenkins and Feuchtwanger, *Hitler's Germany*. London. John Murray.

Rees, L. 1997. *The Nazis: A Warning from History*. New York, NY, USA. MJF Books.

Reitlinger, G. 1956. *SS: Alibi of a Nation, 1922–1945. London. Heinemann*.

Röhl, JCG. 1970. *From Bismarck to Hitler*. London. Longman.

Rothfels, H. 1961. *The German Opposition to Hitler*. London. Oswald Wolff.

Rumbold, H. 1948. Cited in Woodward, EL and Butler, R, *Documents of British Foreign Policy 1919–39*. London. HMSO.

Sax, BC and Kuntz, D. 1992. *Inside Hitler's Germany*. Lexington, MA, USA. D.C. Heath.

Schoenbaum, D. 2000. Cited in Gregor, N, *Nazism*. Oxford, UK. Oxford University Press.

Shirer, WL. 2002. "Berlin Diary: Journal of a Foreign Correspondent 1934–41" in Stackelberg, R and Winkle, S, *The Nazi Germany Sourcebook: an Anthology of Texts*. London. Routledge.

Snyder, LL. 1995. *Encyclopaedia of the Third Reich*. New York, NY, USA. McGraw-Hill.

Speer, A. 1970. *Inside the Third Reich*. London. Sphere.

Stackelberg, R and Winkle, SA. 2002. *The Nazi Germany Sourcebook: an Anthology of Texts*. London. Routledge.

Stephenson, J. 2003. "Fascism and Gender: Women under National Socialism" in Kallis, AA, *The Fascism Reader*. London. Routledge.

Strasser, O. 1940. *Hitler and I. London. Jonathan Cape*.

Stresemann, G. 1982. Cited in Corkery, JF and Stone, RCJ, *Weimar Germany and the Third Reich*. London. Heinemann.

Taylor, AJP. 1967. Cited in www.johndclare.net/Word%20documents/Hitler%20Historiography.doc. *Europe, Grandeur and Decline*.

Taylor, AJP. 1978. *The Course of German History. London. Methuen*.

Turner, HA. 2000. "Nazism and the Third Reich", in Jenkins, J and Feuchtwanger, E, *Hitler's Germany*. London. John Murray.

Ward Price, G. 1939. *I know these Dictators*. London. Harrap.

Wels, O. 1933. http://germanhistorydocs.ghi-dc.org/pdf/eng/English_6.pdf

Wright, G. 1968. *The Ordeal of Total War 1939–45*. New York, NY, USA. Harper Torchbooks.

Revision template: Comparing leaders of different authoritarian states

In Paper 2 there will be no named leaders for you to discuss. The question format will be more like this:

With reference to an authoritarian leader that you have studied, explain fully how important a role propaganda played in their rise to power.

Additionally, examiners will be looking for strong global awareness so it is likely that at least one of the questions on each topic in Paper 2 will be asking you to compare two dictators.

This template can be used to make brief notes concerning various aspects of the rise and rule of different authoritarian states. This, if researched carefully, allows for a quick revision of their key features and characteristics. You may, of course, construct your own template, and adapt this template to the leaders you have studied, using headings of your choosing. Choose headings that will allow you to assess the similarities and differences between the different regimes.

Not all headings will apply to all authoritarian states because of their different natures and situations.

Features of the authoritarian state	Egypt — Nasser	Cuba — Castro	China — Mao	Germany — Hitler
Ideology				
Leadership				
Economic aims and methods				
Party				
Secret police				
Youth and education				
Religion				
Relationship to army				
Media and propaganda				
Women: status and role				
Racial policies/treatment of minorities				
Organized labour				
Coming to power: nature of preceding government				

Index